Where are you now, Manannan Mac Lir?
Where are you now, Son of the Sea, King and Protector?
No more your friends Conchobar and Culain.
No more your magical powers
turning one into a hundred as enemies threaten.
No more your legendary voyages
guided by the heavens you know so well.
Gone and lost in the distance of time.

To whom the Celtic tribute of rushes on Midsummer Eve?
And who is that in the enfolding mist?
Is it you, Manannan Mac Lir — of Mannin, Ellan Vannin, Isle of Man?

HERE IS THE NEWS IN THE YEAR OF OUR LORD 798
MARAUDERS AT LARGE IN IRISH SEA

A war fleet of mysterious origin has appeared in the Irish Sea and attacks on coastal settlements have been reported from Ireland as well as Scotland and Northern England. Villages have been put to the fire and churches looted as the attackers search for church valuables. It seems inevitable that the Isle of Man will shortly suffer a similar fate and the defenceless inhabitants walk in fear and trepidation. Being in a central position the Island could well become a base for these naval excursions. An early report that the monastic establishment on St. Patrick's Isle in the west of the Island had been desecrated has not been confirmed. The report may well be confused with the news from Ireland that the Christian centre of Inis Patrick in Dublin Bay has been similarly attacked. It appears that the monastic buildings have been destroyed and the Shrine of Dachonna broken into and the relics, highly treasured by the monks, removed. Precise information is difficult to obtain but from our Irish friends we have been able to compile this report:

'The situation is not clear at the moment but it seems likely that the raiders are fierce and ruthless fighters with no respect for property or women. After early encounters on the beach around Inis Patrick local forces have withdrawn to regroup. But the raiders are not pressing their advantage. They are also believed to have carried off a number of women. At the moment they seem only to be in search of plunder. The origin of the raiders is not known but eyewitnesses say there have been similar coastal raids in other parts of Ireland where the marauders are known as Gentiles. They are also being called Vikings or Northmen for it is said they come from lands to the north. Their war galleys are unlike anything seen in the Irish Sea before. A coastwatch spokesman said they appear to be clinker built with unusually high prows and stems and are propelled by a single square sail and banks of oars. The ships are very manoeuvrable and can carry up to 100 armed warriors whose battle standards bear a raven as their symbol. Their shields are round, painted black and yellow and they also seem to have unusual skill in working metal. They carry well-made swords and they are protected by iron helmets and coats of chain mail. The other striking feature is that they are clean shaven apart from fierce moustaches which enhance their warlike appearance.'

HOME NEWS : HOUSING DEVELOPMENTS

Plans have been announced for new housing developments in the south east of the Island on the flat ground facing St. Michael's Isle and Langness. A spokesman for the developers said they will follow traditional design and incorporate traditional materials. Each dwelling will be circular in shape and comprise a single room. They will be constructed of stone or wattle and wickerwork and they will have distinctive conical roofs thatched with rushes. While central hearths are still common it is understood that these new dwellings will have the hearth used for warmth and cooking placed to the side of the room against the stone wall.

FARMING REPORT

Agricultural returns for 797 show that the main corn crop in the Island continues to be oats. But there has been some increase in flax production. Otherwise the large amount under pasture remains the same. A Report accompanying the returns says the static nature of the figures shows that there is little sign of modernisation in Manx agriculture. It is being retarded says the Report, by the existing system which encourages farmers to take all they can from the land for their own short term benefit, rather than trying to achieve some long term improvement in productivity.

CRAFTWORKERS

On the industrial front production of stone monuments in the Island has been stepped up. In many cases they take the form of the Cross and a number of intricate designs have been drawn up. Production is concentrated at the monastery established by *Machud* in the north east of the Island where it has been going on since the early part of the last century. A monastery official said the building of churches, or *keeills*, throughout the Island was also continuing apace and it was expected that at least two hundred would be completed eventually. The work of the monastery is a tribute to its founder *Machud* who had a remarkable career. He hailed from Ireland where he was a wicked chieftain who persecuted the followers of St. Patrick. When the two met *Machud* succumbed to the power of Patrick who severely chastised the evil man. As a punishment he was cast adrift in a frail coracle, his hands chained. A day later he was cast upon the headland near to the place of the monastery he was to found following his penance and training for Holy Orders. He rose to be the Island's bishop and today is remembered as Saint Maughold.

MANANNAN — FACT OR FICTION?

Finally, doubt has been cast on the legend of Manannan Mac Lir as the ancient godking of the Isle of Man. It is being said that he was, if he existed at all, little more than a seafaring local trader who had exceptional skills as a navigator but no magical powers. Manannan has hitherto been believed to have been a necromancer or magician who could make one man look like a hundred and throw a mantle of mist around the Island on the approach of enemies. If he should be about today it is certain that we could make good use of his magical powers.

ISLAND HOMES

Although there are no official figures available it is obvious that the population of Manx Celts continues to grow at a steady rate, judging by the number of new homes being built around settlements throughout the Island. After a thousand years the Celts are now masters throughout the land. The new dwellings now springing up are on meadowland ideal for the animals and where good ground is available for crop growing. The style of dwelling follows the traditional style and the one-roomed cottages of about six paces in width are still the most popular. The walls are solidly built of local stone, mostly slate, to the height of the tallest man. Keeping the roof high is an important fire precaution. In the centre of the room a strong wooden post supports the rafters of the conical roof which has a thatch of straw, ling or, sometimes rushes. Great pride is taken in keeping the thatch trim. Illumination is provided by a doorway facing the sun and which can easily be closed at night or in bad weather. Floors are of beaten earth and the stone hearth is a semi-circular platform built against the wall. A hole in the thatch allows the smoke to escape and some hearths are now equipped with baking ovens fuelled by gorse and peat.

Families find these homes quite cosy and they are easily maintained although the thatch can be troublesome, especially in stormy conditions. There is plenty of time, therefore, for working on the land. Each family grows its own crop of corn which is ground into flour on the stone saddle querns. Much time is spent in looking after the animals, these being the local breed of oxen, sheep and purrs (pigs). There is plenty of meat available

A typical Celtic homestead found throughout the Island.

although keeping supplies fresh, or the animals alive, during the long winter months is still a problem. Shellfish, poultry and the occasional wild boar are considered a great delicacy.

Iron is still the most important metal in use and is especially valuable for the making of tools and ploughshares. Iron, in the form of nails and shipbolts, have been a boon to shipwrights who are now able to build boats far superior to the old dug-outs and coracles. It is now quite common to see these new boats around the coast on fishing trips while others venture further afield to visit neighbouring coasts. Bronze is still popular and the womenfolk prize their attractive bracelets and ornamental pins. Strings of beads in various colours and rings of jet or lignite, purchased from traders, are very fashionable. While the men are away the women and children busy themselves spinning and weaving in order to make new clothes for the winter months.

The larger units of the past are no longer fashionable and the ruins of one can still be seen at Ballakeigan in the south of the Island. It measured some thirty paces across and its domed roof was supported on massive oak posts. The family lived in the central area with rooms divided by wattle around the hearth which was made from Pooylvaish limestone. The remaining part of the building was used for the stabling of animals and for storage. The disappearance of such huge structures is the result of the lack of oak trees which were once plentiful. Maintenance was also a problem. There were no fortifications as those were peaceful days. But the recent news of the terror attacks are exercising many minds as to how best we can defend our homes; already ploughshares are being turned into swords.

An artist's impression of the now ruined Celtic round house at Ballakeigan.

HERE IS THE NEWS : 930 A.D.
VIKINGS ANNOUNCE PLANS FOR AN OPEN-AIR ASSEMBLY

Proposals are announced today for setting up an annual open-air assembly for freemen in the Isle of Man for the purpose of law making. It would be based on similar assemblies in the Viking homeland, which are being extended to countries now under colonisation. We have this special report:

'The proposals are set out in a report issued by senior Viking officials in Dublin which points out that an assembly of the kind envisaged is also to be set up this year in Iceland. The concept is that of an assembly where old laws can be recited, new laws submitted for public approval, and judgement given on law breakers. The assembly would be held once a year, on Midsummer Day, June 24th, and the site proposed is at St. John's, as a concession to Celtic feeling in the Island. The village green there has been a gathering place for centuries for the people of the Isle of Man. The report also says there is a practical matter to be considered if, as intended, the assembly is to be used for the judgement of law breakers. It is customary for the death sentence to be carried out immediately — by way of the Barrel of Spikes — and surveyor's reports indicate that the nearby mountain slope has a suitable gradient for this.

The site also has the advantage of a large greensward. The original Viking concept is that of an assembly taking place on what becomes known as the parliament field, or *Thing Vollur*. Work on setting up the Icelandic assembly is already well advanced and should be completed this year. It is hoped that the Isle of Man will follow suit as quickly as possible. But it is acknowledged that it might be several years before this can be achieved.

The Icelandic assembly is to be called the *Althing*. But there is no name for the Manx version as yet, although local officials believe it should have a distinctive name of its own.'

PRESERVING THE GAELIC LANGUAGE

The growing language problems that exist in the Island today have led to plans for preserving the Gaelic language. A spokesman said there was concern in Celtic circles about the way in which Norse is becoming dominant at the expense of Gaelic. Norse is now the main language of government and high society, and inter-marriage between Viking settlers and young Celtic women is leading to Gaelic being used less and less in the home. The spokesman said consideration was being given to raising the matter at the first of the new assemblies to be held at St. John's. He said there was a good deal of grievance over the matter and it was felt that some kind of redress should be sought, perhaps by way of a formal petition. On the other hand there are those who are relying on the fact that Celtic mothers bringing up their offspring will continue to use the Gaelic as the natural 'mother' tongue.

SPOILING THE LANDSCAPE

Environmentalists are complaining that many parts of the Island are being spoiled visually by burial mounds. This is because of the practice among influential Viking landowners of being buried not only with their weapons and other personal possessions, but with their longships. The environmentalists claim that a burial mound planned for Knock-e-Dooney in Andreas is going to be at least eight feet above ground level. An even bigger one has appeared at Balladoole in Arbory and it has been the cause of many protests.

MANX TRADE

New trading figures issued by Government officials show that the Island's balance of imports and exports is being maintained satisfactorily. Imports from the Northland now include fish, hides and furs. But these are more than balanced by exports from the Isle of Man of woollen and linen cloths, along with corn, honey and ale. Sales are spreading as far afield as France and Southern Europe and there have been calls for exporters to use a special symbol or logo which would indicate that their goods were from the Isle of Man. In the meantime there is also a developing slave trade in prisoners-of-war.

CROSS PRODUCTION

A Scandinavian sculptor who has settled in the Island is planning to go into the large scale production of stone crosses with religious and other themes. He is Gaut Bjornson from the island of Coll in the Hebrides and some say he learned the craft of stone carving in Cumbria before setting up his workshop at Ballacooley near Kirk Michael. He says he has developed a unique ring-chain pattern which can be incorporated in the crosses and he is experimenting with other interlacing designs to give Manx crosses a distinctive appearance. Bjornson says he hopes to get exclusive rights for the production of crosses in the Island.

NEW FASHIONS

Finally, on a fashion note, it seems that the wide-skirted gown known as the *kyrtl* is going to be what the fashionable ladies of the Island will be wearing for the next hundred years or so. It will be fastened at the waist with a belt and it will be made of woven cloths like silk and satin, in bright colours, especially scarlet and green. For the men, however, there is likely to be little departure from the traditional warm woolly trousers covering the full length of the leg — especially when the east wind blows.

THE ART OF THE MANX CROSSES

There is a growing admiration for the work of Gaut Bjornson these days and his work is in such demand that other sculptors are being employed to copy his distinctive designs for use on grave stones by well-to-do families. His unique and robust carvings represent a wheel-headed cross standing out in low relief on a rectangular slab of local stone. The decoration treatment is based on the Celtic art tradition of interlacing but also applies stylised Scandinavian 'ringchain' which is now a common feature. The sides of these slabs often bear a Norse Runic inscription giving family details. The letters are made up of straight lines etched into the stone. Less common these days are the Gaelic Ogams where each letter is formed by a certain number of strokes cut on the stone on either side of a central line. This form of writing is very ancient, originating in Ireland, and is the earliest form of the Gaelic language. On the latest designs the form of the Christian cross is often accompanied by carvings from Norse mythology, the one-eyed Odin and his ravens being popular. These representations show that the old pagan beliefs linger on though there is increasing evidence to show that the Norse settlers on the Island now seem to have accepted the ways of our Celtic Church.

When the first Viking settlers arrived over a hundred years ago they brought with them strange beliefs and burial rituals — ship burials for chieftains and warriors and coffin burials for others — accompanied by sacrifices and grave goods for the journey to Valhalla, home of Odin. These burials have been the source of much wonder and witnesses have reported the most extraordinary scenes. At Knock-y-Doonee in the north, for example, a warrior's ship was dragged up the beach with great difficulty to the top of a sandy cliff and positioned in a hollow. In the centre of the ship the warrior was laid together with his weapons and fishing gear, hammer and tongs. In the prow was placed the remains of his horse with harness.

At Balladoole in the south there is another ship burial dating back over a hundred years. There was a great outcry at the choice of site at the time as it had always been respected as a place for burials since earliest times; and our Celtic ancestors also used it for burials for many years. Since our turning to the ways of the Christian monks, burials have taken place here with bodies of the departed laid in cists of Pooylvaish marble. Much of the area was desecrated to contain this ship burial. It is reported the Viking chieftain was a great traveller and was buried in full dress with his weapons. To keep him company a young female was sacrificed and placed beside him. Animals also joined them while flints for fire lighting were provided — all to assist the chieftain on his journey to the after-life. Stones were heaped against the ship and the whole area covered with earth and sods to make a great mound.

Fortunately, such practices have now disappeared and it must be gratifying to the monks of St. Patrick's Isle and those of the monastery at Maughold to know that the Northmen have settled in peace and adopted the ways of Christianity. It is now over 500 years since the first missionaries braved the waters of the deep in their frail coracles to bring the message of Christ. Great arguments continue as to where the first monks came from. There are some who claim it was from the Church at Whithorn, not far to the north of us, which had been established by Ninian in 432 A.D. Others claim it was Patrick of Ireland himself. His name is still widely honoured and many of today's keeills and wells are named after him. There are even more stories that

A priest baptises another member in the grounds of the family keeill.

Patrick came himself but these cannot be verified after so many years. Certainly, there were those sent a little later by St. Columba who was both an Irish royal prince and a priest. Because of local disputes he exiled himself to Iona where he was able to live in peace and continue the work of God. His monastery built on the tiny isle was ravaged by the Vikings but it is good to report that it has been rebuilt and is flourishing again. These early missionaries, wherever they came from, must have made a deep impression on our forefathers and they are now highly revered throughout the Island. Many of the keeills bear their names such as German (reputed to have been our first bishop), Lonan, Conchan, Leoc, Brendan, Santan, Cairbrie, Ronan, and, of course, Machud. The keeills are now more solidly built, being made of stone with a doorway and window set in the walls. Along the east wall can be found the altar stone for use by the priest. The keeill which has been built on the Calf of Man has one of the most beautifully carved altar stones ever seen. It depicts in great detail the Crucifixion of Christ. All keeills are positioned near a well for baptisms while a surrounding wall protects the graves from intruding animals. Most family estates now have their own keeill and it is estimated about 200 have been built. The monks and priests are content to live on water and herbs but through their caring ways for the poor and sick they have won the hearts of all and are highly respected.

It was the early monks who suggested the idea of marking the graves of family members by a small stone slab on which was scratched the form of a cross to show they were Christians. The centuries have seen the designs of these crosses flower into an art form of considerable achievement, now being added to by Gaut and his fellow sculptors. It is likely that their work will endure and be admired by many generations to come.

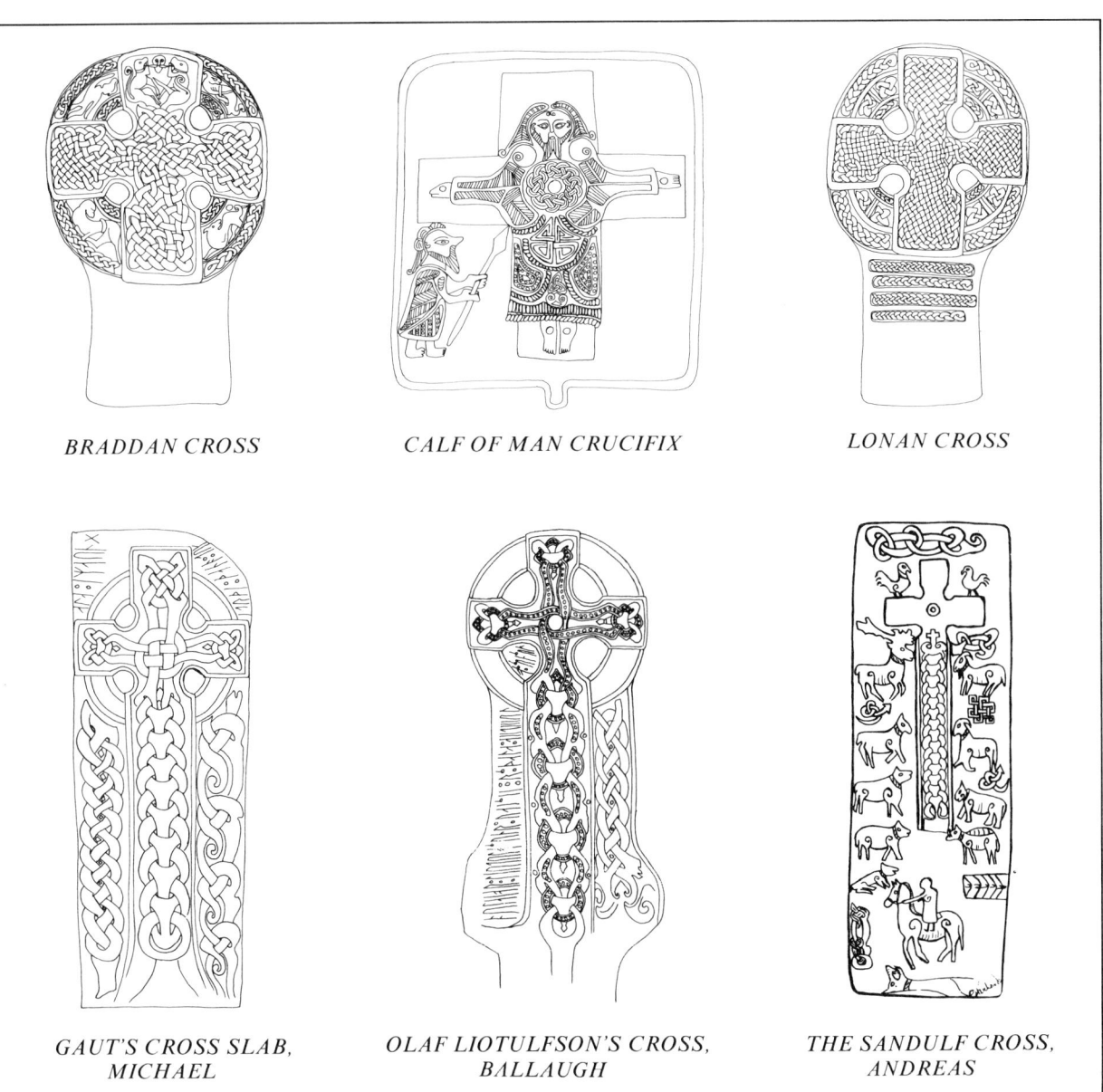

BRADDAN CROSS   *CALF OF MAN CRUCIFIX*   *LONAN CROSS*

GAUT'S CROSS SLAB, MICHAEL   *OLAF LIOTULFSON'S CROSS, BALLAUGH*   *THE SANDULF CROSS, ANDREAS*

GROWING INFLUENCE OF THE NORSE SETTLERS

Further inquiries indicate that there may be some dispute over the site of the proposed open-air assembly. Strong claims are being advanced for sites at Baldalr (Baldwin) and near the small hamlet of Kirk Michael. However, informed opinion has it that St. John's with its important traditions and dry and spacious grassy area will win the day. The ancient mound on the site will also provide a fine vantage point for our rulers.

Precise information about the function of the new body remains hard to obtain. It seems to have a complex mix of legislative and judicial functions and fears have already been expressed that a once a year only meeting will serve only to approve decisions taken by the chiefs rather than as a chance for the freemen to express their opinions. A novel feature to the natives, however, is the idea of 'fencing' the assembly. This means that no trouble or violence is permitted within the confines of the court and so a reasonably peaceful meeting is guaranteed. Interesting also is the important position suggested for the law-givers. It is proposed that all laws should be read out in a language understood by the ordinary people as well as that used by our rulers. This should encourage our Gaelic language group who have been worried about the growing predominance of the Norse tongue. This measure would guarantee the survival of Gaelic in officialese at least, and who knows what the future may bring.

An interesting development for all Manx builders and home owners has been the new style of domestic architecture employed by the Norse. Our traditional round house seems to be ending its day as the new rectangular dwellings gain increasing popularity. The new roof spanning techniques permit a much more straightforward wall construction and the custom of providing benches along the longer sides to act as both seats and beds allows a great increase in comfort. There is a long central hearth but our builders are still wrestling with the problem of smoke-filled rooms.

Of great curiosity, and indeed bewilderment, to the Manx population was the early style of making the long walls of these rectangular buildings slightly curved. It appears that this technique originated in the Norse homelands when, during the winter months, it was the practice to pull the longboats ashore to secure them from the gales. What easier solution was there to overturning them and dropping them over the dwelling house! The boats were secure, the houses better protected and, of course, the walls had to be curved to accommodate the boat! The fine homestead now in operation at the Braaid happily enough contains houses showing both the curved and straight walled constructions.

More and more are finding the new houses attractive, even those ejected from their cliff promontory round dwellings by the new Norse settlers. Sadly, however, most of the new residential sites still find it necessary to build a defensive ditch and an embankment because of the unsettled nature of the times. The Island is likely to be visited by warring Viking factions at any time.

> **THIRD TIME LUCKY FOR GODRED CROVAN**
>
> In 1079 Godred Crovan, son of Harald the Black, returned to the Island, this time to make it his own. Twice he failed but returned a third time having gathered a massive force of ships and men, mostly adventurers from the Hebrides. By night he came to the harbour of Ramsey and hid 300 of his men on the slope of Scacafell (Skyhill). At dawn the Manxmen, both Celts and Norse, formed up in battle order and charged against Godred on the lower ground. The battle raged through the day until dusk descended and Godred, at a signal, called the 300 men from their hiding place at the rear of the Manxmen who began to weaken. With the riverbed at Ramsey filled by the tide they were trapped and began to beg Godred with pitiful cries to spare their lives. Moved with compassion for those with whom he had spent his youth Godred called off his army. He gave his men the choice of dividing the Island among themselves or of plundering the land to enrich themselves. Many chose the latter and returned home. Those who stayed with Godred were granted land in the south of the Island. The northern parts were left to the remainder of the Manxmen though without the right of inheritance. Thus the Island was made the property of King Godred alone and all its dues granted to him. The Gaelic form of Godred is Gorry though he soon became known as King Orry. When he first came to the Island he said he was guided by the stars of the Milky Way. Since then, in Gaelic, the Milky Way has been known as '*Raad Mooar Ree Gorry*' — 'The Great Way of King Orry.'

The changing style of homesteads has been strongly influenced by the Norse settlers. Here our artist shows in detail the more modern type of home now being built in many parts of the Island.

HERE IS THE NEWS : 1229

CATHEDRAL TO BE BUILT ON ST. PATRICK'S ISLE

Stonemasons are moving on to St. Patrick's Isle at Holmtowne today. They are to start work immediately on converting the old and primitive church of Kirk German there into a Cathedral worthy of the newly-created diocese of Sodor and Man. Plans for the new Cathedral were announced by Bishop Symon earlier this year and they indicate the building is to be quite a grandiose construction the like of which has not been seen here before. We have this report:

'The building of the Cathedral will be the next big milestone in the development of the new diocese following on the large part played by King Olaf 1, son of Godred, in cementing the union of Man and the Sudreys — the Southern Isles (Soderenses) of Scotland — before his tragic death in 1153. It was always recognised that a cathedral was needed as a focus for the diocese and the policy decision on building one was taken three months ago at the first Synod, held at Kirk Braddan under the presidency of Bishop Symon. At his palace at Kirk Michael today — which he hopes will become a permanent residence for his successors — he said St. Patrick's Isle was the logical place for it as it is the most sacred site in the Island. He added that it had been decided that the old Kirk German should go in order to make way for the Cathedral, rather than the other church on the islet dedicated to St. Patrick. This is because of its association with St. German, first bishop of the Celtic Church — after whom the Cathedral will be named. Bishop Symon said the other more practical factor that had been taken into account was the large endowment of land that came with it. The Bishop has been in office in the Island for only three years after arriving from Iona and he intends to make the building of St. German's Cathedral his life's work. As a demonstration of his commitment to it he has asked to be buried within the cathedral after his death.'

MORE PIRATE RAIDS

There have been more pirate raids in the south of the Island with much loss of life and destruction of property. The brunt of the attacks has been borne by the followers of the late King Reginald 1, who settled in the south of the Island after their defeat at Tynwald Hill last year by the forces of King Olaf 11, which ended years of civil war. It is thought that Reginald's veterans and their families have been largely wiped out by the pirates. Meanwhile King Olaf is facing problems. Court sources say he is under pressure by the King of England, Henry 111, to provide a strong defence of the Irish Sea area on behalf of the English Crown.

THE TWENTY FOUR SEEK MORE POWER

Leading members of the Twenty-Four are bidding for stronger powers in the government of the Island. They hope to raise the matter at next year's Tynwald assembly at St. John's. In particular they want a new name. As the freeholders traditionally called to advise the King, the so-called 'worthiest men in the land," they want their role to be more clearly defined and they believe a new name will strengthen their public image. One proposal is that they should be called the Keys — as a sign that they are the men who can unlock and declare the meanings of our laws.

MONKS TO WRITE MANX HISTORY.

The monks of Rushen Abbey have been commissioned to write the first history of the Isle of Man. It will be entitled "The Chronicles of Man and the Isles" and will deal specifically with events since the conquest of the Island by Godred Crovan in 1079. Indeed, it is said that it was the great king who suggested the idea originally. It is planned to start this important work soon and it is hoped that it will be handed down from one monk to another in order to maintain continuity.

DECLINE IN MANX ART FORM

Meanwhile there is criticism of Rushen Abbey today for what secular groups in the Island have described as increasing influence over Manx affairs from the Church in Rome. There have been claims that this influence is a direct cause of the death of the only traditional Manx art form, the carving of stone crosses. This is because the Norse runes and the artistic approach in general is being increasingly condemned in Rome as pagan. The cross-carving industry reached its peak, after 600 years of dedicated work and creative endeavour, in the middle of last century.

INCREASING CHURCH AUTHORITY

It is believed in many quarters that the decision to establish the Cathedral of St. German on St. Patrick's Isle is yet another example of the Church's attempt to increase its powers. For centuries the isle has been a political centre organised by our Kings as a military stronghold. The Church it would seem is attempting to reassert its control over this important site.

A more serious matter, however, is concerning the citizens of Holmtowne. The foundations of the new cathedral are disturbing human remains in the ancient burying ground situated in that part of the Isle. Angry townsfolk have already demanded a hearing with Church officials to discuss the problem and Bishop Symon has evinced sympathy with their complaint. Nevertheless, despite the opposition from various quarters, the building is certain to go ahead and the plans that have been released indicate a most impressive structure built largely in the contemporary English style with a substantial south aisle. A particular feature will be the lancet windows of the chancel which will look out across the waters of the bay. There has been a proposal that the west wall should contain a 'leper squint' as is the practice in other parts of Christendom but as the Island remains, fortunately, free of this dread plague no decision on this has so far been announced.

It is interesting to note that when the Island was divided into seventeen parishes in the time of Olaf 1, St. Patrick's Isle was shared between the parishes of St. German and St. Patrick, each with its church built on the Isle. In recent years the church of St. Patrick has been enlarged so will remain untouched with all the attention being given to its near neighbour, St. German's.

Meanwhile, further information about the proposed record of historical events has come to hand. The title will now be 'The Chronicles of the Kings of Man and the Isles'. The previous title omitted the word 'Kings' and it is believed that our ruler objected to the omission. There is no doubt that compilation will be entrusted to a body of monks as they alone have the necessary literary skill and it seems likely that they will be from Rushen Abbey. Measures have already been taken to gather information about past centuries. Obviously the Chronicles will be written in Latin and so the contents will be under the control of the clerics, a matter concerning our political leaders greatly who fear that only events favourable to the Church will be included. A recent discussion at the Abbey indicated that it will be many years before the preliminary work is completed and the work begun, indeed the late 1250's is being put forward as the earliest likely date.

Symon, Bishop of Sodor and Man, who is intent on strengthening the work of the Church and constructing a Cathedral on St. Patrick's Isle.

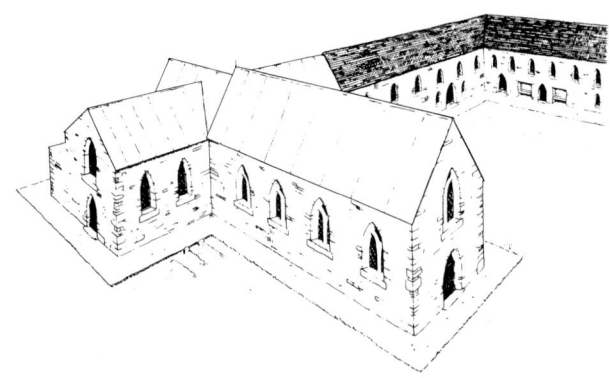

Founded by King Olaf 1 in 1134, the Cistercian Abbey of St. Mary the Virgin in Rushen is now playing an important part in the life of the Island. The Abbot wields considerable spiritual and temporal power, and controls extensive farmlands in various parts of the Island.

KINGS OF MAN AND THE ISLES

Since the Norse colonisation began towards the end of the ninth century local chieftains have fought for supremacy. Some ruled their conquests from Dublin; others from Man itself. Early chroniclers tell of one Macchus (Magnus MacHarold) who paid homage to the English King Edgar ('The Peaceful') and was present when petty kings of the north rowed Edgar on the River Dee at Chester. That was about 973. Then, nearly a century later there was the powerful Sigurd, Earl of Orkney who, followed by his son Jarl Thorfinn, held sway over much of Scotland and the Isles, as well as Man. From that time the Isle of Man became increasingly linked with the Hebrides, the Western Isles of Scotland which, because of their position, were regarded as the 'Southern Isles' by those in authority in Norway. This was the position when Godred Crovan arrived and by his great determination united Man and the Isles under his leadership. He was no stranger to the Island having spent part of his youth here. His return was not at first welcomed and three separate attempts were required by his followers before the Manx Celts and Norse settlers fighting side by side, were finally overcome on the slopes of *Scacafell*. Godred showed compassion and a wish to live in peace. The Chronicles of the Kings of Man and the Isles, now in an advanced state, faithfully record the dynasty founded by Godred Crovan which has survived for nearly two centuries.

GODRED CROVAN (1079–1095) — Son of Harald the Black of Iceland, unites Man and the Isles and spends much time in subduing Dublin. Brings peace and stability and sets up his Tynwald with representatives from the Isles. Rewards his followers with the best lands in the south of the Island. Dies in Islay. Godred leaves three sons — Lagman, Harald and Olaf. Lagman takes the cross of the Crusaders after putting the eyes out of his rebellious brother Harald and dies in Jerusalem. Young Olaf is sent to the court of King Henry I of England during which time there is bitter conflict on the Island with the settlers in the South at war with the Manx in the North. The two sides clashed at Santwat in the west and the Manxmen of the North gained the victory aided by their womenfolk. In 1098 **KING MAGNUS BAREFOOT OF NORWAY** arrives with 160 ships at St. Patrick's Isle determined to claim suzerainty over all Norse conquests. He is killed in battle in Ireland in 1103.

OLAF I (1113–1153) — Olaf returns to the Island and rules for 40 years with much skill and wisdom. Further unites Man and the Isles by creating Roman diocese of *Ecclesia Sodorenses*. Founds Rushen Abbey in 1134 to strengthen work of the Church. In old age is beheaded at Ramsey by one of his nephews from Dublin demanding half his kingdom.

GODRED II (1153–1187) — The son of Olaf is welcomed as King and adds Dublin to his realms but Somerled of Argyll, married to Olaf's illegitimate daughter, seeks to annexe the Isles. They clash in naval battle off Colonsay and Godred is forced to divide the Isles. Further fighting when Somerled appears with his fleet off Ramsey. Godred is forced to leave the Island which is plundered. Godred returns after Somerled's death. He dies at his residence on St. Patrick's Isle and is buried on Iona, made holy by Columba. He left three sons — Reginald, Olaf and Ivar.

REGINALD I (1187–1228) — Born out of wedlock but accepted as King as his half brother Olaf was too young. Reginald was 'a warlike prince who roamed the seas for three years.' Forced to pay homage to King John of England who had inherited the title 'Lord of Ireland.' Olaf, exiled to the Outer Isles, seeks to gain his inheritance with support of the North while the South supports Reginald. At a battle at Tynwald Hill Reginald is killed and his followers routed.

OLAF II (1228–1237) — Now in control of Man but not of all the Isles. Helped by Norway, but promises Henry III of England to defend the Irish Sea against all intruders. Olaf brings Symon from Iona to be bishop of Sodor and Man.

HARALD I (1237–1248) — Son of Olaf II is embroiled in rivalry between Norway and England. Is knighted by Henry III but then marries King Haakon of Norway's daughter. On the return journey is shipwrecked and drowned with his queen near the Shetlands. Is succeeded by his brother **REGINALD II** whose reign lasts but a few weeks, being killed by the knight Ivar and his followers in a meadow near the church of the Holy Trinity, Rushen.

MAGNUS I (1252–1265) — After years of confusion Magnus, youngest son of Olaf gains the Manx throne. Alexander III of Scotland is now a growing force and defeats Haakon of Norway at Largs in 1263. Magnus returns with his fleet hotly pursued by Alexander. A truce made and Magnus retains Man and all the Western Isles. Magnus, last of the dynasty of Godred Crovan, dies in 1265 and is buried at Rushen Abbey. *(Chronica Regum Manniae et Insularum)*

OUR VIKING LEGACY

For some four hundred years the Norsemen and their kings have governed our Island and those few centuries have seen many good times and also many bad times. But what will our descendants many years in the future see as the achievements of our Norsemen, what will they see as their legacy to Man? Their religion? Hardly. We brought them from paganism to Christianity. Still, their Christian crosses, designed at first perhaps under Celtic influence, do mark an artistic achievement without parallel as we know it. Their language? Never! Here too, our Celtic forefathers absorbed and converted them. Our language remained Gaelic but yet there are a few place names scattered about the Island which could well survive for centuries to come as a permanent reminder of the Norse presence. Their farms, their fishing? Not really. Their farming techniques were never revolutionary; their boats were, but now they have been universally copied and developed further. Perhaps, though, Viking blood will in future generations make Manxmen successful fishermen and adventurous seafarers and traders.

But what about our Government? Ah, here at last something can be seen as not only a Norse achievement but a political system that has operated so fairly and successfully that it could well endure for many centuries to come. There is at the top our Tynwald, our annual open-air assembly, to which we all may go and at which our laws must be read out so that all may hear and know them. We can even make our approval or disapproval known, whether our King or Lord likes it or not. There is our House of Keys, our 24 freemen, eight originally from the Sudreys, who share in the government, who can pronounce on law and, perhaps, in the future will even make the law for us all. There is the Lagman who discharges the law one for the Northside and one for the Southside. Then there are our Sheadings, each a 'sixth part' of the Island, that could many centuries hence form our political divisions and parishes. Future generations may well see the political achievements of our Vikings as their main legacy. But, perhaps even more important is the fusion of Celtic and Viking blood which will prove to be the genesis of the Manx as a nation and which may well be seen as the true and lasting legacy of the Norsemen. Only time will tell.

Map showing the six sheadings of Norse administration. Each sheading sends four freemen, or Keys, to the annual Tynwald Assembly. Also shown are the 17 parishes formed from the sheadings for church administration.

SOME VIKING PLACE NAMES AND FAMILY NAMES

Norse 'stadir' meaning 'farm' as in
Ottarstadr (Aust) — Ottar's farm
Also Braust, Leodest, Clypse and Gretch

Kollabyr (Colby) — Kolli's farm
Vardu Fjall (Barrule) — ward fell
Crokaness (Cregneash) — crooked ness
Crossbyr (Crosby) farm of the cross roads
Dalbyr (Dalby) — Dale Farm
Forsdale (Foxdale) — valley of waterfall
Gjarvik (Garwick) — cave creek
Gnipa (Greeba) — a peak
Grenvik (Grenaugh) — the green creek
Ingabreka (Injebreck) — end slope
Langness — long headland
Ramsa (Ramsey) — wild garlic river

Laxa (Laxey) — salmon river
Swart-fell (Sartfell) — dark hill
Skarfakluft (Scarlett) — cormorant's ledge
Snaefjall (Snaefell) — snow mountain
Kirkja (Kirby) — church farm
Kalfr (Calf)
Ragnalsvad (Ronaldsway)
Kverna dalr (Cornaa) Mill Dale

Examples of family names now established are as follows:

Asmundr (Casement); Asketill (Castell); MacOttar (Cottier); Thorketill (Corkill); Thorliotr (Corlett); Olafr (Cowley); Rognvaldr (Crennell) and Thorstein (Costain).

HERE IS THE NEWS : 1313

CASTLE RUSHEN SURRENDERS

The garrison of Castle Rushen surrendered early today after a long and heroic defence against the invading forces of Lord Robert Bruce, King of Scotland. It is a significant victory for the Scottish crown in its continuing struggle with England for outright control of the Isle of Man. We have just received this report from Castletown.

'There is much activity about Castle Rushen and from where I'm standing it is quite obvious that this once powerful fortress, which dates back to Norse rule in the Island, has suffered damage. The final capitulation came suddenly when the defenders, under the command of Lord Dougal Mac Dowyl, could resist no longer. They had put up a spirited resistance during the four week seige. Their long period of hardship had left them no match for the superior numbers of well supplied men, indeed additional supplies had been brought in following a raid on Ireland. This ended a brilliant and rapid campaign by Robert Bruce. It was on May the 18th that his battle fleet anchored in Ramsey Bay and his army was landed. The following Sunday he made a forced march south, pausing only for a night's stay at the monastery just outside the settlement at Douglas and began his investment of Castle Rushen the following day. As this is the main defence complex in the Island his dramatic victory this morning gives him strategic control of the Isle of Man. Bruce's victory is being compared with the comprehensive defeat of the Manx forces at the Battle of Ronaldsway, 38 years ago, when the army of King Alexander III of Scotland landed from the sea on St. Michael's Island. In the pitched battle that followed the Manx were put to flight and Godred, son of Magnus and the last of the male line of Godred Crovan, was among the slain. It is not certain however how today's developments will be received in London by King Edward II.'

The latest news we have from Castletown is that the Scottish forces seem bent on using the castle's defences for their own purposes. These were mainly constructed in the 13th century during the reign of the last of the Norse kings, King Magnus, who died there in 1265. A big question now is who Robert Bruce will appoint to rule the Isle of Man on his behalf. One of his leading commanders has been Thomas Randolf, Earl of Moray, and it is thought he might get the Lordship — and the right to bear the Three Legs of Man.

THREE LEGS SYMBOL MUCH IN EVIDENCE

When King Alexander III of Scotland gained suzerainty over the Island at the end of the Norse period of rule, he adopted the Three Legs as a symbol to represent the Island. It is now widely used and replaces the Viking ship symbol used by the Norse rulers. This most ancient of devices is of Greek origin and is a variant of the four-legged symbol representing the sun. The Three Legs was adopted by Sicily because of its triangular shape and it is thought it came to the notice of King Alexander through his son-in-law, Edmund, who was King of Sicily. The Three Legs is not unlike another symbol based on the triquetra or triple knot once used on coins issued by the King of Dublin as far back as the tenth century.

ISLAND IN DESOLATE STATE

The economic recession in the Isle of Man continues, according to a new survey. And the reason is still the political instability arising from the struggle for civil control of the Island between England and Scotland. This has been going on since 1266. Continuous fighting for the Lordship of Man has left the Manx people impoverished and the land desolate. The latest economic forecast is that the recession will not bottom out this century and that only a long-term settlement of who has the reins of civil power will end it.

BISHOP TO EXTEND TITHES

The Diocese of Sodor and Man has announced that the tithes introduced by Bishop Mark in 1291 are to be extended to include merchants and craftsmen in the Island, instead of the main burden being shouldered by the farmers. A Diocesan official said in some cases the tithe on grain has been avoided by farmers and as this is the most important crop in the Island, action is being taken to stop what is an illegal practice. Farmers are being forbidden to stack any corn without due notice being given to the Proctor.

CHURCH TO TAX FIREPLACES

There is also a new tax being imposed in the Island and this is causing strong protests among householders. The Bishop has decreed that the owner of every house with a fireplace must pay to the Diocese one penny a year. It is already being called "The Smoke Penny" and representatives of home owners throughout the Island have lodged official protests with the Bishop. But he has told them he has no intention of removing the tax for the immediate future — and beyond that.

BID TO BAN SCOTS

Finally, calls for a new law to be promulgated at the Tynwald assembly at St. John's, under which Scotsmen found in the Island might be killed on sight, appear to have been withdrawn. A spokesman for the Twenty-four, or the Keys as they are now known, said it had been thought that this would give Manx people a legal right to self-defence against marauding Scots. But he said the victory of Robert Bruce at Castletown this morning meant that the matter will have to be shelved to await further events.

A CENTURY OF TURMOIL

As we approach the end of another century, the fourteenth in the year of Our Lord, we are still at the mercy of men who, while claiming all the rights of lords and kings, have done little to protect us from the gangs of marauders who come to our shores from Scotland, Ireland and even France. No one has been able to stop them and we seem to have sunk into an age of strife which has followed the golden rule of our Norse kings. Scottish domination was never accepted after the death of Magnus in 1265 and the control of King Alexander III of Scotland led to rebellion. It was necessary for him to send a strong force under John de Vesci and at the Battle of St. Michael's Isle, near the landing place at Ronaldsway, we finally succumbed after 537 of our menfolk were slain. A brief spell of peace followed but the death of Alexander led to a bloody power struggle within Scotland. King Edward I of England took notice of the events beyond his northern border and made it clear that he regarded the 'defenceless and desolate' Isle of Man as an English possession. When the crown of Scotland was finally secured by John Balliol he refused to pay homage to Edward. More warfare followed with Balliol being dethroned and the Island coming into English hands. Anthony Bek, Bishop of Durham and strong ally of King Edward was granted the Island for his own use. He was the first of a long line of rulers who have controlled the Island through this unhappy century.

Arms of Anthony Bek

ANTHONY BEK (1298–1311) — Ambitious and warlike Bishop of Durham, Crusader and defender of the Border lands against the Scots. Quarrelled with Edward I but favourite of Edward II. Never visited the Isle of Man but a seneschal was appointed to receive the Lord's dues.

PIERS GALVESTON (1311–1312) — Infamous boyhood friend of Edward II. Courageous knight but his arrogance brought him universal hatred. Beheaded by Earl of Warwick.

Arms of Thomas Randolph

THOMAS RANDOLPH (1313–1333) — Lord Robert Bruce came in person to claim the Island and captured the stronghold of Castle Rushen in 1313. At the end of that year he granted the Island to Thomas Randolph, Earl of Moray. This was a most wretched period as a succession of Scots and English appeared, though neither stayed long. In 1316 Irish freebooters under Richard de Mandeville landed at Ronaldsway with a large fleet. They put ashore troops, battle standards and large siege equipment. They sent envoys to meet with Tynwald representatives, asking for land, victuals and money. These they were refused and the Irish prepared for battle. They met the Manxmen on the slopes of Barrule and the local forces were put to flight with a large number killed or wounded. The Irish plundered the land of all its valuables and then came to Rushen Abbey, taking all its furniture, cattle and sheep, leaving nothing at all. After a month they loaded their ships and returned home.

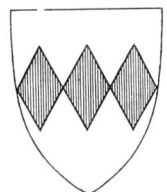

Arms of William de Montecute I

WILLIAM DE MONTECUTE I (1333–1344) — Following Edward III's success over Scotland he reclaimed suzerainty over the Isle of Man which he granted as a kingdom to William de Montecute his ally and later Earl of Salisbury. William drove the reluctant Scots out though they were to return on many a raid, often being bought off to save destruction. Castle Rushen was restored and the keep raised and an outer wall begun.

Arms of William de Montecute II

WILLIAM DE MONTECUTE II (1344–1397) — Companion of the Black Prince. Fought at Crecy and spent much time in France. Did little to defend the Island and Scots continued their raids. The French also attacked but avoided Castle Rushen. The Island was largely governed by an able Manxman, Bishop Donkin. On the death of his son, William sells the crown and rights to Sir William le Scroop.

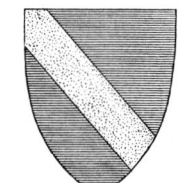

Arms of Henry Percy

WILLIAM LE SCROOP (1397–1399) — Powerful official of Richard II and created Earl of Wiltshire. Entrusted with the imprisonment of the Earl of Warwick who was later removed to the Tower of London. Le Scroop restored St. German's Cathedral and, with Papal permission, built the castle to defend St. Patrick's Isle. Following the defeat of the disliked Richard II Henry Bolingbroke became Henry IV and took possession of the Island following Le Scroop's condemnation for high treason.

Arms of William le Scroop

HENRY PERCY (1399–1405) — The Earl of Northumberland was granted the Island as part of a rich reward for defending the Border lands against Scottish incursions. But Percy was not satisfied and led revolts against the King. Henry IV sent the brothers Sir John Stanley and Sir William Stanley to seize the Island and hold it in his name.

BUILDING CASTLES

Manxmen and women are sleeping more soundly in their beds these days for the first time in many generations. At last our defences seem secure, our places of refuge safe. In the west our compatriots have seen the great new Peele built on Patrick's Holm at Holmtowne. The huge timbers that demanded scores of men to manage them are now formed into an awe-inspiring palisade that even the hardiest foe would be loathe to tackle. These timbers surmounting the rocky cliffs protect the timber-framed buildings inside and such is the space on St. Patrick's Isle, such indeed the more than adequate water supply from the numerous wells, that there can be few more comfortable havens around the coasts of the Irish Sea. The only hazard that can be foreseen is attack by fire and already our master masons have begun building out of sandstone, under the direction of our Lord William le Scroop. A new castle, licensed by the Pope, is being built on the site of the old Gatehouse and will command the vulnerable side of Inis Patrick and make a secure entrance. For some considerable time now small boats have been seen scurrying across the bay from the quarries at Creg Malin at high tide and dumping their dressed stone overboard as near to the castle as they can reach. No doubt other stone towers will soon be built around the perimeter of the isle to strengthen its defences even further.

At the same time William le Scroop has undertaken to repair and alter the Cathedral begun by Bishop Symon. The south aisle is to be demolished and the openings of the Arcade built up with a window in each. The central tower is to be heightened and provided with a parapet. Likewise the transepts, with a new stair turret provided in the south transept. Soldiers will only be able to gain access through the sacred precincts of the Cathedral.

Meanwhile, in the South of the Island, the massive walls of a strength and height that we have never seen before are rising at the mouth of the river at Rushen. The masons, carpenters, quarrymen, carters, and scaffolders have turned the place into a busy hive of activity, a hubbub of noise and endeavour. Some, it must be admitted, are more than a little reluctant to give their day's work to their Lord. The old castle originally built on that site by our Viking Kings when they moved from Peel was, as some may still recall, taken by the great warrior Robert the Bruce when he attacked the Island at the beginning of this century in 1313. Some forty years later the mighty keep, long a landmark, rose higher as both a refuge, a home for the de Montecutes and, for those of us fortunate to walk the topmost battlements, a place to view and perhaps subdue the surrounding countryside and its rich farmlands. Now we can see the extensions being built to this powerful place. The marvellous new curtain wall, the ditch and the embankment will surely make our Castle Rushen the most powerful of fortifications. The Castle, with its huddle of houses around its wall, is likely to remain the centre of Manx political life for many centuries to come.

And yet travellers to our Island bring tales of destruction caused by the use of gunpowder and guns that will cause great explosions which propel objects of stone and iron over great distances. Some say that these inventions will mean the end of castles as impregnable fortresses. Perhaps, after all, the craftsmen toiling over their huge blocks of limestone on the scaffolding around Castle Rushen are toiling in vain. Only time will tell.

William de Montecute, King of Man and first Earl of Salisbury, and his son William de Montecute II, have done much to improve the defences of Castle Rushen.

Whilst work is in progress on constructing a castle for the defence of Patrick's Holm, the Cathedral of St. German is also being repaired and altered. The illustration shows how the south aisle has been removed and the openings of the Arcade built up with a window placed in each. The central tower has been heightened and provided with a parapet. The transepts have also been heightened and a stair turret provided in the south transept.

THE POWER OF THE CHURCH

Grumbling and the use of choice language is much in evidence in hamlets and crofts throughout the Island these days. The subject of complaint is the ever increasing demands of our church leaders which place a heavy burden on families struggling to keep body and soul together. Having to part with a tenth share of everything they produce brings considerable hardship, especially in times of plague and famine. Conditions are wretched enough without having to pay a high price for the ministrations of the parish clergy and their masters. The traditional payment of tithes dates back to Norse times and the generous grants of land form the basis of the Church's power which these days seems to be growing annually, bishop and abbot becoming increasingly influential as they rule their baronies and exact their dues from the general populace. And behind them is the power of the Popes who are constantly striving to exert their authority over Christendom.

It was Bishop Symon who first regularised the position of the Church at a diocesan synod held in Kirk Braddan church in 1229. Here the laws of the Manx Church were written down for the first time and rigorously applied. (It seems strange no such attempt has been made to record the ancient laws of Tynwald which are still administered as 'breast law'.) The zealot Bishop Mark at another Synod in 1291, also held at Braddan, introduced fresh tithes which he also applied to merchants and craftsmen. Caught up in the attempts of Edward I of England to curb the power of Rome it will be remembered Bishop Mark was expelled from the Island in 1299. The fury of the Pope resulted in the Island being placed under an interdict which lasted for three years. It was a dreadful punishment and all church services ceased. The return of Bishop Mark in 1302 saw the introduction of a tax of one penny a year on every homestead with a fireplace. It was the Bishop's way of stamping his authority over the diocese and the hated 'smoke tax' is still with us.

Tithes at present are paid to the church to cover grain, beer, animals, geese, poultry, eggs, butter, cheese and fish. The collection of these dues is the responsibility of the parson or his agent called the proctor, while the Bishop has his own sumner for enforcing payment. Grain is by far the most important crop and the farmer cannot stack his corn without notice to the proctor. Failing to do this results in the sumner and two neighbours calling with authority to pull the stack down and take a tenth part. Certain tithes such as butter, cheese and eggs have to be brought to the church on Sunday and presented at the altar. Sacrament can be refused in cases of non-payment of the full tithe. More serious offences were dealt with by the church courts, the Vicars-general having the right to commit offenders to the crypt of St. German's cathedral as the ultimate punishment.

Of all the tithes paid nearly half goes to the Bishop who holds the chief power. Of the rest half goes to the religious houses, chief of which is Rushen Abbey. The remainder is divided among the parish clergy. Rushen Abbey now controls scores of farms, mills and cottages mainly in its lands in Lezayre, Michael, German, Onchan and Lonan. The Abbey has also been granted all mining rights and the Abbot rules his lands through his own courts and has the power of life and limb. No one denies the benefits brought by the monks and much has been learned in agriculture and animal husbandry, particularly with sheep. The trackways to the Abbey lands have been much improved for the packhorses who can now cross the river at Rushen by a new bridge recently built by the monks. The Abbey is our only centre of learning and the monks give free instruction to the children and administer to the poor and sick. Their knowledge of herbs is of great benefit.

It will be recalled that Abbot William Russell, a Manxman, was elected by the clergy as the Island's bishop and he resided at Kirk Michael from 1348 to 1374. He was consecrated by the Pope at Avignon thus ending the ancient practice of Manx bishops being consecrated by the Archbishop of Trondheim in Norway. He proved to be one of the ablest of bishops and at the Synod held at Michael in 1350 he issued further instructions to the clergy regularising the preaching of God's word, the instruction of children and the administering of the Sacrament on Sundays and Holy Days. Just before his death he acquired a site in the parish of Arbory for the newly arrived Franciscan Friars to set up an oratory.

Bishop Russell was succeeded in 1374 by John Donkan, another Manxman. He, too, was consecrated by the exiled Pope at Avignon. On his way home he was caught up in the skirmishes between the English and French and was imprisoned in Picardy for two years, only being released on payment of a ransom. He seems to have got himself into trouble with the Pope, after complaining about the greed and aggression being exercised by the Church. He will be remembered as the last effective Bishop of Sodor and Man. At his death the clergy of Iona elected a bishop for the Western Isles only though the full title of our own bishop is likely to be retained. However, the plight we are in today is symptomatic of the power of the church far exceeding the governorship of our absent rulers. When will this cease? Not until someone will come and take direct control at Castle Rushen and give us firm and fair rule whilst keeping the ambitions of the ecclesiastics in check. It is our fervent hope that this will come about as we enter a new century.

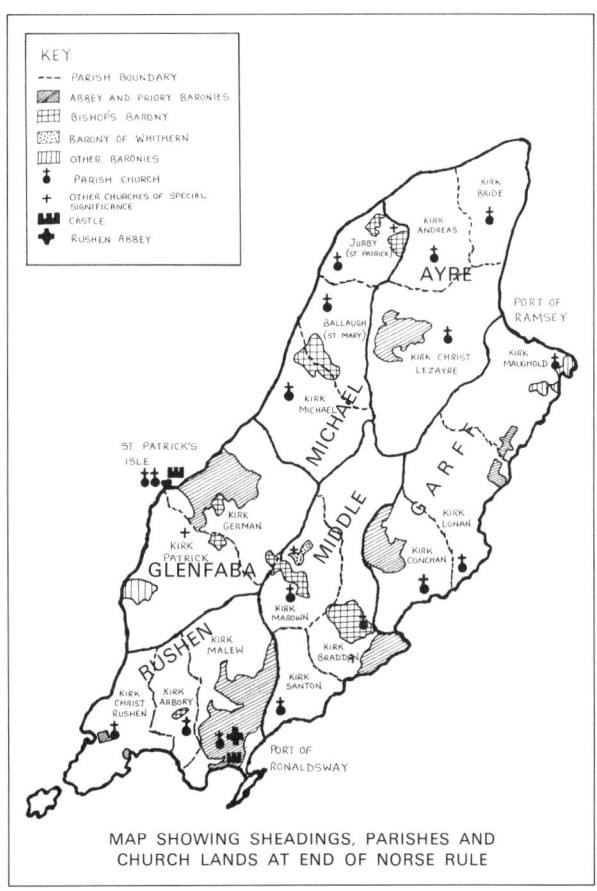

MAP SHOWING SHEADINGS, PARISHES AND CHURCH LANDS AT END OF NORSE RULE

HERE IS THE NEWS : 1405

NEW LORD OF MAN APPOINTED

The court of King Henry IV in London today announced the appointment of a new Lord of Man to take effect later this year. He is 55 year old Sir John Stanley, head of an English noble family with extensive lands and estates in Staffordshire. We have this report:

'Little is known in the Island about Sir John. But he is understood to have rendered sterling service to the Crown of England, serving in Aquitaine and in Ireland over the last 20 years and also on the Welsh and Scottish borders. The appointment will consolidate English control over Manx affairs, now that the Scots have conceded final defeat. But the Lordship of Man is no sinecure. William le Scroop, Earl of Wiltshire, who held office from 1392 was beheaded by order of King Henry on the latter's accession six years ago. His successor was the Earl of Northumberland, who was displaced last year on being accused of high treason. Sir John Stanley, however, appears to have the King's full confidence. The gift of the Island has been made to him on the simple condition that he does homage and gives two falcons to succeeding Kings of England at their Coronations. Sir John is unlikely to visit the Island during his reign and he will appoint a Governor, or Captain, to represent him. A spokesman for the Keys said it was hoped that stabilisation of civil control will enable the State to get back some of the immense power now held by the Church in the Island. He said the power of the ecclesiastical barons like the Bishop of Sodor and Man and the Abbot of Rushen, was too great and allowed the Pope clear domination of the Island. It is expected Sir John will consider having Manx laws written down in future, instead of the Deemsters and Keys having to administer them from memory. It is the fact that the Church has had its laws in writing since Bishop Symon's synod at Kirk Braddan in 1229 that has given the Church ascendancy over the State for so long'.

BETTER JUSTICE DEMANDED

In the meantime social reform groups in the Island are calling for a major overhaul of the administration of justice. They want alleged offenders and wrong-doers to be called for trial in future by what is described as 'God and the country.' In practical terms this means trial by a jury. The reform groups say the time for abolishing trial by ordeal and combat, which has been in existence since Viking times, is long overdue.

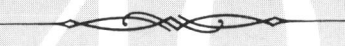

CORN IMPORTS

There have been further shipments of corn into the Isle of Man from Ireland. This is the fifth year the shipments have had to be made in order to combat the starvation resulting from the continuing recession in the Manx economy. A Treasury report says the base of the economy needs to be broadened considerably. Too many Manx people's efforts are concentrated in the farming, fishing and labouring sectors and diversification into new areas of endeavour is badly needed.

FRIARS TO DEPART?

The oratory established by Franciscan friars in the south of the Island 32 years ago appears to have closed down. The buildings they occupied at the village of St. Columba in Arbory are now deserted. Some of them have been taken over and incorporated into the smallholding that is to be known as the Friary Farm at Ballabeg. Some of the friars are understood to be still on the Island but for how long is not known. The Franciscans are known as Grey Friars — or Begging Friars because of the non-ownership of property — and they set up their main oratory, for 12 brethren, in 1373. It is thought that they hoped to rival in influence the Cistercian monks at Rushen Abbey.

COMPULSORY MILITARY SERVICE

Officers and men from Lancashire, North Wales and other of the Stanley strongholds have been brought to the Island to strengthen the defences of Castle Rushen. At the same time it has been announced that compulsory military service is to be reinstated in the Island. All men aged 20 to 26 will have to train as militiamen under the Parish Captains. They will also have to kit themselves out with bows and arrows, sword and buckler at their own expense.

SCOTS TO BE EXPELLED

Finally, a new law is to be drafted to counter any further Scots attempts at infiltration of the Island. Under this all Scotsmen on Manx soil will be obliged to take the next boat home to Scotland, on pain of forfeiture of their goods, along with a period of imprisonment. Before the English Crown gained its present supremacy over the Scots following the long struggle for control of the Island, it had been suggested that Scotsmen should be shot on sight. But the Deemsters have ruled against this.

THE STRENGTH OF THE STANLEYS

The news of the granting of the Island by Henry IV to Sir John Stanley was received with the usual mutterings about absentee rulers. Sir John belonged to one of the most important and powerful families in England with huge estates in Staffordshire. He married the heiress to the Lathom estates at Knowsley, Liverpool. There were many ribald comments when his fifteen year old son, also called John, arrived at Castle Rushen but he soon showed he meant business. He summoned all the worthiest men and commons before him and proceeded to proclaim his father king and demanded homage from all. This proved to be the resurrection of Tynwald which had rarely assembled since Norse times. Castle Rushen and Peel Castle were re-garrisoned and a Captain and officials from Lancashire installed to administer the Island in the best interests of the Lord.

Following the death of his father in 1414 Sir John returned to the Isle of Man three years later as King John II. He reasserted his position following much dissatisfaction among the settled Manx. There were those who were accused of treason and condemned to death unless they submitted to the Lord's rule. His most important visit to the Island came in 1429 when he summoned the two Lagman (Lawmen or Deemsters) and the faithful 24 Keys to a meeting of the Tynwald Court at Castle Rushen. They listened as he introduced new statutes which replaced trial by combat with trial by jury; protected property against unlawful confiscation; held every man responsible for his wife's debts and introduced fixed weights and measures. Additionally, and for the first time ever, Sir John decreed that all the law as exercised by the Lagman, should be set down in writing so that the ancient 'breast law' be replaced by a strict legal code. Turning his attention to the excesses of the Church barons he forbade them to give sanctuary to offenders and he wanted proof of all their rights to lands and holdings. The bishop and abbot were required to pay homage to the King, but Furness, St. Bees and Whithorn were not present and were called to appear within 40 days or to forfeit their lands.

Three quarters of a century passed before the visit of another Stanley, the Island being left in charge of a succession of responsible Governors who ensured that the Lord's privileges and revenues were not neglected. The Lord of Man has rights to the choicest game and fish while each quarterland division has to supply large quantities of free beeves, corn and fish for the castle garrisons. Thus the farmers, their labourers, fishermen, and artisans have had to bear a heavy burden in return for stern administration and protection. Military service was introduced for all men between 20 and 26 who trained as militiamen under the captains of the parishes. There was much expenditure on the castles as well, with a huge curtain wall surrounding Peel Castle.

In 1485 the Stanleys were promoted to Earls and took their name from their Derby estates in Lancashire where they are now the paramount family. The second Earl Derby (1504-1521) gave up the title of King in favour of Lord of Man preferring, as he said, 'to be a great Lord rather than a petty King'. The Earl arrived at Castle Rushen in 1507 following a show of force off the Scottish coast in the wake of more raids from that quarter. During his visit he decreed that the Island's main landing place should be called Derbyhaven rather than Ronaldsway.

The third Earl (1521-1572) responded to certain grievances concerning the church and he abolished the tithes on ale and marriage presents, while reducing the death dues. Earl Edward was a devout Roman Catholic but he carried out the orders of King Henry VIII and supervised the dissolution of Rushen Abbey, Bemaken

The Arms of the House of Stanley, including the Eagle and Child. When Sir Thomas Lathom and his Lady were out walking they came to a wild part where it was known an eagle had her nest. On hearing the cries of a young child, seemingly from the nest, they sent for their servants to investigate. They reported that a young male child, dressed in rich swaddling clothes, was indeed in the nest. Being childless, Lord and Lady Lathom regarded the child as a gift from heaven and cared for the child as their own. He grew up and eventually came into possession of the wealthy Lathom estate and left an only daughter, Isabel. She became the wife of Sir John Stanley who adopted the Eagle and Child as his crest which is still in use by the Earls of Derby today.

Friary and St. Bridget's Nunnery. Protestanism was slowly accepted with little disorder within the seventeen parishes though the clergy are still not free to marry as in England. The third Earl again strengthened the Island's defences building a series of gun forts at Peel, Ramsey, Douglas and Derbyhaven. At Castle Rushen a sloping stone bank, or glacis, has been built as a protection against cannon fire.

Following the sudden death of the young fifth Earl in 1594 there has been much dispute with the family as regards his successor. Queen Elizabeth has seen fit to take control of the Island because of its important position and has shown much interest in its well being. Her gift of a clock to Castle Rushen, although within the walls and not seen by the public, has been a source of much wonder to the townsfolk who can hear the regular striking of its bell. Since the death of Good Queen Bess, King James has reinstated the Stanleys as rulers with William, sixth Earl of Derby and his Countess jointly in control. The Earl has shown little interest and has recently resigned his responsibilities to the Countess Elizabeth who has taken up residence in the Castle. Occasionally she is visited by her young son, Lord Strange, who is being educated at Lathom House.

Lord Thomas Stanley, First Earl of Derby. Present at the Battle of Bosworth in 1485 and the defeat of King Richard III, Sir Thomas retrieved Richard's crown from a hawthorn bush and placed it on the head of his stepson Henry Tudor and hailed him as King Henry VII. Later that year Sir Thomas was created Earl of Derby, making the Stanley family one of the most important in England.

HERE IS THE NEWS : 1620

MANXMAN LEADS EXPEDITION TO AMERICA

A group of Calvinist religious dissenters who set out from England three months ago in search of a new life in the Americas have made a safe landfall in what is known as New England. In military command of the expedition aboard the sailing ship 'Mayflower' was soldier/adventurer of Manx connections, Captain Myles Standish, whose leadership is being credited with ensuring a successful voyage. We have this report:

'Captain Standish, who is 36, belongs to an ancient Lancashire family which has had a branch at Ellanbane in Lezayre for many years. He was accompanied on the voyage by his wife Rose. She is actually his cousin and they married in the Island two years ago. Her sister is Miss Barbara Standish and they are the daughters of Mr. John Standish, a member of the House of Keys. Captain Standish himself spent his youth in the Island and was educated at Castletown Grammar School. He left the family home 19 years ago to take up a military career. Captain and Mrs. Standish do not follow the Puritan faith of the Calvinists who hope to establish the first successful English colony in the Americas. It was while he was campaigning in the Low Countries during the war against Spain that he became acquainted with Puritan refugees from England and this resulted in his commission to take military command of the 'Mayflower,' which set sail in the autumn. Large numbers of Puritans have been fleeing the country because they say being forced to worship in the Anglican way is religious persecution. The Mayflower made landfall after a journey in which the women and children who accompanied their menfolk suffered considerable hardship and privation, worsened by the Atlantic storms. Even now their troubles are far from over. New England is an inhospitable place and the settlers face a long, hard struggle for survival. But a spokesman for the Standish family in the Isle of Man said today they were delighted to be represented on what would be regarded as an historic voyage by future generations in both England and the Americas'.

CAPTAIN EDWARD CHRISTIAN

A Manxman who is carving out a distinguished career for himself at sea has just been appointed commander of the 34 gun English frigate 'Bonaventure'. He is Captain Edward Christian, second son of the Reverend John Christian, Vicar of Maughold, who left the Island originally to sail as Master with the East India Company. Last year he became a courtier in the Duke of Buckingham's suite at the English Court. It is this position which has led to his latest preferment. Captain Christian has always made it known that he intends to settle in the Isle of Man eventually.

RUSHEN CASTLE CLOCK

Clockmakers from London have been brought to the Island to examine the great clock of Castle Rushen, that was a royal gift from the late Queen Elizabeth. There have been claims that it has not been keeping good time since it was installed shortly before her death 16 years ago. The clock commemorates the decision of the late Queen to assume control over Manx affairs in 1594 because of a dispute in the Derby family over succession to the Lordship of Man. Derby rule in the Island has now been restored for nearly 10 years and a spokesman for the Lord said everything would be done to maintain the clock in good condition in memory of Queen Elizabeth's reign.

PRAYER BOOK IN MANX

A new attempt is to be made shortly to get the Manx translation of the Book of Common Prayer published and finally made available to the people of the Island. It will be the first book to be printed in the Manx language. The translation was completed nine years ago by Bishop John Phillips, a Welshman whose spelling of the Manx has raised a few eyebrows of local linguists. Since completion there have been difficulties in finding a publisher. One of the problems has been that it is not regarded as an economic proposition to publish a book of substantial size which will have a very limited circulation.

MANX CLERGY AND MARRIAGE

It has been announced by the Diocese of Sodor and Man that increasing numbers of Manx clergy are now seeking permission to marry. This privilege has been available to them for the last 10 years and it is a direct result of what is being referred to as the Reformation, the controversial decision of the late King Henry the Eighth to break with the Church of Rome and proclaim himself head of the Church of England in 1534. This was followed 15 years later by the introduction of the right of clergy in England to marry. But it was some time before the reform, like so many others, was extended to the Isle of Man.

LIVING STANDARDS IMPROVING

Finally, it seems that living standards for working class people in the Island are rising. Tynwald Court has been responsible for the regulation of wages for the last decade, and wage rates have risen considerably since then. Artisans can now expect to be paid at least fourpence a day, with meat and drink included. Masons and blacksmiths are getting as much as sixpence a day. But there are claims that common labourers have not been doing quite so well. They are still getting only twopence a day — and that is without meat and drink.

THE ILLUSTRATIONS OF DANIEL KING

It is good to know that the artist Daniel King (a pupil of W. Hollar, a leading English illustrator) has visited the Isle of Man recently and completed a series of drawings which form the first pictorial record of important buildings and places. Two of his collection are reproduced below depicting Castle Rushen and the settlement around Douglas harbour. Others will appear in later pages. (Manx National Heritage)

Castlerushen as it appeares on the south east side. A The Counter-Scarpe. B The Round towre on the Counter Scarpe. C The wall of ye Castle. D The houses of ye town. E The wall about the Castle.

The Landskipp of Douglas Towne as it doth appeare from ye west. A The Towne. B The Chappell. C The Sand D The Sea that ebbes & floes. E The Rocks & Mountaine that goes to the Beacon. F The Bridge yt comes from the Nunnerie. G The Sand that they passe over. H The hill yt is on the west side of the towne.

HERE IS THE NEWS : 1651

EARL OF DERBY EXECUTED

The Lord of Man, James, Seventh Earl of Derby, was executed early today, 15th October, at Bolton in Lancashire for his resistance to the Parliamentary forces of Oliver Cromwell. His death leaves the Isle of Man open to invasion and a Parliamentary force under the command of a Colonel Duckenfield who is reported to be preparing to set out from Chester Castle in the next few days. We have this report:

'His Lordship, who had ruled the Island for 24 years and earned himself the Manx title of *Yn Stanlagh Mooar* — the Great Stanley — had always been a fierce supporter of the Royalist cause. He refused to surrender the Island earlier this year and it was shortly after this that he took a force of 300 Manx foot soldiers to England to join the Royal standard in the attempt to restore the monarchy. But he and his men were attacked by a superior force near Wigan two months ago and scattered. His Lordship escaped and managed to join Prince Charles but he was captured following the defeat at the Battle of Worcester last month. After confinement and court martial at Chester Castle he was sentenced to death on the block, with Cromwell himself insisting on there being no reprieve. This will leave the Isle of Man in a state of some uncertainty over the immediate future — there are mixed feelings among the populace. Lord Derby, for all his autocratic style of rule and his hard and hotly-disputed attitude to the ownership of Manx land, is acknowledged to have had the welfare of the Island at heart and this is reflected in the many social and other reforms that he has put through. At the same time the House of Stanley is one of the great feudal English clans and it was inevitable that its members should have strong Royalist sympathies. His campaigning for the royal cause has cost the Isle of Man dearly in wealth and men in a fight which is not of its own making. As a result there is known to be a lot of sympathy in the Island for Cromwell and Parliament.

The administration of the Island in his absence was left by Lord Derby to his wife Countess Charlotte. It is understood that she has not yet been informed of his death. The Parliamentary force at Chester is expected to sail shortly and make for a landing in Ramsey Bay. One of Colonel Duckenfield's priorities will be to effect the release from Peel Castle of Captain Edward Christian. This great Manx seaman and adventurer, who was originally Lord Derby's Lieutenant Governor in the Island, has been imprisoned for the last eight years for allegedly leading a Manx revolt against His Lordship. He is known to have strong Parliamentary sympathies.'

PRICES ARE RISING

Figures published today show that the cost of living in the Island is continuing to run at a low level. But there are signs that prices are beginning to rise sharply, mainly because of the presence of so many garrison troops who are having to be quartered free of charge. In particular wheat has risen in price from 20 to 32 shillings a quarter. As a result the House of Keys is advocating that price control should be introduced as soon as possible.

ILLEGAL CORN GRINDING

Action is to be taken against farmers in the Island found grinding corn illegally. It is laid down by the Office of the Lord of Man that all corn must be ground in the Lord's mills. But some farmers have been avoiding this obligation by using illicit handmills, known as *braainyn-laue* or querns. A warning has been issued that these will be seized and destroyed when found. The move comes as tithe levels in the Island fall and taxation by the Church is replaced by new taxes imposed through the civil power. Taxes already accruing to the Lord include those payable for the right to fish for herring and to import and export goods.

MYLES STANDISH TO RETURN HOME

It is hoped that a distinguished family with Manx connections which has been in the Americas for nearly 30 years might be able to make a homecoming trip in the near future. They are Captain and Mrs. Myles Standish who live with their family at the settlement in New England. Captain Standish, now 67, was military commander of the Puritan expedition which sailed from England in the "Mayflower" 31 years ago. His first wife Rose, who was his cousin and also a member of the Standish family of Ellanbane, Lezayre, died shortly after the landing. Her sister Barbara went out three years later to become his second wife. They have four children.

CHANGING SURNAMES

Manx surnames, without many people being aware if it, are gradually changing. The old Celtic, Irish, Scots, Norse and Anglo-Saxon surnames that had the age-old prefix "Mac" have been disappearing for the last two hundred years or more. In many cases the Mac has disappeared completely. McCorleod has become Corlett, McCosten Costain, McLucas Clucas, and McAllister Callister. But philologists say there are some old names surviving like McYlrea, McYlchreest and McYlcarrane. But one wonders, for how long.

YN STANLAGH MOOAR — THE GREAT STANLEY

James, seventh Earl of Derby, will, no doubt, go down in history as one of the more memorable Lords of Man. Whilst most unpopular because of his attempts to claim all rights to land tenure against traditions going back to Norse times, he has become known as *Yn Stanlagh Mooar*, the Great Stanley. After the death of his mother in 1627 he arrived on the Island as a young Lord Strange of twenty years to take control of the Isle of Man and was a frequent visitor in the years that followed. In 1626 he had married Charlotte de la Tremouille, some five years older than him, whose family had connections with most royal families of Europe. Indeed the wedding took place in the Palace of the Prince of Orange at The Hague in the presence of the King and Queen of Bohemia. It was a great marriage for the heir to any earldom and James brought her to the Island with high hopes of providing his bride with a life style befitting her birth. The accommodation built last century against the rampart wall within Castle Rushen was re-designed during the next twenty years to provide a spacious dining room and other accommodation for the use of the Lord and his family. The most resplendent room in the whole Castle is the State Reception Room brightened by choice Arras tapestries of the Samson story, gleaming shields and weapons, and colourful pictures. Here is placed the Lord's Chair of State covered with velvet laid with gold lace and fringes. Derby House, as it is now known, was also extended to give views above the ramparts over which windows open. The Earl also had a fine Bath House (Bagnio) built on the edge of the town where he spent time with his closest friends. Appearing gentle and considerate when it suited him, James could also be artful and devious in his dealings with his adversaries, always adopting the air of an autocratic ruler whose word must always be final. This was to lead him into considerable problems over such

James Stanley, 7th Earl of Derby, with Charlotte de la Tremouille, his Countess, and one of their children. From an engraving of the original oil painting by Van Dyck.

The Prospective of Castle Rushen on the South eastside. A The innerward of the Castle. B The wall of the Castle. C The wall aboute the Castle. D The Counter-Scarpe. E The new building wherein ye Earle of Derbie lived. F The new Worke. G The Burne that the Sea comes in. H As the Towne appeares

(Manx National Heritage)

matters as the right of land tenure, tithes and the demands of the church, free billeting of his men-at-arms brought from England, and his deafness to the clamour for an elective system for the Keys. To add to his Lordship's worries matters in England were causing him considerable anxiety, the struggle between King Charles I and the Parliamentarians finally ending with the outbreak of the Civil War in 1642. This was the year in which Lord Strange succeeded his unambitious father as Lord Derby and became the seventh Earl. Being one of the most ardent supporters of the Royal cause he answered the call by providing 40,000 and arming 5,000 men from his English estates. Such was his enthusiasm he was even under suspicion as a rival to the King himself and was forced to return to Knowsley. He later returned to the Island following news of the unrest which had developed in his absence.

The Earl hastened to the Island bringing a number of cavalry with him to deal with the disturbance led by Edward Christian. James had left his Countess and family at Lathom House believing them to be safe. But early in 1644 news was received that Lathom House was being battered and besieged by Lord Fairfax and it only held out because of the stubborn resistance of the Countess. He immediately set sail and arrived in time to support Prince Rupert in relieving the eighteen week siege. After the rout of the Royalists at Marston Moor later in the year, the Earl returned to join the Countess at Castle Rushen where he was able to experience a brief spell of comparative peace. He was able to give time to Island affairs introducing a few legal reforms and exercising the spiritual power in the absence of a bishop and, indeed, lived himself at Bishopscourt during the summer months. He and the Countess also hosted the occasional revelry at Castle Rushen in an attempt to maintain the spirits of their Royalist friends who had sought sanctuary on the Island.

Above all, James was determined that his Island possession would never fall into the hands of the Commonwealth enemies. Castle Rushen was strengthened; a hundred years before a glacis had been constructed around the curtain wall to counter the effect of cannon and now a platform was built in front of the barbican to take the big defensive guns now available. The Earl became more unpopular by raising further forces with all able-bodied Manxmen being armed with dirks and trained as foot soldiers, and being constantly drilled for an expected invasion. The garrisons of Castle Rushen and Peel Castle were increased and a troop of 288 cavalry was raised. Seven camps were formed throughout the Island and new forts were constructed around the coast including those at the Point of Ayre and the Royal Fort at Ramsey. The Douglas fort was strengthened as was the Derby Fort on St. Michael's Isle to protect Derbyhaven, the main port to the Island. The most impressive of all was the great earthwork at Ballachurry, Andreas, which acted as the centre of protection for the north.

A small navy of five ships was also assembled, one of the ships being lost in action against a Commonwealth force which was driven away. Three merchantmen were captured off Castletown and a landing on the Calf of Man, which was protected by a detachment of the Castle garrison, was prevented. But the increase of armaments had to be paid for and was a heavy burden on Manx people who had little interest in the affairs of England. They could see little advantage in supporting the cause of Earl James and there were many who thought they would fare better under the new Commonwealth. The position was aggravated by the news of the execution of King Charles in 1649.

Earl James had now lost all his estates in England, though he was offered them back by Cromwell's General Ireton in return for surrendering the Island to Parliament. This the Earl flatly refused to do (see letter below) and when news of a Royalist rising was received the Earl took 300 of his local men to assist but they were overwhelmed at Wigan. The Manx, having little desire to continue to fight, made their own way back to the Island. The Earl also escaped, but shared in the final defeat at Worcester. Taken prisoner, he was court-martialled and died on the scaffold at Bolton in 1651.

The seventh Earl had sought to rule the Island as the 'petty King' which he considered himself to be, claiming the right to deal with his subjects as he himself thought fit — dealing on occasions with fairness when it suited him, though not averse to using force to quell the aspirations of his subjects. He was, without doubt an outstanding man of his time, earning the name '*Yn Stanlagh Mooar*' — the Great Stanley

---

Castletown,
July 12. 1649.

To Commissary-General Ireton

Sir,

I received your letter with indignation and scorn, and return you this answer, that I cannot but wonder whence you should gather any hope from me that I should, like you, prove treacherous to my Sovereign, since you cannot but be sensible of my former actings in his late Majesty's service, from which principles of Loyalty I am in no whit departed.

I scorn your proffers, disdain your favour and abhor your treason, and am so far from delivering up this Island to your advantage, that I will keep it to the utmost of my power and your destruction.

Take this for your final answer and forbear any further solicitations; for if you trouble me with any more messages on this occasion, I will burn the paper and hang the bearer. This is the immutible resolution and shall be the undoubted practice of him who accounts it his chief glory to be, His Majesty's most Loyal and obedient Servant.

Derby.

RELEASE OF EDWARD CHRISTIAN

It has been difficult to keep abreast with the happenings at Castle Rushen during the past few months. Colonel Duckinfield, in charge of the Commmonwealth occupying forces, has established his Headquarters in the town. But one of the most heartening developments has been a Statement issued by the Colonel which declares that Edward Christian is to be released from Peel Castle where he has languished for the past eight years within its dank walls. What delight this announcement has brought to his many friends and supporters throughout the Island. And what a relief for Edward who has sacrificed some of his prime years because of the enmity of the seventh Earl.

To many Manxmen, and indeed Manxwomen, Edward has been the champion of their rights and their hopes to a far greater extent than any other leading Manxman of our age. And yet his initial appearance on the political stage resulted directly from the patronage of the then Lord Strange. In 1628 it will be recalled that James, the seventh Earl of Derby, appointed Edward as his Lieutenant Governor. This, at the time, was no surprise. Edward was from Maughold where his father, a brother of Deemster Christian of Milntown, was vicar. Edward had sought his fortune abroad and had returned to the Island a very wealthy man with a distinguished career behind him. He had owned and captained an East Indiaman; he had commanded a naval frigate, the 'Bonaventure'; he had been a notable member of the courtly suite of the Duke of Buckingham. Our Edward was no rude, unlettered country yokel but a man of proven ability and this Derby recognised. Meanwhile, Edward's acquisition of the mines at Bradda consolidated his position as a man of substance. Certainly, Derby believed that he was getting his Lieutenant Governor at cut price. He was heard to remark at the time that Edward didn't really want any pay, but would be content with whatever he, Derby, felt like giving him.

There are few of us who would argue that Edward ruled our Island well for the next ten years or so. In 1639 the sacking of Edward surprised us all. The reason given was that, far from being content to work for next to nothing, Edward expected a decent reward. Derby claimed that the more he was given the more he wanted.

However, Edward was not out of favour for very long. The outbreak of the Civil War forced Derby to look to his defences and Edward was a man of proven abilty. In 1642 many Manxmen found themselves under the command of Edward when James put him in charge of the Manx forces. The training camps then set up, especially the one at the Lhen, had effects not anticipated. Manxmen from all over the Island found themselves thrust together and, not surprisingly, they talked about their lives and they discovered that they shared many of the same grievances, particularly the obligation of the tithe. Edward, to his credit, supported the people in their complaints and in June of that year the Governor at Tynwald was dismayed to find the people bearing arms. So alarmed was he that he took immediate steps to summon Lord Derby to return to the Island,

It took the Earl nearly a year to arrive but the meeting called by him at Peel will long be remembered. Lord Derby was an affable and a very cunning man. He sprinkled observers among the crowd. He noted the speakers and turned away wrath by soft and reasonable statements. By the end of the meeting the Keys and the four chosen men from each parish were well under control. But Edward had, in Derby's mind at least, been identified and isolated as the ring leader.

The authorities prepared their case. Edward was arrested and charged. And the charges were so extreme as to show that Edward was well acquainted with the revolutionary political notions extant in our time, so revolutionary that only afar in the future might they be fulfilled. He was charged with attempting to overthrow the Government; intending to make the House of Keys an elected body; to have Deemsters chosen from the Keys every three years and finally to force the Deemsters and Keys to repeal all laws not in favour of the people. Clearly Edward, despite his widespread popular support, had no chance. In December, 1643, he was fined one thousand marks and sentenced to imprisonment for life in Peel Castle.

Now he has been released; and those who have seen him have been dismayed at the way in which he has aged. But his spirit burns as brightly as ever and his reputation as the true champion of ordinary Manxmen and women remains firm and unsullied. Perhaps someone in the future will take his place and voice, once again, our aspirations.

Peell Castle as it doth appeare from the east. A The hill is farr higher than the Castle. B The Sea that comes round about the castle, When the tide is at highest the greatest ships maie runne about it & come into ye harbor and when ye tide is out maie goe drie to the Castle. C The Rocks. D The hill within the Castle. E The wall aboute the Castle. F The Cathedrall Church. G Two other Chappells. The rest are Lodgings. The Hills are the Landskipp of Wales and Ireland.

(Manx National Heritage)

LIFE UNDER THE COMMONWEALTH

These last few days of May, 1660, have seen great rejoicing throughout the Island. Crowds have been gathering at the Crosses in Peeletown, Castletown, Douglas and Ramsey to greet the proclamation of King Charles the Second with much shouting, shooting of muskets, beer drinking and general enthusiasm. There are few, it would seem, who lament the passing of the Commonwealth. Yet the more reflective among us might wonder, was it so bad? Was it in fact any different?

What stayed the same? Though Parliament deemed the Island to be part of England, our government remained unaltered; our constitution, our laws, our officials or most of them stayed the same. To many of us little changed. Our lives spent tilling the land or harvesting the sea stayed hard and demanding. Few of us enjoyed the luxury of contemplating changes when all our energies were devoted to wrenching a living for ourselves and our families from a tough and harsh world. Yet there were differences, and some affected even the lowest of our society. We noticed that our Governors, particularly James Chaloner, took a deeper and more learned interest in us than any Governor before. Governor Chaloner has even made a searching enquiry into the constitution of the Manx Courts and the condition of the people etc. His findings are contained in a history of the Island called 'A Short Treatise of the Isle of Man'. The new men have ruled firmly but they were fair and fairness was important when it came to collecting rents for Thomas, Lord Fairfax who took over the title of Lord of Man from the deceased seventh Earl. Oddly enough, it is said that Lady Derby received her moneys more regularly from the Commonwealth than under the monarchy!

Best of all, for many of us, we noticed that we had no bishop as all of these had been abolished! And we saw our Governors live at Bishopscourt. Best because much of the Bishop's moneys went to our poor parish clergy and best because Governor Chaloner used it also to set up Free Schools in our four towns. And what benefits to the children from all classes these schools have brought. At last for many there would be a chance to better themselves.

Yet, although we lost our Bishop, we suffered none of the extremes of religion practised by those who dressed in sober blacks and greys, proudly describing themselves as Puritans although, even before the destruction of the Monarchy, there had been hints of their influence in Kirk Michael. So there has been much rejoicing at the return of the King but perhaps also a hidden wish that the good things for the people that were experienced will be continued, and that the oppressions of the past will not be restored.

> *THE LAST HOURS OF*
> *GOVERNOR CHALONER*
> *Thomas Chaloner, as a Yorkshire Member of Parliament, was a signatory for the Death Warrant of Charles I. After the Restoration of King Charles II he was excluded from Indemnity but he remained in charge of Castle Rushen. Here he kept a pretty Wench that was his Concubine; where when News was brought to him that there were some come to the Castle to demand it for his Majesty, he spake to his Girl to make him a Possett, into which he put, out of a paper he had, some Poison which did in a very short time, make him fall a vomiting exceedingly; and after some time vomited nothing but Blood. His retchings were so violent that the Standers by were much grieved to behold it. Within three hours he died. The Demandants of the Castle came and saw him dead: he was swollen so extremely that they could not see any eye he had, and no more of his nose than the tip of it, which showed like a Wart, and his Coddes were swollen as big as one's head.*

The Landskipp of Bishopscourte as it appeares on the south by east. A The Hill. B The Brooke. C The Chappell. D The Square Tower. E The Orchard. F The mudd wall to the garden. G The Barnes. H The Kitchen. The rest is the Countrie that lies above the howse.

HERE IS THE NEWS : 1663
EXECUTION OF WILLIAM CHRISTIAN

In spite of a last minute appeal for a reprieve sent to King Charles in London, sentence of death was carried out today, 2nd January, on 54 year old William Christian of Castletown. Before a large crowd he made a brave end to his life with a speech in which he declared he had acted in the best interests of his fellow Manxmen as well as Charlotte, Countess of Derby. We have this report from Hango Hill:

'Christian went to his Maker in front of a firing squad. But there was little heart in the men behind the muskets and some could be seen aiming into the air above Christian's head. The original sentence of the Court of General Gaol Delivery last month was the usual one for treason – to be hung, drawn and quartered. But this was commuted to death by shooting on account of his wife's severe distress.

Christian bore up nobly to his fate and refused the blindfold before the musket balls struck him down. Now it will be for history to decide whether this Manxman known to all as Brown-haired William, or Illiam Dhone, was traitor or patriot. He held the office of Receiver of Revenues and was Major General to the Countess Charlotte when her husband, the seventh Earl of Derby, Lord of Man, The Great Stanley was beheaded twelve years ago at Bolton for his support for the Royalist cause against that of Parliament. It was a meeting at Christian's family home at Ronaldsway that nearly 800 Manxmen took oath to turn against Countess Charlotte, who had been left in charge of the Lord's affairs, and surrender the Island to the Parliamentary forces under Colonel Duckenfield which landed at Ramsey after the execution of Lord Derby and captured Castle Rushen shortly after that. In his final speech this morning Christian said he had been aware of his duty to Countess Charlotte. But he had believed his greater duty had been to his fellow Manx. It was the restoration of the Monarchy that led to Christian being brought to trial on the orders of the present Lord of Man, Charles, eighth Earl of Derby, son of Countess Charlotte and the seventh Earl. But he denied the right of the court to try him and refused to plead, so that he was virtually condemned without trial. He was sentenced to death, but three other leaders of his alleged rebellion against the Lord were imprisoned.'

William Christian was a son of Deemster Ewan Christian – and a distant family connection of another Manxman of destiny, the late Captain Edward Christian. Captain Christian was serving a life sentence for rebellion against the Lord when he was released by Colonel Duckenfield from Peel Castle after the latter's capture of the Island. He was imprisoned again eight years later, this time for plotting against Governor Chaloner, and died in Peel Castle eighteen months ago. His great demand had been that the Keys should be democratically elected, and that Keys and Deemsters should swear an oath to repeal all laws not in the interests of the Manx people.

LIQUOR LICENCES

There are new moves to control the sale of strong liquor in the Island. The House of Keys has decided that the sale of beers, wines and spirits should be done by licence in future. The issue of licences will be limited to responsible people who will be called upon to pay a recognizance as well as the annual licence fee of four pence. Meanwhile persons found drunk will be fined – and punished in the stocks in default of payment. For a second offence they will be tied to the whipping stocks, as a warning honly. For a third offence they will actually be whipped.

POOR RESPONSE TO LIBRARY

Officials of the Public Library in Castletown have expressed disappointment over the number of books being read. But they admit that the reason could be the fact that many of the books in the library are serious religious works – and they are in Latin. The library, the first in the Island, has been in operation for the last six years. It was founded by Lord Fairfax, when the Island was granted to him by Parliament following Colonel Duckenfield's expedition. There are 217 books in the library altogether, all of them sent to the Island by Lord Fairfax.

LORD DERBY'S DEMANDS

Petitions for redress of grievance are to be presented at Tynwald Hill over what are condemned as highly progressive rights now being claimed by Lord Derby following his restoration as Lord of Man. Human rights activists say he is trying to interfere with the personal freedom of Manx people by involving laws which forbid tenants to leave the Island without a special licence. Offenders can be treated as felons, and have their property forfeited. It is also claimed that it is wrong for the Lord to demand such considerable tribute of provisions for his castles at Castletown and Peeletown. This now involves each quarterland in providing one beef per annum – which amounts to a total of 600 beeves per year.

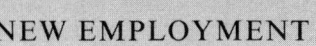

NEW EMPLOYMENT CONDITIONS

Finally, new rules have been drawn up by the Deemsters for the hiring of farm labourers and servant maids by the gentry. The hiring of men is to take place in November and of women in May. If they fail to give good service they will be liable to whipping or to imprisonment. But there are compensations for good workers, in the quality of their food for instance. The Deemsters have decided that people in enforced service who serve their masters well should be entitled to have their porridge made so thick that the pot stick will stand upright in the pot.

THE CHRISTIANS OF MILNTOWN

The execution of William Christian, youngest son of Deemster Ewan Christian, has come as an untimely blow to the prominent Manx family who for a long time have been leading members of the Council and Keys and yet, at other times, adversaries of those appointed to rule the Isle of Man. The origins of the Christians of Milntown date from the time when the early Norse settlers arrived in the north of the Island. They moved round to the confluence of the Auldyn stream and the Sulby river. Here they built their stronghold named Altadale from the original Norse Alptadair meaning 'Swan's Glen.' This gave way in more recent times to Milntown which is the modern name given to the Christian estate in the north. One of their ancestors became known as McCrystyn 'Son of the Christian' when the new religion was gradually being adopted. The name became permanent and the McCrystyns became pre-eminent providing a long series of Lagmen (now called Deemsters) to represent the northern half of the Island. The first recorded was Deemster John McCrystyn who was party to a Declaration, dated 1408, protesting against the claim of English kings to grant the Manx crown to their appointees. It was a protest the McCrystyns were to continue for many years leading to the events of recent times. Deemster William, who died in 1593, was the first to sign his name as Christian thus dropping the prefix Mc or Mac a habit which has now been generally adopted by Manx families though still lamented by some.

Deemster Ewan Christian will long be remembered as the protagonist of the late seventh Earl. He had advised his three legitimate sons John, Edward and William to settle themselves off the Island because of the uncertainties of the times. This they did and married into prominent families in the north of England William became involved in the growing coal mining industry of Lancashire, but he hankered for home and arrived back at Milntown with his wife, Elizabeth and children in 1637. His father had come into possession of the small Ronaldsway estate and it was here that William settled, extending Ronaldsway House to accommodate his family that grew to nine children.

Lord Strange had his policy that the Christians could not be ignored and his new neighbour became a visitor to Castle Rushen on social occasions. Before long he was appointed a Member of the House of Keys and was given the post of Steward of the Abbey lands which had been granted to the Stanleys in 1609. In 1643 came the widespread unrest and rioting, the boisterous return of Lord Derby and his soldiery, the trial of Edward Christian and the bargain over the prison sentence struck with Deemster Ewan Christian. Immediately after that, Ronaldsway was given into William's possession, and with his father's doleful concurrence, William agreed to take a 'lease of three lives' on the insistence of his Lorship. In 1648, having proved himself eminently reliable, William was appointed Receiver General and placed in charge of all the Lord's revenues.

The Royalist rising of 1651 saw the Earl disappear with his ships and militia leaving only a token force which he placed in charge of William. When news of the Earl's capture was received the Countess proceeded to make terms with Colonel Duckenfield to surrender Castle Rushen in return for her husband's release. When this became known locally the Mustering Cross (Crosh Vushta) was sent round the parishes-two pieces of crossed mountain ash passed from one home to another. On October 19th of that fateful year 800 Manxmen gathered at Ronaldsway and took a rather vague oath about withstanding the Countess's designs. The business of taking over all the forts, except Rushen, was set about next day and completed with the surrender of Peel Castle by October 28th.

With the arrival of the Commonwealth forces under Colonel Duckenfield it was William Christian who was given the unenviable task to call upon the Countess to surrender. No doubt he wished he had never been born

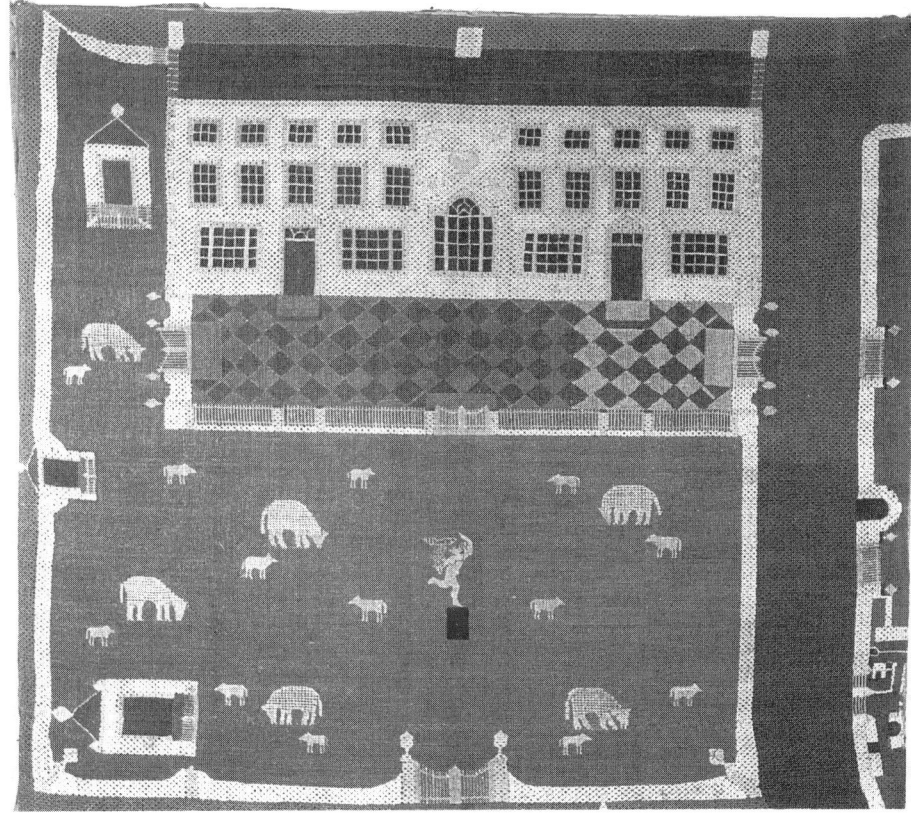

Ronaldsway House, home of William Christian (Illiam Dhone), where 800 Manx men assembled in the uprising of 1651. The sampler shows patterned pebbles and elegant plaster work on the front of the house, paved garden, gateways, statue of Mercury, and summer houses in the sheepfold where sheep are grazing to keep the grass down. On the right is Ronaldsway Farm.

when he found himself before the formidable lady esconced on the Chair of State. The letter he read from Colonel Duckenfield made reference to 'the late Earl' the first intimation the Countess had received of her husband's execution. The unhappy envoy's retreat before a show of passion and anguish was with haste as he heard the clanking of the portcullis being lowered and the drawbridge raised.

Castle Rushen was well stocked for a siege and no doubt could have withstood the battering of the guns now being placed in position. But the Countess feared treachery from within and knowing her cause was lost she agreed to the terms of surrender. She and the younger members of her family were given safe passage from the Island and never returned.

The government of the Island was placed under Lord Fairfax, Royalist rule being replaced by the 'no nonsense' of the Parliamentarians. Still the Christians held sway, William being appointed Governor whilst remaining Receiver General. His father, Ewan of Milntown, had died and the two Deemsters were now William's eldest brother, John and his nephew, Edward, John's eldest son. Never had the Christians held such power though it was obvious they were anything but popular. Members of well known Manx families had their ears cut off for slander while there were growing symptoms of animosity against the Christians.

The Christians were also soon to clash with Commissioner Chaloner who was determined to maintain the Commonwealth influence after the death of Cromwell in 1658. All the Christian appointments were cancelled. William and his family vacated Ronaldsway and returned to Lancashire in time for the Restoration of the monarchy and the arrival of Charles II. The Act of Indemnity passed by the British Parliament suppressed all acts of retribution which could have been catastrophic. But the leading Royalists must have envied Charles Stanley, now the eighth Earl of Derby, who contrived to have William Christian seized. Tried for treason by the House of Keys he was found guilty and executed upon a site at Hango Hill within sight of Castle Rushen and Ronaldsway.

The enigma of William Christian will, no doubt, endure for centuries. To our Derby rulers he will never be forgiven for his traitorous acts. But to the Manx he will long be remembered for his burning desire to control the Island's destiny from within, and without interference from beyond our shores. To them he will always be Illiam Dhone the patriot 'Brown-haired William.'

THE TRIAL OF 'ILLIAM DHONE'

Upon the succession in 1660 of Charles as eighth Earl of Derby, every attempt was made to bring to boot those who had taken part in the rebellion of 1651. William Christian had left the Island to visit London where he was detained on a charge involving £20,000 in connection with the Abbey lands of which he had been Steward. Upon his release from Fleet Prison he ventured to return to the Island upon advice that the Act of Indemnity secured him from any action that might result from his part in the Manx rebellion. But his offences were not against the Crown, but rather the Lord of Man, and Charles was determined to avenge the wrongs against his family. In September, 1662, William was arrested on a charge of treason and imprisoned in Castle Rushen.

Charles referred to the House of Keys concerning the charge and while advising him that under the Statute of 1422 the prisoner could be tried without a jury, it was recommended that a jury should be applied. A jury of six was consequently chosen and charged with the duty of the trial. The six chosen were all of humble rank, three being dependents of the Earl and all were too ignorant of the English language to understand the pleadings submitted to them. At the Court of General Gaol Delivery held on 26th November, Christian refused to appear, not being obliged to by law. But his refusal to appear, and remaining silent, was tantamount to admitting his guilt. Deemster Norris applied for the advice of the Keys. (The other Deemster was William's brother, John, who with one of William's sons, had sailed to England to petition the King to stop the trial.) The Keys declared that when a person refused to plea he is 'at the mercy of the Lord for life and goods.' However, seven of the 24 Keys refused to sign the declaration, some having themselves been involved in the rebellion. As Charles wanted unanimity, the seven were replaced by those of his own choosing and unanimity was secured by the Court on 29th December. The Deemster was ordered by the Deputy Governor to pronounce sentence although consideration was to be given to an earnest petition by the prisoner's wife, Elizabeth, and, 'in consideration of her very disconsolate condition' the usual punishment for treason of hanging, drawing and quartering should be commuted to 'shot to death that his life may depart his body.'

The sentence was carried out on 2nd January, 1663, at Hango Hill and the body was taken to Malew Church the following day for burial in the chancel. The Church Register records that 'Christian died most penitently and most courageously, made a good end, prayed earnestly and made an excellent speech.' In his last words, William Christian complained bitterly of his unjust trial by a 'prompted and threatened jury' and a 'pretended Court of Justice.' He reminded those present on that chilly morning that his part in the uprising of the people was 'not against the Derby family but merely to present grievances to the Countess'.

The petition borne by his brother resulted in an Order for Lord Derby to present his prisoner. But it was too late. A general amnesty was applied to the Island though three did not escape prison sentences for treason. They were Ewan Curphey, a Member of the House of Keys, Samuel Radcliffe, also of the Keys and Captain of the Patrick Militia, and John Caesar, Lieutenant of the Malew Militia. An Order in Council dated 5th August of that year restored their freedom and gave them compensation.

Portrait of 'Illiam Dhone'

HERE IS THE NEWS : 1688
MANX COINAGE TO HELP TRADE

In what is hailed as a major step forward in the economic development of the Isle of Man, the first ever Manx coinage is to be minted later this year. The man behind the idea is Douglas merchant Mr. John Murrey, after whom the new coins are named. We have this report:

'Mr. Murrey, who is also a farmer with extensive lands at Ronaldsway, intends to produce brass coins and they will be known as Murrey Pence. The next step will be to have them made legal tender, which will require an Act of Tynwald. This is expected to take some years, but when it is achieved an official Manx coinage should bring order to what is getting to be a confusing situation in the Island, which has been holding back the development of trade and commerce, both domestically and as far as export business is concerned. There is actually no coinage in circulation at the moment which has true legal standing. There are many Irish coins, known as St. Patrick Halfpennies and Limerick Tokens. There have also been a large number of base coins left in the Island by people passing through and Mr. Murrey says the genuine article has been conspicuous by its absence. He says a reliable and independent coinage in the Island, with the force of Manx law behind it, will give a tremendous impetus to trade generally. Certainly the need for such a coinage has never been more pressing, now that the practice of trade by barter has been more or less in disuse for the last quarter of a century or more. The reason for this has been the English settlers who have moved into the Island and their practice of making payments in cash instead of farm produce like the Manx. It was also the increase in cash transactions that led to the introduction of legislation in 1649 to limit the interest payable on loans to 10 per cent under Usury Acts. At the same time it has become more common for wages, which have been controlled by law for the last 60 years, to be paid in coin. Mr. Murrey says with money needed to this degree in normal life in the Isle of Man, it was time for the coinage to be stabilised and legalised.'

BISHOP BARROW CRITICISES

The Lord Bishop has hit out at what he calls the loose, vicious and irreligious lives being led by many people in the Island. Bishop Barrow, who has now been head of the Diocese for five years, also attacked the ignorance of the clergy, pointing out that they are underpaid to a degree that they have to resort to spare time work, which includes the keeping of alehouses. But he puts the main blame for godlessness on the lack of understanding of the English language by Manx people. Bishop Barrow has announced that he is to take over farmland at Hango Hill and Ballagilley in Malew, which will be administered by Trustees who will be responsible for supervising the training of the two ablest scholars from the Castletown Grammar School to prepare them to become clergymen serving in the Isle of Man.

WILLIAM CHRISTIAN'S ESTATE RESTORED

The estates of the man who is coming to be regarded as a Manx patriot and martyr, William Christian, better known as Illiam Dhone, are to be restored to his family. This includes his house at Derbyhaven, within sight of where he died before a firing squad five years ago for alleged rebellion against Derby rule in 1651. The move follows the grant by King Charles of the appeal for a reprieve, which was sent to London when the death sentence was passed at a Court of General Gaol. The reprieve was granted – but the royal warrant did not arrive in the Island until after Christian's execution. His alleged fellow conspirators have already been released from imprisonment, and their estates restored.

ALIENS TO BE WELCOMED

There are growing demands for the relaxation of the laws relating to aliens in the Island. Under the Act of 1422 in the Customary Laws, Scotsmen and Irishmen and other aliens can live on Manx soil only by swearing fealty to the Lord and paying for a residential licence. Otherwise they can be sent to prison. But many members of the House of Keys believe it should be free to anyone to live in the Island. They point to the large number who want to become so-called 'free denizens' of the Island, many of whom are recognised to have skills as well as other assets which would be advantageous to the Manx community as a whole.

REGULATIONS FOR BAD SERVANTS

The Deemsters have come under heavy criticism for new regulations drawn up in relation to the punishment of bad servants. These lay down that 'if any master draws blood upon the servant, he is to be spared.' Social reform groups say this is an infamous attempt to give employers protection under the law to abuse their servants. There has been a welcome, however, to proposals by the Deemsters for protecting women's rights in the Island. The intention is that when an unmarried woman suffers outrage at the hands of a man, a Deemster can give her a rope, a sword and a ring – so that she might either hang him, cut off his head, or make him marry her.

LORD DERBY'S HORSE RACE

Finally, Lord Derby has announced that a horse race is to be held on an annual basis in future as part of a programme of improving the breeding stock in the Island. It is hoped that the first can be staged next summer. The provisional date set is 28th July. A spokesman for Lord Derby said there was a large open stretch of land across the bay from Castletown which would be suitable for running such a race. It will be confined to Manx horses and there will be a prize for the winning owner, donated by Lord Derby, of £5.

AS OTHERS SEE US

A eventful century has given way to a new one and, of late, several distinguished visitors from England have frequented our shores and it has been an education, sometimes an annoying and sometimes an amusing education, to listen to their comments. The practice of most of us going barefoot causes much amusement but, to be fair, when they saw the carranes we were wearing on Sundays or in the fields their laughter was even more uproarious. Our houses, cabins they call them, of sods thatched with ling seem to have reminded them of Ireland. Mind you, many of us have now managed to replace the sods with straw for thatching the roofs which is a great improvement. We still have a very limited diet of mainly herring and oatcake with an occasional meat dish, skilful housewives managing the flavouring with herbs very well. It can, of course, be washed down with jough, or mild ale with its quality guaranteed as even an occasional clergyman runs an alehouse. But the welcome news is that the new century has seen the arrival of the potato which will greatly add to our meagre diet. Everyone is keen to try this new food and soon the crop will be grown throughout the Island.

Our towns too, have raised both smiles and eyebrows. Small in area, meanly housed, few chimneys, very often dirty and not much to boast about at all. But are they worse than towns in other countries? At least here householders are made to sweep the streets outside their houses; they can't keep cows in the streets and their pigs are not allowed to stray. Of late, even the middens have been removed from the streets. From what is heard about conditions in the great city of London, perhaps the Isle of Man is not so bad. Still, sad to say and perhaps understandable, smallpox, flux and dysentery rage in the towns and there seems little that can be done to stop their ravages.

Our visitors wonder about these conditions. Perhaps the Manx wonder too. Some years ago The Great Stanley said that the Island would never prosper until trading became an important part of Manx life. Why then hasn't it? The reason is that the English Government refuses to allow it. Their Navigation Acts prevent us carrying our goods, such as they are, in our own ships though we are protected, somewhat, in our own crafts and industries. Nevertheless, there seems to be some hope. The essential requirement, an accepted coinage, appeared some years ago in 1688. John Murrey from Douglas produced his pennies and at last we found ourselves with a regular and accepted coinage. So important has this been that the tenth Earl Derby in 1709 replaced the Murrey coinage with his own. It is now that steps can be taken so that our own trade can flourish.

Yet, listening to our learned visitors, one aspect of our Island ways has intrigued them mightily. In the old days the Manx farmers held their lands by what became known as the 'tenure of straw'. When a farmer wanted to sell his land or change its ownership he passed a straw from the land to the new tenant in the presence of the Lord's Steward. The passing of the straw was accepted by our Courts. The only thing wrong was that the Lord of the Island did not reckon that the land was the farmer's to sell in the first place! He believed it was his and last century he tried to replace the straw by a system of leases for twenty one years. This meant that a farmer could have his rent altered and, most important, a farmer could not guarantee that his son would work the farm after him. As very nearly all farmers pass the land to their sons it can be imagined the dismay this caused. Indeed there are many who claim that it was this that caused Illiam Dhone and his 800 supporters to leave the side of the Derbys in the Civil War over fifty years ago. What does now seem certain is that the sorry state of the land recently, the empty farms, a lack of tenants and bad husbandry was because of the dislike of the Lord's claims.

But now all that is likely to be improved by the 1704 Act of Settlement passed by Tynwald with the support of James, tenth Earl. The Act is already becoming known as the Manx Magna Carta. By this, the old straw tenure is recognised, the farmers really becoming owners of the land and possessing the rights of inheritance and sale. They now pay a fixed Lord's rent and at last there seems to be a real chance for the agriculture of the Island to settle down to a stable and, it is hoped, a prosperous period.

Our visitors writing in their journals, commenting on our customs and conditions, no doubt thought mainly of the edification and, perhaps, amusement provided for their readers in England and elsewhere. They would not suspect that as they poked and prodded, questioned and queried, we in our own quiet Manx way were deriving perhaps even greater edification and amusement from them!

AS BISHOP BARROW SAW US....

"I found at my coming that the people were for the most part loose and vicious in their lives, rude and barbarous in their behaviour, and which I suppose the cause of this disorder, without any true sense of religion and indeed in a position almost incapable of being bettered, for they had no means of instruction or of being acquainted with the very principles of Christianity. Their ministers, it is true, took it upon themselves to preach, but they were themselves much fitter to be taught being very illiterate, and wholly ignorant having had no other instruction than what that rude place afforded them ... they had no books ... their very poverty gave rise to such merchandise (their livings not amounting to £5 or £6 per annum) ... as the keeping of alehouses."

Thus wrote Bishop Isaac Barrow upon his arrival in 1663, no doubt with some exaggeration and glad to belittle the efforts of the Puritan rulers.

CARING FOR OUR SOULS

It was the Stanleys who were the first to curb the power of the Island's Church, and the dissolution of Rushen Abbey and the other religious orders further weakened the ecclesiastics. Nevertheless, the seventeenth century has seen a remarkable upsurge in the influence of Bishopscourt throughout the Island. Tithes are strictly enforced, an intolerable burden for many, while the ecclesiastical courts punish those who fall foul of the Church's laws. Imprisonment within the crypt of St. German's Cathedral is the dreaded punishment for misdemeanours such as adultery. Other offences, such as non-attendance at the parish churches, means penance at the door of the church for a number of Sundays.

The Reformation passed peacefully enough though in 1594 it was necessary to legislate against such popery as carrying banners and bells before the dead, praying upon the graves and eating meat during Lent. The children of clergy were legitimised and the right to marry granted in 1610. The changes from the ways of the primitive Church of our forefathers to the doctrine of the Church of England took many years. This is little wonder because there were few books in the Manx language and the clergy had to translate as best they could while congregations learned the responses off by heart.

Earl James, a devout churchman, ruled for many years without a bishop diverting the income for more pressing purposes though he ensured that the discipline of the Church was not neglected. When Lord Fairfax of the Commonwealth replaced Lord Derby in 1651 there was little difference though the Book of Common Prayer was withdrawn and the Deemsters exacted discipline in place of the Vicars General. The Governor during this period appointed four from each parish, usually including the Captain of the Parish, to ensure that such things as profanities, games and sports on the Sabbath, interruptions of services, swearing and blasphemy, working or visiting ale houses on the Sabbath were severely dealt with.

Following the Restoration, Earl Charles took steps to reorganise the Church and in 1663 appointed Isaac Barrow as both his Bishop and Governor. Bishop Barrow was the son of a famous mathematician at Cambridge and he brought with him great ability, an iron will and tremendous energy. He soon made it clear he was not impressed with what he found – a people irreligious and a poor lot of clergy. To him education was the answer and with the help of the Earl he took immediate steps to provide schools in each parish so that youths could be tutored in the English language. To achieve this he leased from Earl Charles the tithes from the Abbey lands. A Royal Bounty was also obtained from the English king. Thus he was able to form a Trust and provide schools still not provided in England. Also with this Trust he established an Academic School for more able pupils. This he established in Castletown at the Chapel of St. Mary built by the monks of Rushen Abbey who were amongst the first to bring education to the Isle of Man.

Bishop Barrow then turned his attention to improving the standard of his clergy and for this purpose set up another Trust. To provide an income, he acquired the lands of Ballagilley and Hango Farms. The former was vacant at the time but Hango Farm was occupied by the Laces who stubbornly refused to leave their land, their rights being upheld after an appeal to the Keys. The bishop then showed he could be a harsh and cruel man when determined to achieve his object. With the support of the Earl he had the Laces evicted. The roof of their home was removed and the livestock driven on to the beach. Lace was imprisoned within the gatehouse of Peel Castle and his wife confined within Castle Rushen. The Trust that was secured enabled two or three scholars either to be attached to the Academic School, whose Master received additional remuneration for giving them instruction in the classics and theology, or they were sent to Dublin University to qualify for ordination in Holy Orders and acceptance in the Manx Church.

The Earl has given great support to the parish schools and all his tenants are compelled to send their children with fines or dismissal from his service for non-attendance. Recalcitrant clergy who fail to give proper instruction are liable to forfeit part of their stipends. And so the efforts of the bishop has set alight a Lamp of Learning for the people which is still not to be seen in England. Mention must also be made of a sum of money which was left by Philip Christian, a native of Peel. He went to London and prospered becoming a member of the Clothworkers Company. He wanted the money to be used to found a school in Peel but it was not until 1689 that the school house was completed. This was achieved with the help of Bishop Levinz.

Bishop Levinz, of the High Anglican school, did much at the end of last century to maintain the church discipline and responded to the many complaints from his clergy about the poor attendance at the parish churches on Sundays and Holy Days. He proclaimed that families not represented at the morning and afternoon services are to be penalised by the forfeiture of four pence on each occasion. In 1690 he issued further proclamations concerning working on the Sabbath. Fishermen are now banned from going to sea from Saturday night to Monday morning while millers should stop their work from Saturday noon. Punishment for not complying can be 14 days in the crypt of St. German's. A determined effort through the church courts is being made to stamp out the rising number of cases involving adultery, slander, bad language, assault and drunkenness. Even soldiers and their officers of the garrison at Castle Rushen and Peel meekly submit to sentences for showing disrespect for the ways of the Church

While it has not been necessary to take action concerning the growing number of Noncomformists we hear about in England, there being none on the Island, the Quakers have been severely dealt with by the bishops. No one is permitted to receive them in their homes and the Quakers are not permitted to hold meetings in the fields or outhouses on the Lord's Day. Many have suffered because of this and have spent long spells under St. German's. Imprisonment and heavy fines follow failure to pay tithes and Church dues. The children are baptised against the parents wishes and their dead are refused Christian burial. A growing number of Quaker burials is taking place in an ancient burial ground at the deserted and ruined chapel on the slopes above Maughold.

News of the decline of the influence of the Anglican Church in England is much talked about these days, many wishing that the decline would spread to the Island. But there appears to be little chance of that happening judging by the words of Bishop Wilson who has been in power since 1698. But there are many questions being asked. How long will the Church be able to remain omnipotent throughout the Island? When will the people be freed from the intolerable burden of the tithes and live their lives without being continually pried upon by our spiritual masters? There are many who ask : Is this the way to take care of our souls?

'THE CLOSE' AND THE COWLEYS

With the Island's population now approaching 20,000, more and more land is being brought into cultivation as most families are still heavily dependent on the crofting way of life which has existed since earliest times. Cottages and farmsteads are now dotted everywhere about the Island and are also found on much higher ground where, by dint of hard labour, the peaty soil aided by the mild climate is now producing the staple crops of rye, barley and oats. Much of this new land is called 'intack' (enclosed from the waste) and permission has been given to farmers by the Earl to bring these areas into cultivation. An example of what can be achieved can be found on the high ground overlooking the valley of the Great (Sulby) River. Typical of the mountain farmers are the Cowleys of The Close, Braddan, whose farm covers some fifty acres. This is in the Rheast Mooar area between the streams of Druidale and Crammag which feed into the Great River, and where the northern extremity of Braddan parish meets that of Lezayre.

The present occupier is John Cowley whose family branches are well known in the area. It appears that The Close was chosen in preference to the Kirk Michael estate of the White House, the attractions being a good supply of peat for fuel, an abundance of the purest spring water and extensive pasture for animal grazing, especially for the sheep. Crops can be grown on the well-worked fields which are tilled by the breast plough aided by one of the sturdy little Manx ponies.

The farm buildings are typical in being built of rough slate taken from the hillside and thatched and tied with suggane (straw rope). The kitchen hearth and chimney – chiollagh – is made of heavy beams of slate bound with clay mortar. For baking, a pot oven is placed over the fire of peat and gorse. Sleeping space for the children is provided on a boarded floor above the parents' bedroom. One of the doorways to the kitchen has been filled in now that the winnowing of the crops has been transferred to the barn built at a later date. Next to the farmhouse is the stable which is dated 1706 following reconstruction. Here are kept the ponies used as pack animals and for drawing the wooden cart sledges. The barn is positioned close to the haggard where eight small round platforms provide bases for the thurrans (cornstacks) while a longer base is for the haystack used for feeding the animals in winter. Attached to the barn is the mucklagh (pig sty) which has a flag and sod roof. The thatched cowhouse is separate and has six tethering stones positioned in the wall.

To the north of the farm buildings is a stone walled enclosure which is the main garden where fruit trees survive and where conifers have been planted to give some protection from the north winds. Another garden has lazy beds for the growing of household vegetables and herbs. The fields beyond are ridged in long broad butts and reaping the crops is by the traditional toothed-sickle. The Close has its own lime kiln to provide vital fertiliser for the soil. Flax is also grown to provide the household linen, dresses and nets for the herring fishing. The dub for steeping the flax plants has been formed partly from the small quarry working. Sixty yards to the north is the corn kiln – downstream from the flax dub and a safe distance from the thatched buildings. Here, in the small rectangular building the corn is parched before being taken further downstream by pack pony to the mill for crushing. The horizontal mill stands on the Druidale bank of the Great River opposite The Close and water is supplied to the wheel by a lade. A horizontal mill, usually called the Little Mill (Mwyllin Beg) has a horizontal wooden wheel, or 'twirl,' struck by the water entering the building down a chute. The wheel drives directly on to a vertical axle which is fastened to the upper mill wheel on the floor above.

The Cowleys live in one of the most isolated communities on the Island and, being so far and remote from the parish church of Braddan, they have to pay their tithes in Kirk Michael which ministers to their spiritual needs. The family, of necessity, are almost self-supporting. Communications are most difficult with just a pony track joining the lonely Druidale road leading northwards to Ballaugh Glen, or southwards via Brandy Well to Kirk Michael. There is also a zig-zag pony track across the lhergy (ravine) to Sulby Glen by way of the Crammag farm (the nearest neighbours) or down the lhergy itself past the corn-mill.

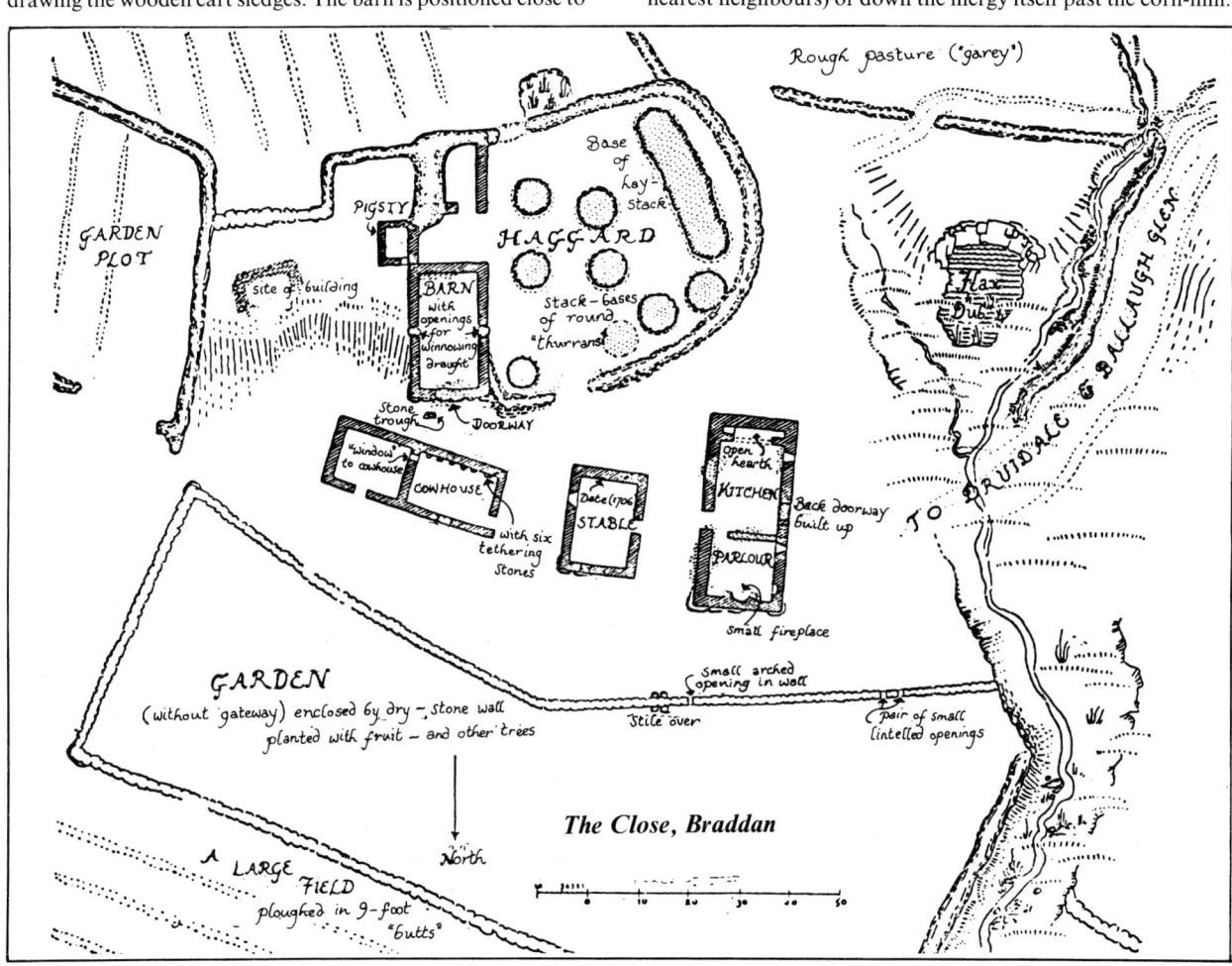

The Close, Braddan

WATCH AND WARD and THE MANX MILITIA

Whilst we may chafe at having to pay the Lord's tithe to victual the professional soldiery at Castle Rushen and Peel Castle, it behoves us all to be prepared to play our part in the defence of the Island. From earliest times in most societies all members, especially the males, had an obligation to defend their communities by undertaking military duties, by becoming soldiers. The Isle of Man is no exception and Manxmen, too, accept their military responsibilities, though not always willingly. In Viking times the Sheading provided the basic organisational unit and from these times, perhaps, comes the task of the Sheadings to furnish, and man, a ship in time of war. But it was from the twelfth century that our parishes derive the present and much criticised system of Watch and Ward which the Stanleys insist we still maintain 'upon pain of lyfe and lyme.' Another Norse system is the lighting of beacons on North and South Barrule (*Warool, Wardfell*) so that the whole Island can be quickly alerted in time of danger. Nevertheless, as all men from sixteen to sixty know to their cost, we have to leave our homes and take our turn and climb to the tops of the Day Watch mountains such as Cronk ny Arrey Laa (Hill of the Day Watch) or, what is worse, trudge along to the Night Watch shores or creeks where ships could land unknown in the darkness. This is not an easy task when most of us have work to do on our land or on our boats. But penalties are severe should a man not attend to his duties 'for whosoever faileth any night in his ward forfeiteth a wether (castrated ram) to the warden; and a second night a cowe; and the third night lyfe and lyme to the Lord.'

Now, however, we find an extra imposition becoming more and more accepted. Over the last fifty years or so there have been several occasions when the Island seemed in danger. It was reasonable then to look to its defence and, thus, what we know as the Militia, became established. But the Manx Militia has now become a permanent feature of our life. There are 22 Companies of Militia, 18 in the country areas and 4 in the towns. The Captains of the Parishes and the Towns are the Commanders and we are expected not only to be militiamen but also to provide our own weapons! Pikemen and shotmen we are all to be, with 15 foot pikes or 4 foot muskets to carry around. In addition the practice of troops of Horse Militia, first introduced in the mid-seventeenth century, by recruiting four men from each parish and adding four officers seems to be developing into something more decorative. Now each troop or so, it is rumoured, not only has to wear a rather smart uniform but has to have the same coloured horses – bays, blacks or greys! The practice seems to be causing the greatest indignation throughout the country, as is the annual camp. A fortnight or even 20 days in little tents in the fields around St. John's Chapel is not everyone's idea of gainful occupation.

For centuries the *Crosh Vushta*, or Mustering Cross, has been the means of mustering the country and severe penalties are imposed on those who fail to pass on the cross to his neighbour. It was the *Crosh Vushta* in 1651 that summoned the country to rally under *Illiam Dhone* in the Manx Rebellion. However, in more recent times the Captains of the Parishes are favouring the *Drum Vushta*, Mustering Drum, as being more efficient. Certainly it worked recently when, in 1715, it was rumoured that the Old Pretender was likely to invade. Dan Bodaugh of Ballaugh was accused of playing the parish drum one Sunday evening, to the scandal of the Church and the great alarm of the parishioners who rushed to arms. But he was found innocent of the charge, and the ecclesiastical court came to the conclusion that the Sulby drum was the culprit!

Still, despite our complaints about doing this national service, these remain turbulent times. As we are all aware the political situation in England is not yet totally stable and perhaps it behoves us all to look to our own defences yet awhile.

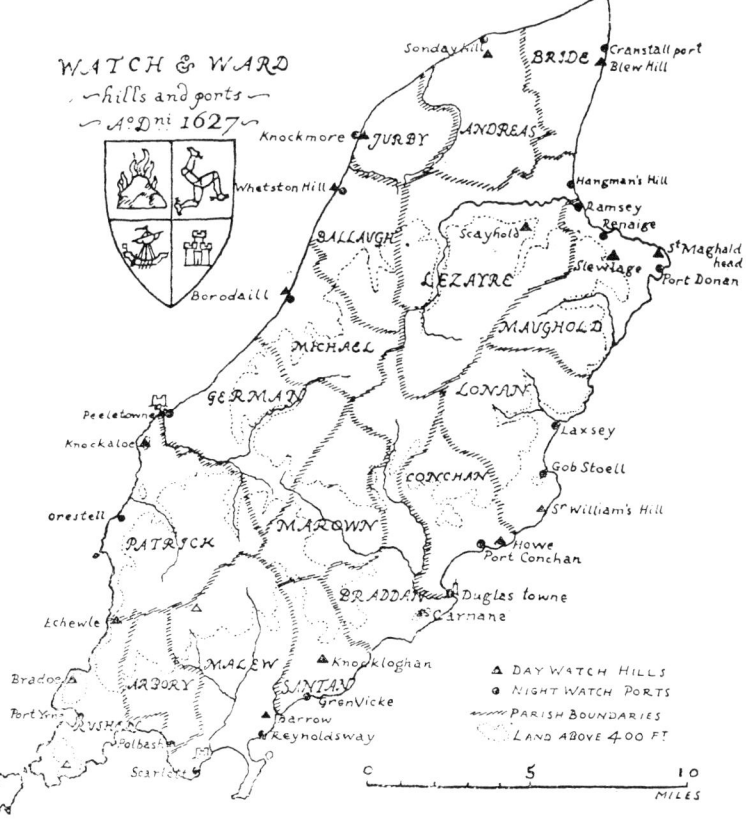

Crosh Vushta

Map showing the position of the Day and Night Watch Stations which have been used for centuries to give warning of the approach of hostile forces. In charge of manning each Station was a Warden but now the responsibilty is being undertaken by the Captains of the Parishes who are commanders of the local yeoman forces. The Coat of Arms is interesting in that it shows a beacon hill ablaze, the Legs of Man and a war galley of the Lord of the Isles. It belongs to the MacLeod family of Cromarty who claim to be descendants of the Kings of Man and the Isles.

THE GOOD WORKS OF BISHOP WILSON

The name of our Lord Bishop is now much revered throughout the parishes. Since Bishop Thomas Wilson D.D., arrived on our shores he has won the hearts of the people through his kindness, devotedness and understanding. He had been Chaplain to William, the ninth Earl Derby and tutor to James, the tenth Earl our present Lord since 1702. On his arrival in 1698 Bishop Wilson was shocked at the degree of poverty he found wherever he went. It is well known his personal income of £300 was often used to help the poor and he was tireless in directing food to the needy after poor harvests such as the wet harvest of 1708. This was followed by the almost complete disappearance of the shoals of herring for many seasons which brought more distress. The Bishop introduced new prayers to suit our needs including the petition: '*That it may please Thee to give and preserve to our use the kindly fruits of the earth and to restore and continue to us the Blessings of the Seas so in due course we may enjoy them.*' He attaches great importance to the clergy attending the boats of the herring fleet so that they may bless the endeavours of the fishermen. He has also introduced prayers for the consecration of churches, chapels and churchyards while the form of worship in the churches has been modernised. This has been especially appreciated by the growing number who are familiar with the English tongue, now about a third. He has revived the custom of parish perambulations whereby the priest is required to go around the boundaries on Ascension Day to bless the fields and denounce the use of charms. We have also seen what is hoped will be the last case of a woman being tried in a Church Court for witchcraft. The Bishop was quick to realise that the insecurity of tenure as the result of the Lord laying claim to his land rights were ruining the Manx and he persuaded Earl William to allow the Keys to draw up proposals. The Keys commissioned the Bishop, Ewan Christian of Milntown, Ewan Christian of Lewaigue and John Stevenson of Balladoole to proceed to England and meet the Earl's representatives. There was little delay and the Act of Settlement has brought many great reforms, the abolition of irritating services and an improvement in agriculture now that tenants have security of tenure. Soon after his arrival Bishop Wilson rebuilt much of Bishopscourt and planted many trees being something of a pioneer in this respect. His reforming interests in agriculture have seen his farm become a model for others to follow and he has distributed much farming literature to help others.

The Bishop has done much to improve the status of the clergy through better stipends and restoring the rectories and vicarages which had fallen into a ruinous state. The parishes are now better organised with registers kept to record visits to families and their condition so that steps

Thomas Wilson D.D., Bishop of Sodor and Man.

can be taken to assist those most in need. Besides births, marriages and deaths, confirmations have also to be recorded as this has now been made a condition of marriage. The parochial schools have been further encouraged with the vicar or rector relieved of their teaching duties. Licensed masters and mistresses are charged with instructing the children in learning and good manners, teaching the Catechism and prayers, and to bring the children up in the fear of God. The clergy are required to visit the schools regularly and to report regarding numbers, attendance, books the children read and their proficiency. The good Bishop has also set up parish public libraries for those wishing to improve themselves. In Castletown a new building, opposite the entrance to the Castle, was completed in 1710, and the upper floor has been reserved for the library, many of the books being transferred from the Castle. The ground

St. John's Chapel, German, restored in 1704.

Parish Church of Kirk Christ, Lezayre. Built 1704.

floor of the building provides a new meeting place for the House of Keys.

Like his predecessors, Bishop Wilson has seen education as the answer to many of our problems and the key to the future. With the accumulated monies of 'The Academic Fund' set up by Bishop Barrow last century, he has been able to spend considerable sums on the grammar schools and offer better salaries to the masters in charge. In 1700 star pupil of the Academic School, William Walker was appointed master of the Douglas Grammar School at the age of 20. Three years later, and old enough to receive Holy Orders, Bishop Wilson appointed him to fill the vacancy of Ballaugh rectory. The Douglas Grammar School in Bond Street is now to be placed under the charge of the chaplain of the new chapel dedicated to St. Matthew completed in 1708. In Castletown, work began on building a new Chapel of St. Mary in 1698, largely at the expense of Earl William. This has enabled the old chapel to be devoted entirely to educational purposes. The building, dating back to the thirteenth century, has been altered and an annexe added on the seaward side. It now accomodates the Castletown Grammar School founded in 1675 besides the Academic School set up by Bishop Barrow to train clergy for the Manx Church.

We have seen the Bishop's zeal for building spread throughout the Island. In 1704 St. John's Chapel, for long used in the Tynwald Ceremony, was renovated. It combines the Manx style with the cruciform, resembling two long barn structures intersecting at right angles. The west end has a step-ladder tower of timber supporting three bells. Lezayre Church was also built in 1704 followed by the restoration of St. Catherine's, Ballure. The parish of Patrick now has its own church to take the place of the more inaccessible one on St. Patrick's Isle. St. Mary de Ballaugh has been extensively restored with a large chancel added and fronted by a square based tower supporting an octagonal belcote. On the top is a dome on which has been placed a weather vane with the date 1717 to mark the year of the restoration. A new church is to be built for Lonan and Malew church is to be extensively repaired. Bishop Wilson has made it known that it is his policy to stop the practice of Quarterland farmers having to provide their own seat in church, with the right to be buried in the space beneath.

In addition to his many good works the Bishop is desirous that his church should lose none of its power and influence. True, he has mitigated much of the harsh

The converted old Chapel of St. Mary, Castletown. An annexe has also been added and the building now accommodates the Academic School and Grammar School.

treatment meted out by the church courts but he has not relented in any way when it comes to payment of church dues. In fact he is quoted as saying: '*Lastly I have often complained of the evil practice of paying their customs in the very worst grain and goods they can get, so that I am forced to return it or fling it away...*' At the Convocation held in Kirk Michael in 1712 it will be recalled that the increasing amount of land being given over to potato growing should become tithable and a just amount of the crop be given to the rector, vicar or proctor. The fish tithe was also confirmed and the custom of the proctor dividing the fish landing into five portions continues with one share taken by the clergy and another share for the Lord's Governor and officials and the garrison soldiers. The fishermen have appealed on many occasions against this exaction but without success so there is much grumbling heard in the ports and on the beaches.

Nevertheless, Bishop Wilson is much loved by all, from the Keys to the poorest in the land, because of his goodness and example. But there are signs of a conflict developing between Governor Horne, representative of James 11, the tenth Earl, and the Church authorities. In 1716, for example, the Governor upheld the appeal of an unfortunate woman who refused to do penance and was consequently excommunicated. The Bishop fought the case and his decision was upheld. More recently the Governor has refused the use of soldiers to take offenders to prison after being committed by the ecclesiastical courts. This has been followed by charges against the Bishop and Vicars-General who are accused of assuming powers beyond the laws of Tynwald. Officials at Castle Rushen say the situation is becoming increasingly delicate and reaching crisis proportions.

St. Matthew's Chapel, Douglas. Built 1708.

Parish Church of Ballaugh. Extensively restored and enlarged in 1717.

TRADE : OUR HOPE FOR THE FUTURE

Of late, few residents in Douglas can fail to have noticed the arrival of stranger merchants and traders in their midst. Many of these come-overs hail from Liverpool and most, if not all, have a very sharp eye for the main chance. Two of these richer merchants, Richard Maguire of Dublin and Josiah Poole of Dublin, have been granted the licence to collect Manx dues on imports on behalf of Lord Derby, James the tenth Earl. While the dues are low, he is happy to benefit from this trade despite remonstrances from Whitehall.

The Manx have long complained of the evil effect of what are described as the 'Navigation Acts' passed some years ago by the Westminster Parliament. These Acts state that goods can only be traded into Britain or her colonies in British ships and our ships apparently, despite our allegiance to the Crown, do not qualify as British! The result has been that our traders have failed to prosper, our harbours remain primitive through lack of funds and our general prosperity has been curtailed.

Now we are seeing, first in Douglas and then in other parts of the Island, vessels arriving from many strange lands – from Spain, Portugal, from lands bordering the Black Sea, from Norway and Sweden, from the West Indies and it seems likely that this trade will continue to increase. New warehouses are being built along the river banks in Douglas and elsewhere old ones are being extended. Cellars in our houses once often unused are now bulging with barrels of wine and spirits ond other trading commodities such as tobacco and tea. With high duties on imports entering British ports (for example, an enormous five shillings a per pound for tea) it is not surprising, dare we say it, that local merchants find it more than profitable to receive commodities into the Island and then run them across the Irish Sea into welcoming hands for dispersal without incurring the exorbitant duties collected by British Customs and Excise officials.

This trade seems likely in the future to have important consequences. It is likely to lead to a local ship building industry to supply vessels capable of sailing the deep oceans. Already there is a need to build fine houses for the rich merchants and all this means that there will be work aplenty and at decent wages as well for our people.

Until recently Manxmen and women were required by law to seek the permission of the Governor before they could leave the Island. By such means our rulers hoped to secure their labour supply and so keep down wages. Needless to say, many of the more enterprising got hold of licences – or left the Island without them. Perhaps this recent development of what is politely known as the 'running trade' will keep more of our young people at home and greater efforts will be made to increase the more usual trading enterprises. It is anticipated that shortly our own products – fish, beef, hides, corn, fowl, beer and so on – can be exported without hindrance and it may well be that to concentrate on this might be the best way to avoid incurring the anger of the Imperial Parliament at Westminster, the political consequences of which might be disastrous.

Fine houses are being built along the quaysides in Douglas by the merchants now settling here. Many have fine doorways as shown above.

THE MURREYS : MERCHANTS OF DOUGLAS

The Murreys have now established themselves as the most prominent of local families belonging to the growing merchant class in Douglas. The most famous member of the family was the late John Murrey who had a lease on all the Manx lead and copper mines from Lord Derby. It will be recalled he issued the first Manx coinage which had the legend 'Iohn Murrey 1688 His Penny I.M.' and the Manx motto 'Quocunque Cesseris Stabit' on the reverse. The family residence has been established at Murrey's Court close to the busy market in Douglas.

John Murrey's son, also called John, married Susanna Patten, a first cousin of Bishop Wilson's wife, and in 1706 he presented a clock to the chapel of St. Matthew being built in Douglas, and, later, gave a large silver flagon which is still in use. They live in Murrey's Court, close to the market in Douglas, where their son, another John, was born. He went to England and became a member of the English Bar. He has recently been appointed Ambassador to Constantinople while his sister, Elizabeth, is married to the British Consul in Venice.

Other branches of the Murrey family are also well established on the Island and are playing a leading part in developing the trading activities of Douglas. David, a cousin to John of Murrey's Court, died in 1702. He dealt in timber and tobacco and was regarded as the richest man on the Island when it was revealed that his estate amounted to the considerable sum of £3,396. Main beneficiaries of his will were his sons John, David, Robert, James and William, and his daughters Susan and Margaret. The son David mentioned above continued the timber and tobacco interests but he perished at sea in 1709.

In his father's will a sum of £20 was left for the poor of Kirk Braddan and Douglas. 'Also, I remit such debt owing to me by the poor in the corn book or what may not be collected by Mr Samuel Watleworth of Peele.' (Mr Watleworth became Archdeacon of Mann in 1703. He died in 1718 at the age of 72 and is buried in St. German's Cathedral). An amount of £5 per annum was left to the Rev William Walker for the care and education of any children of his, and for the chapel of Douglas, St. Matthew's, a silver sacramental cup. The Rev Walker, a witness to the will, was then only 23 and was master of the Douglas Grammar School.

David Murrey's cousin, another John, also prospered and in about 1720 bought the Ronaldsway estate where his family still live. It was John who had the Smelt House at Derbyhaven built in 1711 to continue the family interests in the long history of lead mining on the Island. The substantial building in local limestone is a large rectangle of 74ft by 23ft used as a warehouse and for smelting. On the south side of the building a 7ft wall encloses a yard for the storage of ore awaiting smelting. So it can be seen that John is continuing the family interests started by his grandfather in the middle of last century.

John Murrey's warehouse at Derbyhaven. Part of the building contains the smelting-hearth in connection with the lead-mining industry, the ore being stored in the attached yard.

HERE IS THE NEWS : 1722
BISHOP WILSON IMPRISONED

The Lieutenant Governor today, 29th June, 1722, signed an order committing the Bishop of Sodor and Mann, Bishop Wilson, to imprisonment in Castle Rushen, after what has been the most dramatic conflict between Church and State ever seen in the Island. It is understood that Bishop Wilson is to make an immediate appeal to the King in Council. We have this report:

'The situation has come about through a personal confrontation between Bishop Wilson and Governor Horne, and it is the climax of a long period of conflict between the Diocese and the civil power in the Island. The Bishop is known for his strong belief that the Church should regain many of its old powers, particularly by way of its ecclesiastical courts. But Governor Horne has consistently refused to allow troops to be used to arrest pesons sentenced by the Vicars General, and remove them to the Bishop's prison in the crypt of St. German's Cathedral. He has also denied the ecclesiastical courts the right to punish members of his castle households and garrisons – and he has allowed persons sentenced by these courts to appeal to a civil court. The matter reached a personal level a short time ago when the Bishop sentenced the wife of Governor Horne to make public acknowledgement that she had slandered another lady. In reply the Govenor ordered the sentence to be set aside – along with a series of other sentences passed this year in the ecclesiastical courts. The Bishop and the Vicars General refused to do this and were fined by the Governor. Now we have today's order of imprisonment made because they have refused to pay. What happens now depends on Bishop Wilson's appeal to the King. At 58, with 24 years in office behind him, he is renowned for his saintliness and his kindness, and his belief in universal education. His downfall has only come about because of his resistance to the growing power of the State at the expense of the Church, and his belief that people should be punished if they do not lead a more godly life. Legal experts believe the King will allow him to take his case to appeal, in which case he could be released from Castle Rushen in a matter of weeks to await a hearing.'

ALARM OF BRITISH CUSTOMS OFFICIALS

Customs officials have hit out today against the rapid growth of smuggling in the Isle of Man which is making it a centre of what is known as the 'running trade.' In a report they say it has been growing for nearly 30 years with dutiable goods being shipped in from France, Spain, Portugal, Norway and Sweden. After the paltry Manx duties have been paid the goods are then run secretly to quiet creeks and bays in other parts of the British Isles, to avoid the duties payable there. The goods are mainly wines, spirits, tobacco and tea. The report says the Manxman's aptitude for seafaring is making him a daring and skilful practitioner of the smuggling trade.

MANX COINS ONLY LEGAL TENDER

Coinage minted by Lord James is now increasingly used in the Island and it is hoped that in future it will be declared the only legal copper tender in local use. There have also been demands for a new issue to be struck at Castletown and produced to a higher standard than the first pence and halfpence minted 13 years ago by the Government. But this is expected to be of similar design, with the Derby family crest, the Eagle and Child, on one side and the Latin motto 'Quocunque Jeceris Stabit' on the other. The first coins to be minted in the Island were an historic private issue made by a Douglas trader, Mr John Murrey, as long ago as 1668. There are 14 Manx pence to the English shilling.

FIRST POPULATION CENSUS

Plans are being made for carrying out the Island's first population census. This follows the increasing immigration that has been taking place since the controversial Manx restrictions on aliens were abolished 25 years ago by repeal of the 1422 Act of the Customary Laws. Officials believe that with people from outside the Island – particularly Scotsmen and Irishmen – no longer having to petition the Lord of Man for special residential licences, many hundreds of new settlers have moved into the Island.

EMIGRATION INCREASING

While immigration has been increasing, emigration from the Island by Manxmen and women has been stepped up as well. Numbers of young people in particular have been taking advantage of readily available permissions to leave, obtainable from the office of the Lord. This has effectively ended one of the causes of long-term and extreme unrest among Manx people and the growing opposition to the rule of the Derbys. It was always considered that their ban on people leaving the Island on pain of imprisonment and the confiscation of personal property, was a gross infringement of personal freedom.

GROWTH OF DOUGLAS

Finally, there is a growing dispute between Castletown and Douglas over which is the most important town in the Island. Castletown is still the official residence of the Lord of Man and his Governors, as well as the House of Keys. But Douglas has grown into a bigger settlement and, according to some observers, the richest in the Island. This is because of the fine haven for shipping in Douglas Bay. It also has the biggest market in the Island, with increasing numbers of farmers sending produce to it. Castletown says the pre-eminence of Douglas is leading strangers to mistake it for the capital of the Isle of Man.

GOVERNOR CURBS CHURCH AUTHORITY

The release of Bishop Wilson and his Vicars General brought great jubilation throughout the Island. They had endured nine weeks of incarceration in the damp cells of Castle Rushen, receiving rough prison treatment and isolated from friendly company. The Bishop, through the opening in his cell, was able to give his blessing to all who flocked to receive it. Popular feeling ran high but the garrison soldiers quelled any signs of tumult. The Bishop was released at the end of August, 1722, following the action of the Archbishop of York to bring the case before the Privy Council in London. The fines, £50 for the Bishop and £20 for his Vicars General, were lodged pending the appeal. It took two years before the documents prepared by the two sides were presented to the Privy Council. The result, announced in July 1724, clearly favoured the Bishop with the charges dropped and the fines returned. The arrest of Governor Horne had been ordered but this was not effected as he had already left the Island. The Bishop did not see fit to retaliate in any way though his imprisonment brought on a complaint resulting in the loss of the use of his right arm.

However, those stirring events are long past and the apparent victory of Bishop Wilson is now seen to have failed to resolve the issues. Who deals with appeals against the ecclesiastical courts – the Lord of Man or Archbishop – had still not been settled. Nor had the liability of the Earl's household and soldiers to church censures, and the question of the use of the military to enforce church discipline, been mentioned. Nevertheless, the Keys remained loyal to the Bishop and at the July Tynwald of 1725 a petition by Bishop Wilson for the use of soldiers to enforce his discipline was granted.

This uneasy peace between Church and State only lasted until the arrival of Governor Horton at the end of 1725. He made it abundantly clear that he intended to limit the power of Bishopcourt once and for all. It was claimed that the Bishop was centuries behind his time (some have compared the situation similar to the struggle between Henry II and Thomas Becket) and that he has been responsible for keeping the Manx people in a backward state of ignorance and fearful superstition. On behalf of Lord James, the tenth Earl of Derby, he claimed that the Island's spiritual laws should have been abolished two centuries ago when the Isle of Man became part of the province of York in the time of Henry VIII. One of Governor Horton's first acts was to relieve the military of all ecclesiastical duties.

While this was a great blow to the Church there had been a growing feeling, among both clergy and laity, that the laws of the Church should be revised and modernised. Consequently an interim draft of amendments and alterations was sent to the Earl pending a complete revision of the spiritual code of law. This the Earl was quick to approve, but he then shook everyone by suspending the whole code until it could be revised by the Legislature. The Keys remonstrated that this would lead to an immediate disintegration of church discipline and an increase of vice and immorality. Such remonstrations fell on deaf ears and the Governor and his officials at Castle Rushen were instructed to prepare a report on the future of the spiritual courts.

The Governor seized the opportunity to promote the civil courts above those of the church which, he said, were too exalted and have led to the ruination of many Manx families. In his report he claimed that 'church power is utterly destructive of, and, inconsistent with, the liberties and properties of the inhabitants, and with the Protestant religion itself.' The report further stated that the spiritual customary laws were merely 'absurd arbitrary practices' used by the ecclesiastical courts at their own pleasure without the sanction and authority of the Island's Legislature. The report concluded by saying the civil laws are sufficient to govern the Island while protecting the rights of the individual without interference from the Church.

The report was accepted by Earl James and it soon led to a series of rebuffs to Church authority such as the remission of an excommunication order which the Governor had published at Kirk Braddan despite strong protests from the Bishop. Governor Horton replaced those members of the House of Keys who were against him so he was able to introduce new legislation which virtually ended the conflict between Church and State.

During the past ten years, since 1726, there have been several convictions for robbery, previously a rare crime on the Island, and for smuggling which is rapidly becoming the chief business of the inhabitants. Bishop Wilson cries out against the 'surpassing growth of wickednesses' which he blames on the 'the great contempt that of late has been put upon the discipline of the Church.' But the good Bishop cries in vain – such matters are now in the hands of the civil courts and the Deemsters.

THE VICARS GENERAL AND CHURCH DISCIPLINE

The two Vicars General who were imprisoned with the Bishop are two of the Island's most able scholars. They are William Walker and Mathias Curghey. Imprisoned together, they were able to share their common interest in translating the New Testament into Manx completing the Gospels and the Acts. They have not yet been published.

William Walker has been Rector of Ballaugh since 1703. As a boy he worked for John Stevenson on his farm at Balladoole, Arbory. He shone as a scholar at the parish school and Bishop Wilson enrolled him at the Castletown Academy after which he took Holy Orders. A constant companion of the bishop he undertook to plead the Bishop's case and travelled to London on various occasions before the matter came before the Privy Council. For his zeal and ability the Archbishop of York conferred the degree of Doctor of Laws upon the rector.

Until recently, it was the Vicars General who were responsible for implementing the Bishop's strict policy of punishing offenders who strayed from the ways of the church. Cases were brought before one of the Vicars General who used the parish church of the offender to hold court. Penance was the usual form of punishment where those found guilty were obliged to stand within the church clothed in white and acknowledge their repentance before the congregation. Alternatively they had to stand in the market place with a horse's bit between the teeth and a bridle over the head. Simple women deemed to be wicked were dragged behind a boat through the sea, the owners of the boat being liable to imprisonment should they refuse to carry out the sentence. The crypt of St. German's Cathedral was used as a prison and kept for serious offences such as adultery. There were usually one or two held there under the miltary guard of Peel Castle. This, too, was where the Quakers were punished but there have been fewer cases in latter years owing to the Bishop's more tolerant attitude towards them.

HERE IS THE NEWS : 1736
END OF DERBY RULE

After 331 years of rule by the Earls of Derby, the Isle of Man officially came under a new Lordship today, that of the Dukes of Atholl. James Murray, the second Duke, was given a tumultous welcome by the Manx people at Tynwald Hill, with troops and the Manx Militia formed up to fire a resounding volley. We have this report from St. Johns.

'The welcome given to the Duke, who is 46, demonstrates more than anything else the relief of the Manx people at having seen the last of Derby rule. Since the Stanley family became Lords of Man in 1405 there has been growing weariness and resentment of its highly oppressive nature. Now they are going – and the Duke of Atholl, whose appointment was announced a short time ago by King James in London, has made a splendid start to his family's tenure of office, wasting little time in coming to the Isle of Man personally. Many of the Derbys never visited the Island at all, and they ruled largely by way of Lieutenant Governors. But in presiding over Tynwald this morning the Duke of Atholl enraptured the crowds, and followed up with the announcement of reforms. He said next year there would be a new Act of Tynwald, a Manx Bill of Rights, to regulate the courts and to assure all people of the right to a hearing before a jury before they could be remanded. It will also enable the Lord to fix Customs duties in future only with the consent of Keys, Council and Deemsters.

The Atholls are the new Lords because the 10th Earl of Derby, the last Stanley Lord, died this year without issue. Neither did he actually visit the Island during his 34 years in office, being mainly occupied with service in the Army, in which he was a brigadier. In the absence of a natural successor the Lordship went to James Murray, the second Duke of Atholl. His grandmother was the third daughter of the seventh Earl of Derby, the Great Stanley, who was beheaded in 1651 for his support for the Royalist cause in the Civil War. The new Lord comes of a distinguished Scottish noble family. He has been M.P. for Perth since 1715 and succeeded to the Dukedom in 1724. The Manx people now look to his family for greater freedom and better government for themselves and the Isle of Man.'

DRIVE TO STOP SMUGGLING

The Government in London has launched a new drive against the smuggling trade in the Island. This follows a Treasury report which puts the annual loss to the English Exchequer because of the Manx trade at a third of a million pounds a year. Increases in tobacco duty have led to a big upsurge in activity, and Customs officers based in Douglas have been accused of conniving with the smugglers, allowing them to land goods openly in the bay before running them by night to the mainland. A new Act of Parliament just brought out seeks to ban the export of all goods from the Island. It also has a clause giving the Treasury power to contract for purchase of the Dominion of Man.

INCREASED DRUNKENNESS

Meanwhile the smuggling is being blamed for worsening drunkenness among the Manx people, mainly because it gives them ready access to ardent spirits in addition to beer. Under Act of Tynwald the number of licences issued for the sale of beer, wines and spirits is limited to 200. But this has not been strongly enforced. In a pastoral letter Bishop Wilson says tippling is a cause of the wicked behaviour of the Manx people. But the ecclesiastical courts' power to deal with it has been limited since the Bishop, who is now 72, was imprisoned 14 years ago in a clash with the Lord's Governor over the power of the Church to punish offenders.

NEW CENSUS

A second population census is to be carried out in the Island. This is because the first, which was held ten years ago, has since been condemned as highly inaccurate. It showed an all-Island population of 14,426 persons, with most living in rural areas and only 2,500 living in the towns. Douglas was the most populous settlement with 810 people – just 25 more than its rival for pre-eminence in Island affairs, Castletown. Officials now say a further census would measure population growth, if any, and migration. It is expected to be carried out in a few years' time.

EDUCATION

Bishop Wilson's zeal for education is earning him recognition of being the pioneer of universal education in the British Isles, the Isle of Man being the only place where parents are compelled to send their children to school until they can read fluently. Brighter pupils are able to extend their education at the Grammar Schools at Castletown and Douglas. However, a Diocesan spokesman has said there is no intention to usurp Manx as the dominant language. To encourage this the catechism in the Manx language is to be made more widely available. Meanwhile, an extended translation of the Scriptures is also being undertaken.

HEALTH

Finally, bad sanitary conditions in the towns are being blamed for worsening epidemics and dysentery in the Island. Regulations are to be drawn up by the House of Keys and the Deemsters for keeping the streets to a higher degree of cleanliness. Medical authorities also say poor diet leaves people in the Island open to the spread of infectious diseases, and they welcome the wider introduction into Manx markets of a vegetable which first appeared at the beginning of the century, the potato. They are now universally grown and are said to go particularly well with the great Manx staple food, the salted herring.

SOCIAL CONDITIONS OF TODAY

As we reach the middle of the century great alarm has spread once again throughout the Island as the dread disease smallpox has claimed more victims. As yet there is no sign that this awful, often fatal and always disfiguring illness has taken on the character of the epidemics that have ravaged our people of late and filled our churchyards and emptied our villages. Learned men have spent years trying to discover the roots of this disease, and indeed of the flux and dysentery, but all to no avail. Indeed there are some, fools perhaps, who claim that we should look no further than the conditions in which people live.

Our towns, it is true, are still somewhat noisome smelly places in which to live. Cows roam the streets in company with pigs, middens block the thoroughfares and make walking, especially at night, a hazardous undertaking. Many of our wells, our only source of drinking water both in the towns and in the parishes, are no longer sweet. With the development of our trade, and our slowly increasing population, our towns are growing in size. In the past thirty years Douglas has grown from 810 souls to 1,814; Castletown from 785 to 915; Ramsey from 460 to 805 and Peel from 475 to 805. The numbers in the parishes have also shown an increase so that the total population of the Island in 1757 is now reckoned to be 19,144 compared with 14,426 some thirty years ago.

The narrow crowded streets in the towns are pushing further and further away from the harbours and the disposal of waste is becoming an increasingly serious problem. The animals already mentioned have graced our streets for many years as the distinction between life in our towns and in the country remained slight. But now, unless our towns are radically improved, future generations will be confronted with a health and safety problem almost impossible to solve. The new streets need to be paved and, where possible, lit in some way. Drains to run off the sewage need to be constructed, and the sewage led to somewhere other than the harbours which, as many can testify, smell mightily in the summer. Our water supplies must be kept clean – too many wells are now fouled with refuse. A proper system of running the towns will, sooner or later, have to be devised.

And what of the country folk? The farmers are still the backbone of the Island community providing our food, manning our defences and providing members for the House of Keys. Even so, they live frugally on herring, potato, porridge and oatcake preferring to sell the bacon, butter and eggs or exchange them for iron, starch and soap at markets. They also trade in beer, yarn, flax, hemp and honey. Every hour of the day is one of toil and the farm labourers, who are the majority of the community, live in constant poverty. But there is always help at hand thanks to the hospitality of those who are better off. Some farmers have provided lodges for beggars and wanderers. Craftsmen, especially smiths, masons and carpenters enjoy greater freedom as their skills are in demand on the quarterland farms whose houses are roomy, some with two storeys, and expertly built. More and more of these are now boasting slate roofs.

For many others, especially the labourers and those young and wishing to settle down and start a family, it takes years of spare time to build their own little cottage using stone from the hillside or pebbles from the beach. Less demanding are those built of sods and mud with rafters of rough timber or driftwood. Strangely, they keep to the same pattern of a rectangle divided by a partition into a living room and a bedroom for 'Himself' and 'Herself.' Above is a loft for extra storage or for sleeping space for the children. Families often consist of ten or more children. All cottages have a thatch secured by *suggane* and with a hole for the smoke to escape from the *chiollagh*. This is where the peat burns to keep the pot bubbling. Some have portable pot ovens which are surrounded by burning peat; others have the wall oven under which 'bons' (gorse sticks) provide the heat. It is here where the family huddle when the nights are drawing in and the cold weather arrives. If the means of the inhabitants enable them to keep a cow an extension to the roof provides cover for the cowhouse, with a connecting door so that the animal can be attended to without going outside. Sanitation is provided by dry closets in a small building (*thie veg*) situated well away from the cottage and often attached to the pigsty (*mucklagh*).

Moving about the Island is limited to the narrow lanes or tracks just wide enough for a horse with rider or laden with *creels* (baskets) to pass. There are still no roadways as such and little need as there are few wheeled vehicles to use them. Bishop Wilson has the only carriage on the Island which he uses in his declining years but only on the sands of Kirk Michael. Keeping the lanes clear and drained by ditches is paid for by taxes on the occupiers of the land or requiring others to provide horses, carts, sledges and men. The Captains of the Parishes have been overseeing the work until recently. But now Tynwald, in the Act of 1753, has appointed a Highway Committee to supervise road improvements. Further money is being raised by appropriating the sum of three shillings and sixpence from the licences of each public house.

With there being few wheeled vehicles there has been little call to build proper bridges across the rivers and streams although petitions have been received for one across the river at Braddan Church and across the Sulby river at Ramsey. As one observer has noticed it is still the custom for women to carry the men across the streams on their backs. Tynwald is still deliberating the matter of building bridges.

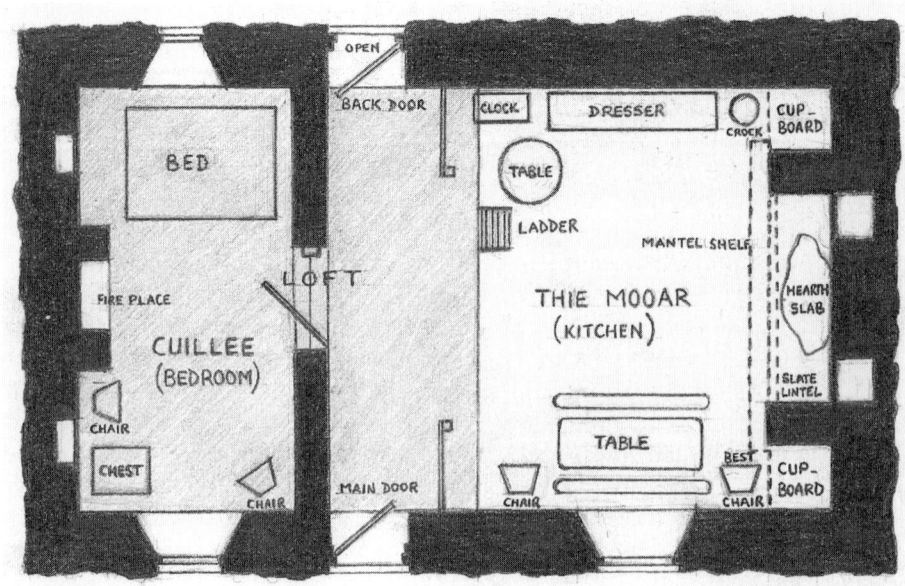

Plan of a typical homestead occupied by cottagers around the Island. Shaded area denotes loft.

HERE IS THE NEWS : 1760
SEA BATTLE OFF JURBY HEAD

After a fierce engagement at sea to the North of the Island this morning the squadron of French navy ships which has been maurauding in the Irish Sea for some weeks was beaten into submission by vessels of the Royal Navy under the command of Captain John Elliott. The commander of the French squadron, Commodore Francois Thurot, was killed in the fight and his body has been lost at sea. We have this report:

'28.2.60. It was a fair contest with three British ships against three French and as might be expected the Royal Navy won a comprehensive victory. Commodore Thurot, one of the most brilliant and famous of the French navy's young commanders, is thought to have been killed in the second or third British broadside. It was not long afterwards that the French ships all struck their colours. They are to be escorted into Ramsey some time tomorrow. Captain Elliott had been pursuing the Frenchmen since four o'clock this morning and it took five hours to bring them to battle in the seas between the Isle of Man and the Mull of Galloway. The sight and sound of the conflict could be clearly discerned from the Manx shore, Bishop Hildesley being one of the many who watched the engagement. The three French ships are the 'Mareshal Belle Isle' of 44 guns, 'Blonde', 32 guns and 'Terpsichore', 26 guns. They carried more than 1,200 men in all, and at least 300 are said to have been killed or injured. The British ships 'Aeolus' under Captain Elliott, 'Pallas' under Captain Clements and 'Brilliant' under Captain Logie, had only five killed and 31 wounded. It was in September last year that the French squadron set sail from Dunkerque and slipped past the British blockade. In spite of losing three of his six ships Thurot was first successful in his harrying mission, sailing up Belfast Lough and capturing Carrickfergus Castle. After that he planned to raid the Isle of Man for fresh supplies, attack British shipping off Liverpool and Whitehaven, and then return to France. But Captain Elliott and his ships, which were stationed at Kinsale, had been waiting for him to reach the open sea. After a stern chase they brought the French into action at nine o'clock this morning and in $1\frac{1}{2}$ hours victory had been secured.'

Commodore Thurot was only 35 – and he knew Manx waters well. When he was 15 he left France to join the Manx smuggling trade, running cargoes to Anglesey for 10 years. On his return to France he found further employment in smuggling until war broke out between Britain and France in 1755 and he joined the Dunkerque privateers harrassing British shipping. But the French Government recognised his courage and seamanship and enlisted him in their navy, and this led to his fatal command of the squadron which has now been lost. His popularity was such in French society that a number of ladies of fashion helped to fit out his force – including Madame Pompadour.

CALL FOR LIGHTHOUSES

Shipowners operating on sea routes to and from the Island have called for the Lord of Man to consider the establishment of what are known as lighthouses on Manx coasts. They say the lack of warning lights on dangerous headlands is creating a serious risk to shipping. Sea traffic in Manx waters is increasing rapidly and the new supervisors of harbours appointed by Tynwald are stepping up improvement work in ports and harbours in the Island. The work is funded by the imposition on the shipping companies of harbour and anchorage dues payable to the Lord.

ANOTHER SMALLPOX EPIDEMIC

A new epidemic of smallpox, the third in the last half a century, is raging in the Isle of Man. Smallpox is now regarded as the most serious of all the killer diseases to which the people of the Island are at risk. It is more commonly known as '*Breck Willy Killey*' after the man who was first to suffer from the disease. The last epidemic was only eight years ago and there was one before that in 1704. But in spite of a large number of deaths being reported the population continues to increase in number. The latest census figures show just over 19,000 people are now living in the Island compared with 14,000 in the last census, in 1726. Douglas has 1,800 people – twice as many as Castletown.

HIGHWAYS TO BE IMPROVED

Major highway improvements are now being undertaken throughout the Island – and under Act of Tynwald householders are being made to pay for them. The money is being raised through a levy on people whose property adjoins the road side. It is being assessed at present at three shillings and fourpence per householder. The improvement in the roads has led to wheeled carriages making their appearance on Island roads. To continue the overall improvement in the internal communications system there are also plans for building bridges over the River Bright between Douglas and Kirk Braddan, and over the Sulby River at Ramsey.

BISHOP CONDEMNS ENGLISH DEBTORS

Finally, Bishop Hildesley has publicly condemned the presence within Manx shores of increasing numbers of debtors from England and elsewhere. They are in the Island because they are able to escape payment of their debts by establishing Manx residence. The Bishop says such people by their nature are dissolute and unprincipled, for all that they have much money to spend to the advantage of Manx traders and farmers. Their conduct in private life is leading the simple-minded Manx into bad ways, he says, at a time when their moral integrity is already undermined by the smuggling trade.

THE LAST VOYAGE OF FRANCOIS THUROT

The departure of the battered hulk of the 'Belle Isle' from Ramsey Bay, together with the captured 'Blonde' and 'Terpsichore', has brought general relief to the Island, and much gratitude for the protection of the Royal Navy. The Isle of Man had come perilously close to being involved in the present war between the old enemies – France and England. Francois Thurot fought bravely to the end and was much respected by all who came to know him as a smuggler, privateer and adventurer, and also as a man of honour and humanity. He had great knowledge of the Irish Sea and the defences around the coasts of England and Ireland. News of his expedition, under the auspices of the French Government, struck fear into the hearts of many a port.

Departing Dunkerque, with 1,500 French and Swiss soldiers, the squadron sailed first to Goteberg in friendly Sweden, then to Bergen in Norway from whence he sailed, via the Faroes, to strike Northern Ireland. He arrived with three of his original squadron of six armed merchantmen. Londonderry was his target but unfavourable winds brought the ships to Belfast Lough. Thurot entered and landed 600 able-bodied troops under the command of the aristocratic Brigadier de Flobert. The ancient castle of Carrickfergus was quickly taken and saved on condition that supplies were provided for the French. These could only be provided by a terrified Belfast; four hostages were held until all demands were met. The 'Belle Isle' and the other frigates were loaded with fresh water and large quantities of wine, brandy, peas, onions, beeves, butter, vinegar, biscuit, tobacco, candles, rice and sugar. The heavily laden ships withdrew on February 26th, escaping the arrival of the English squadron under Commodore Elliot who had taken two days, because of gales, to sail from Kinsale. The three French ships crossed the North Channel and came up against the coast of Galloway at Luce Bay where Thurot veered south. Instead of reaching the shelter of Ramsey Bay he came down the west coast and, making use of favourable winds, it is believed he was heading for Peel which he had visited some years before to collect a cargo of rum for importation to France. It was also during his visit that he bought the negro butler of Mr. George Moore. The negro was called Douglas and had been dismissed following misconduct with one of the maidservants. Whether or not Douglas was still with his new master is not known but it appears that Thurot was making for Peel with the intention of robbing Mr. Moore who resides at Ballamooar, Patrick. There was also the possibility of hostages being taken until more provisions were obtained. It is well known that George Moore, Speaker of the House of Keys, is one of our leading merchants and heavily involved in smuggling and, like many other Manxmen, admires the activities of Francois Thurot, calling him 'King of the Smugglers.' The outcome of any confrontation between Thurot and The Speaker will now never be known.

However, luck was running out for the adventurous Thurot. Commodore Elliot was in sight of the French whom he found just off Jurby Head early on the morning of February 28th. Thurot, gallantly and without support, advanced to make battle with the 'Aeolus'. Work on the crofts stopped as the ships thundered at each other while the puffs of smoke from the cannon could clearly be seen. The 'Belle Isle' suffered terrible damage as Thurot manoeuvred to get his troops aboard the 'Aeolus'. The engagement lasted over an hour until Thurot was struck by an English bullet from a swivel gun. His body was thrown overboard so Commodore Elliot did not have the satisfaction of rendering the last rites to his brave adversary. It has since been reported that Thurot's body, along with others, was washed ashore on the coast of Galloway. He was buried with due ceremony in Kirkmaiden churchyard; his dagger and snuff box have been preserved.

The sea battle over, the hulk of the 'Belle Isle' could well have sunk had it not been for the assistance of local fishermen. The remains of the ship, and the surrendered 'Blonde' and 'Terpsichore' were moved round to Ramsey Bay. The bodies of over 300 French, killed and injured, were attended to but the main problem was what to do with the prisoners – sailors and soldiers – said to number over a thousand. Commodore Elliot was for putting them ashore at Ramsey but Governor Basil Cochrane rigorously opposed the plan fearing the Island would be overrun with plundering, and ships in Manx ports seized to make an escape. There was also the fear that some of the Manx who had a passion for independence would join the French in an insurrection and destroy the Manx Government. The plan was aborted and the Royal Navy moved the prisoners to ports in England and Ireland for repatriation. The three French ships have now left for Portsmouth. Letters have been sent, via Whitehaven, to inform the Duke of Atholl of recent events.

At home, Bishop Mark Hildesley has issued special prayers to be said in churches and chapels to give thanks for our safe deliverance The Bishop has procured the bowsprit of the 'Belle Isle', with two of her guns, which he intends to mount on a mound on his estate at Bishopscourt. The mound is to be named 'Aeolus' (son of Neptune, god of the wind) in honour of Commodore Elliot's ship. With a shortage of timber in the north, timbers from the Belle Isle washed up on the shore at the Lhen are much sought after for roof rafters. And so it is with great relief that the Bishop is able to proclaim that the Island 'has escaped unmolested and free to get on with the herrings and potatoes.'

The Gallant Action off the Isle of Man, where the brave Capt Elliott defeated & took the Marshal Belle Isle, Commanded by the famous Thurot, & two other French Ships of War, the 28th of Feby 1760.
Printed for Carington Bowles, Map & Printseller, N.º 69 in St Pauls Church Yard, London.

BISHOP HILDESLEY : A SHINING LIGHT

The much revered Thomas Wilson died in 1755 in his 93rd year after being our Island bishop for 58 years. He had many opportunities of advancement but preferred to stay with his people whom he felt needed him as they are so poor. In his later years he gave over half his income to feed the poor and he will be remembered by many for his charity during the terrible famine between 1739 and 1741 when he gave corn to the poor or sold it at half price. He was able to do this because of his knowledge of farming and his success in running the Bishopcourt estate which became a pattern for other farmers.

To the end he was unpopular with Governors and officials because of his strict discipline and his determination to defend the position of the Church in Island affairs. He was as stern with his clergy as with the laity and gave frequent admonition to those who were lax in their spiritual duties. He placed his clergy in the forefront of his fight against the evils of the day, especially those arising from the smuggling trade. The clergy are now less haranguing in their sermons and relate better to the real and present necessities of their flocks. Conducting services in both Manx and English has also improved, and his successor Bishop Hildesley since arriving on the Island, has seen fit to compliment all parishes on the high standard of the clergy and the way in which the parishioners respond both in punctuality and attendance. He is particularly pleased with attendance for the Sacrament noting that, 'There were not less than 600 at the Communion in a country parish at Easter.'

Bishop Mark Hildesley, after being consecrated by the Archbishop of York, was installed as bishop in St. German's Cathedral in August 1755. It was noted by those present that this may be the last such occasion as the fabric of the cathedral is giving much cause for concern, the roof being in a particularly dilapidated condition. Resources have, of course, been used to rebuild or enlarge the parish churches and creating new chapels. That many of the churches are too small for the growing population has been observed by Bishop Hildesley who has taken steps to rebuild or enlarge three of the parish churches while he, himself, has funded the new chapel of St. Marks. Work has also started on a new church for Douglas which will be by far the biggest on the Island.

Bishop Hildesley has shown great zeal in church organistaion and one of his first acts was to require all his clergy to produce their Letters of Orders and licences pertaining to their duties. He has also introduced new attire for the clergy so that they can be distinguished from the laity. Now they are required to appear in black or dark gray and to wear a wig. He has enhanced the stipends with the rectories, in receipt of all tithes, worth £100 and vicarages worth between £30 and £50. These increases have been made possible by the bishop appointing his clergy as his proctors in the collection ot tithes and church dues.

Above everything, it has been noticed the Bishop Hildesley is making a determined effort to see that all churches are equipped with Bibles in the Manx language for the better understanding of congregations which predominantly still only understand the native language. He has acquired a knowledge of Manx himself. While the great work of translation goes on a Manx Prayer Book appeared in 1765 and is now in general use for the benefit of all. The task of translating the Bible has been divided between the clergy who are working under the supervision of the Rev. Philip Moore, headmaster of the Douglas Grammar School, and his pupil John Kelly. Use has been made of results of new learning made available since the English translation of 1611. One commentator who has seen parts of the translation considers it to be very good and 'the beautiful expressions of the Manx language, superior to the Irish, is visible to every Celtic scholar.' However, great difficulty has been found in funding the printing costs. Approaches have been made to the Society for the Promotion of Christian Knowledge and they have agreed to provide £100 while Bishop Hildesley has gained the support of other charitable persons in England. Thus, progress is being made and the printing of the Old Testament has now been completed. It is hoped that the New Testament will follow in the near future. As one woman in Kirk Michael was heard to remark: 'No longer will we have to sit in darkness!'

Less stern than his predecessor, and making less use of the church courts, Bishop Hildesley has won the hearts of Manx people by his kindliness, understanding, humour and wisdom. The bishop is, indeed, a shining light to us all.

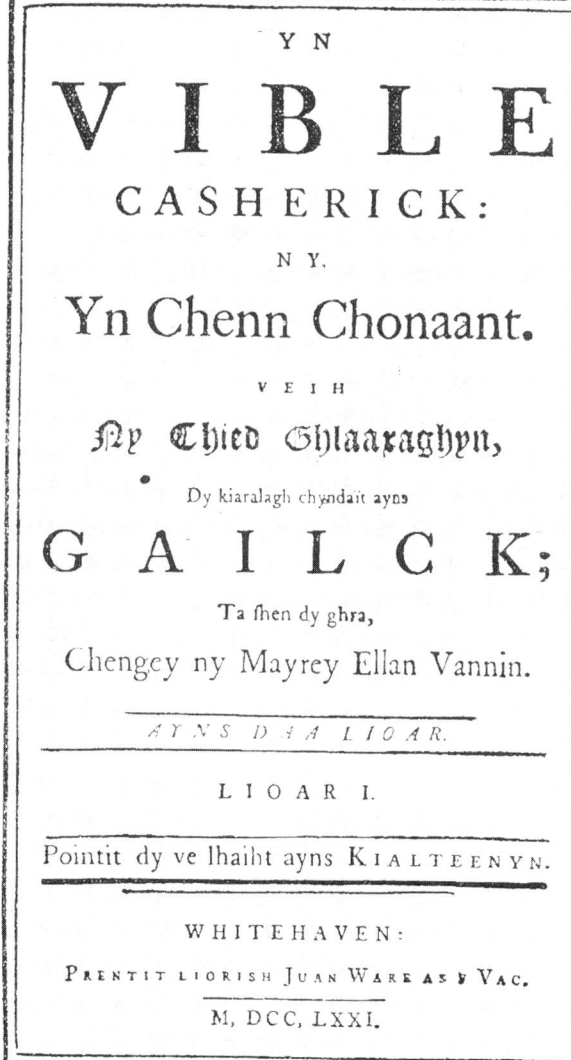

THE 'HILDESLEY' MANX BIBLE 1771
edited by Rev. Philip Moore.

THE MANX MISCHIEF

Whilst smuggling is usually thought of as avoidance of paying duty, the lucrative business in which many Manx families are now involved is more generally known as 'the running trade' and in other places as 'the mischief.' Such terms have slightly less illicit overtones and, in any case, the vast amount of goods being handled have already paid custom dues to the Lord of the Island. The practice was first encouraged by the Lords of Derby and more recently by the Duke of Atholl, the latter, by the 1737 Act of Tynwald, granting asylum to all who fall foul of British law. They are benefiting greatly from the expanding business. Having paid dues on arrival in Douglas, Ramsey, Peel or Castletown, there is no compunction in running the goods across the sea to welcoming hands on the surrounding coasts of England, Scotland and Ireland.

To many Manxmen it has proved to be the most remunerative career open to them — better than the Bar, far better than the Church, both of which demand an expensive education, and offer but a meagre reward. To others there is little else save the farming and the fishing so why not use their maritime skills to benefit their families and help pay the Lord's rent? The whole Island is involved and it has become a way of life despite the dangers. There are those who have fallen to the guns of the customs cutters out at sea while others have been fined, gaoled or had their boats and goods confiscated.

Situated in the Irish Sea the Island is an ideal centre for the distribution of goods and is free, so far, from any effective intervention from the Westminster Parliament. Merchants from Liverpool, Glasgow, Belfast and Dublin have been quick to seize the opportunities afforded by the tariff differences and have settled on the Island creating a vast warehouse of goods to be run into Great Britain and Ireland. Douglas has flourished amazingly while throughout the Island most of our leading families have seen fit to add their names to the merchant class. George Moore, who resides at Ballamoar, Patrick is a leading member of the House of Keys in line, some say, to become Foreman one day. But, first and foremost, he is a merchant who has pressed heavily for a harbour to be built at Peel. He owns two ships which ply with the Americas and the Continent bringing home goods to join in the running trade.

There is now a honeycomb of caverns and passages underlying the narrow streets of Peel and under the waterside taverns and merchant houses in Douglas. Bridge House, Castletown, home of the Quayles, holds numerous dark passages as does Ronaldsway House which is situated conveniently close to the waters of Derbyhaven. Ballaquane House, near Peel, is also known to be heavily involved, an iron-studded door leading to an enclave for the contraband. The leading farmers have secret cellars under their outbuildings while freelance smugglers have their hideouts among the hills and glens. Goods awaiting transit can be hidden in the many caves around the coast. Those at *Gob ny Deigan* are much favoured by traders working from Peel. It is all a smugglers' paradise. Come darkness, the movements begin with carts being loaded, the horses' hooves and cart wheels being craped so they can make their silent way to rendezvous with the awaiting boats in some sheltered creek. Across the sea, in whatever direction, there are those ready to receive the fresh consignments with lamps to guide the sailors.

Apart from its position and being beyond the jurisdiction of the Westminster Parliament, the Isle of Man has been able to benefit from other factors. The wars in Europe against 'the old enemy' have proved costly affairs sending up taxation, and import duties have risen steeply. These, together with certain prohibitions and restrictions, charters and statutory monopolies, have made smuggling generally a much more attractive proposition and, because many of the measures are so unpopular, rather less reprehensible. The design of ships has also improved whereby the old square-rigged ships at the mercy of wind direction have been replaced by ships now with sails fore and aft so that, close-hauled, they can progress in all conditions making it possible to enter and leave ports undetected by the custom men.

Since the days of Charles II the collection of custom duties has been in the hands of Boards of Commissioners first appointed in 1671. The difficulty with the Isle of Man soon became apparent and inspectors were sent by the Liverpool Board to survey the situation in Douglas, Peel and Ramsey. They reported that something would have to be done 'in order to prevent the evil of the practices of the merchants in the Isle of Man.' It was noted that the Irish Commissioners were also at a loss. Negotiations were opened for a 'treaty' between the Crown and Lord Derby. The latter replied by declaring in a Book of Rates (1692) the insular dues on 200 imports and 80 exports, ensuring that such rates were favourable to the merchants he had encouraged to operate from the Island. The negotiations soon ground to a halt and the clandestine running increased by leaps and bounds.

The legislation of 1706, in the days of Queen Anne, which prohibited goods shipped in the East Indies from being landed elsewhere than in Great Britain was directed specifically against this illicit traffic. In 1725 further legislation was introduced to prevent all exports from the Isle of Man, apart from home products. Such measures have had little effect as enforcement was not possible on the Island or within three miles of its coast. Huge quantities of tea, brandy and tobacco are being run across to the mainland. The Liverpool Board reports that the Ribble 'is the place of the greatest smuggling in the country' and that the 'vast fraud would continue unless officers were placed almost within sight of each other and the troops likewise to their assistance.'

Custom officers placed on the Island are powerless to act. In fact their presence is vehemently opposed and open hostility shown to visiting Custom cruisers. Captain Richmond has remarked that his crew were obliged whenever they went ashore 'to go armed as if in an enemy country.' He has also been threatened with imprisonment if he dares to make a search of any vessel in a Manx port. Such threats have not proved idle.

A most serious incident occurred recently when Captain Dow brought the cruiser *'Sincerity'* of Whitehaven into Douglas on Midsummer Eve, 1750. The following morning Dow spotted the Dutch ship *'Hope'* at anchor off Douglas

Customs cutter giving chase to one of the many boats involved in the 'running trade.'

Head and reckoned the ship was loaded with East India goods. The *'Sincerity'* was made ready to investigate when Captain Paul Bridgen, governor of the fort at Douglas, appeared on the quay with 300 men armed with swords, pistols, bludgeons and stones. Words were exchanged and an armed boat belonging to the cruiser was forcibly taken away and four of the custom men captured and imprisoned. The *'Sincerity'* eventually escaped and pursued the *'Hope'* which went ashore on Ramsey Sands. Captain Dow sent his mate and ten men to rummage the vessel but when the hatches were opened they found 150 Manxmen lying in wait! Ramsey's Governor Matthew Christian ordered the boarding party to be taken and marched off to prison. The locals then unloaded the valuable cargo of tea, silks, chintzes and pepper. Some of the prisoners languished in Castle Rushen for many weeks in dungeons 'not fit for a Christian' as the Liverpool Commissioners reported to London which could offer no advice.

That was some years ago and the amount of contraband handled on the Island continues to grow and it must now be accepted that the Westminster Parliament will be forced to take some drastic action. Enquiries and investigations are being made and the recent report by Captain Webber ('An Impartial Enquiry,' 1760) seeks to provide details of the different branches of the trade. He mentions that on a moderate computation 700,000 lbs weight of tea are annually consumed in Ireland yet the importation from England is but 200,000 lbs so that the difference of 500,000 lbs is known to be brought from Gottenberg, Copenhagen and Holland to the Isle of Man, and from thence run into the ports of Ireland between Waterford and Derry. This tea thus escapes the one shilling and eight pence per pound duty so that the Revenue there suffers a loss annually of £41,666 13s 4d., not to mention the deprivation to the English Revenue and the East India Company of providing the 500,000 lbs of tea.

A more searching enquiry has been ordered by the Treasury and the Commissioners of Customs have proof that the several millions of pounds worth being handled by Manx merchants is resulting in an annual loss of £350,000 to the English Exchequer and something like £200,000 to the Irish Revenue. Against this they calculate that the Duke of Atholl receives £6,000 annually from insular duties, a profitable position he is loath to part with. But he is a Privy Councillor and he cannot protest too strongly at the approaches being made to him that he should relinquish his rights and pass control to the Crown. Westminster is applying further pressure by increasing the number of Royal Navy revenue cutters which are now in Manx ports and keeping a watchful eye around our coast. An announcement from Blair Castle is expected any day now.

SMUGGLERS' TALES

When the wind is up and the doors are shut, many are the tales told round a jar of jough. There was Dollan Radcliffe of Andreas whose lugger ran brandy from the Lhen to Kirkcudbright creek until he was captured by a cutter and taken in tow. In the night he surprised his guard and threw him overboard. He cut the tow and vanished into the darkness with his illegal cargo.

There was John Clarke described as 'one of the greatest and most cunning rogues from the Isle of Man.' He landed his weekly cargo near Whitehaven until discovered after being given away by someone he had sacked. Robert Copley was another local smuggler until he was intercepted near Whitehaven having on board 200 gallons of brandy and 20 gallons of Canary wine.

And then was was the famous Thomas Stowell of Ramsey. He died aged 22 in 1755 after being shot during a chase by a Custom boat. He lies buried in Bowness chuchyard. Beside him under the same yew tree are the unmarked graves of six other Manx smugglers who perished in a storm in 1762.

(An extract from the Universal Dictionary of Trade and Commerce by Malachy Postlethwyatt, 1755.) 'The Isle of Man is, and has been for many years, a common storehouse for all manner of goods and merchandise that pay high duties in Great Britain or Ireland, or are prohibited into these kingdoms.

The merchants in that Island have constant supplies of tobacco, both in leaf and roll, tea in chests, with all sorts of East India and Dutch goods from Holland. They are likewise supplied with tobacco and other things from Dunkirk, Ostend, Norway and even some parts of Great Britain; with tea and India goods of all sorts from Gottenburg and Denmark; with vast quantities of brandy and wines from France, and with rum from America; the Scotch and others send vessels to our plantations on purpose for that commodity and land it there, contrary as is supposed to the Act of Navigation.

These goods are all warehoused in that Island, and afterwards put into packages of lesser quantities and weights for running into Great Britain and Ireland. There are nine or ten large wherries and many smaller boats constantly employed in the smuggling trade, if the weather permits, laden with high duty or prohibited goods. The boats from Peel-town supply the east and north parts of Ireland, the Highlands and West of Scotland; those from Douglas and Derbyhaven supply Wales, Cheshire and Lancashire; and those from Ramsey, Cumberland and the country on each side of the Solway Firth, the chief trade being into the Scottish border near Annan, the country being all ready to assist and protect them in such numbers as no officer dare offer to molest.

These cargoes, which generally consist of brandy, rum, tea, and silks, are afterwards brought out of the Scottish border on horseback in the night, under an armed force of men into England till they have passed all the preventative officers on the English border. Thus all the northern counties are supplied with these commodities at a cheap rate, for the smuggler from that Island generally buys his brandy and rum there at two shillings the gallon, or under, and by paying no duties is enabled to undersell the fair trader.

The yearly loss to the revenue of Great Britain and Ireland is now computed to be over £200,000, not to mention its carrying away the coin, to the detriment to the honest merchant, landowner and even ruin to the labouring people; for being constantly supplied with brandy, rum and Dutch geneva at so cheap a price, induces them to drink much as not only weaken their constitutions but corrupt their morals. All methods of prevention have proved ineffectual.

For the year to July 1754 a manufacturer of tobacco with eight working men shipped to Ireland 175,358 pounds of neat tobacco. There is now in the Isle of Man several workhouses in which are employed 50 men upwards, all workers of Irish roll tobacco. A manufactory of such proportion in England would produce over 50,000 rolls — 1,000,000 pounds of neat tobacco — which must all be run chiefly into Ireland. Such an amount represents a loss of Irish duties amounting to £24,000 16s 7d. This tobacco imported into the Isle of Man makes a considerable article of the Lord proprietor's revenue to bring him £1,500 per annum.

In the ports of Cumberland it is complained that not one merchant has imported and paid duty for any French brandy for seven years past, the country being glutted with the same by the smuggling boats and night-carriers from the Isle of Man though for the last four years that Island has been chiefly supplied with coarse Spanish brandy from Cette and Barcelona which they purchase at 10 pence a gallon and sell out again to the smuggling boats at 18 pence a gallon, the duty on importation of the same but 1 pence to the Lord of the Isle.'

HERE IS THE NEWS: 1765
DUKE OF ATHOLL SELLS OUT TO WHITEHALL

In spite of a last minute protest in London by a deputation from the House of Keys, the Duke of Atholl has given in to pressure to sell his sovereign rights as Lord of Man to the British Crown, and bring the Isle of Man under direct rule from Whitehall. The action is being taken because of the worsening effect of the Manx smuggling trade on revenues accruing to the Treasury. We have this report:

'The British Government has been showing increasing frustration over the freedom with which the 'smuggling trade' has been operating in the Island since the latter part of the 17th century. The drain on Treasury revenues is now estimated to have been millions of pounds. There have been accusations that attempts to impose control have been thwarted by corruption among Customs officials based in the Island — and by a deliberate lack of supervision on the part of the Lords of Man. The intention now is that King George III and his successors, will be Lords of Man, henceforth with power to send officers to enter and search Manx ports under what will be known as 'the Mischief Act.' This will mean imposing British taxes and duties on Manx goods, and making them payable directly to the Treasury in London. At the same time dutiable goods bound for the Isle of Man will have to be imported into Britain first, and taxed there. The Crown is, in effect, imposing an enforced takeover upon the Isle of Man. It will be carried through in law by what is to be called 'the "Isle of Man Revesting Act" under which Britain will buy out the Atholl family's rights of Lordship. A proposal in these terms was put by Prime Minister George Grenville to the third Duke of Atholl only last year, when he succeeded the second Duke. At first he was reluctant to sell, but was told that if necessary he could be compelled. This will not go so far as to take over the Duke's rights as Lord of the Manor — in other words he retains his personal property in the Island. It is the rulership that now passes into Crown hands — and there have been forecasts already that there will be a complete shutdown of economic activity in the Island, legal and illegal. This was why a Keys deputation was rushed to Whitehall to try and avert the disaster. But it has become clear that they were virtually ignored by the British Government. The Revesting Bill has already been introduced into the Parliament at Westminster. It is expected to have a speedy passage and become law by proclamation under the Great Seal of England before the year is half over. The Mischief Bill, which gives British Customs men absolute control over the trade in goods to and from the Island was introduced into Parliament in January. This is not expected to get the Royal Assent until next year, but its provisions will apply before then. A spokesman for the Keys said today that what was taking place would come to be regarded as the greatest disaster ever to befall the Isle of Man.'

NEW COINS NOW IN USE
The new issue of Manx coinage is now in general use in the Island and fulfilling the intention that it should, with the remains of the 1733 issue, supplant the use of any other copper coinage from other countries. One of the last acts of the late second Duke of Atholl was to authorise the issue. It consists of pennies and halfpennies bearing the Ducal crown on one side and the Three Legs of Man on the other. The exchange rate is one of 14 Manx pence to the English shilling. The Act providing for the issue says that henceforth: 'no person shall be obliged to take any other brass or copper money'.

MINING PROSPECTS
Mineral prospectors say there are good long-term prospects for the mining industry in the Isle of Man. It is already known that there are lead deposits; in the 13th Century Manx lead was used in the roofing of King Edward I's castles in Wales. But there are also deposits of iron and even silver and copper. The most promising areas are understood to be at Bradda and Foxdale. There has also been some prospecting in the Island for coal, but without any result so far.

THE BIBLE IN MANX
Work is progressing rapidly under the supervision of the Lord Bishop on the translation of the Bible into Manx. Bishop Hildesley plans to have it printed alongside the Manx Prayer Book and other religious works in the language that is still spoken by two-thirds of the people of the Island. The task of translation is divided among the Clergy and their work is revised by the Reverend Philip Moore, headmaster of Douglas Grammar School, and his pupil John Kelly. It will be recalled that while Kelly was taking some of the manuscripts to Whitehaven for printing his ship was wrecked and he was in the sea five hours before being rescued. But he managed to keep his manuscripts dry.

REVESTMENT: A BLEAK PROSPECT

'All the babes unborn will rue the day
That the Isle of Man was sold away'

This piece of doggerel is being heard with increasing fervour not only in our alehouses and taverns but even in some of our more genteel drawing-rooms about the Island. The purchase of our Island and the sovereignty of the Island returned to the king of England by the Revestment Act has initiated enormous changes in our lives, changes the extent of which few can as yet fully understand. It is clear already, however, that in place of hereditary Lords who at least took a personal interest, albeit in some instances a fleeting one, in our affairs we have seen substituted a group of faceless officials from England owing their first allegiance to the Treasury. These grey clerks have but one object in view — to extract as much revenue as possible for their masters and to do this with no concern for our Island's present or future prosperity. What will happen to the surplus moneys collected here? When the costs of our governing have been met where will the extra money find its home? The £70,000 paid to the Duke for his rights of Lordship in the Revestment Act seems adequate, remembering that he retains all personal property as well as his manorial rights. Those rights may well be disputed both by the Manx people and the English Government. The Mischief Act, to receive Royal Assent shortly, will intensify the grip of Westminster. Taken together, these laws could paralyse all forms of economic enterprise for years to come. So, the rhyme is perhaps already more true than any of us would wish.

And yet on July 11th all seemed fair. Then it will be recalled Mr. Wood, the first Governor selected by an English ministry, assumed office supported by the 42nd Regiment of Foot. At Castle Rushen it was for many a sad occasion. The venerable stones had seen the Manx flag raised that morning, as it had been for the past 300 years or so. But later that same day three volleys were fired, Mr. Wood made a speech and the Manx flag was lowered as the English colours were hoisted to announce that the reign of George III, King of England and Lord of Man, had begun. Sadness, however, could not be allowed for long. The bonfires prepared were lit, the demonstration of joy proceeded with and, in the Castle itself, the leaders of our society drank deeply of the new Governor's claret.

On a more serious note concern is already being voiced in all quarters of the Island about our representatives in the Keys and the members of the Council. Some suspect that already several see it as their duty to represent the interests of the English Government; others to see to the continuing interests of the Duke of Atholl. Who, it is asked, is left to protect the interests of the people of the Isle of Man? It will be instructive to see where George Moore, the Foreman of the Keys, will place himself; perhaps the recent fashion of describing him as 'Speaker' as in the House of Commons is significant. It will be recalled that he has occupied that position since 1758 and has the distinction of being the first of the merchant class to hold this high office.

Mr. George Moore of Ballamoar, Patrick, is the best known and most successful of the new class of Manx merchants. To many he is seen as the champion of our rights; few are better fitted for the task. His trading interests range all over the world, his business acumen is vast and he is well versed in dealing with the official interest of national governments. It is also notable that the merchants are increasingly challenging the traditional supremacy of our landowning families. Herring and barrels of wine may not possess the same cachet as quarterland acres but they seem undoubtedly to point to our future. His fine new mansion at Ballamoar, with its new trees, shrubs and variety of plants regularly imported from England and sometimes from

The Manx flag no longer flies over the ramparts of Castle Rushen now that Governor Wood represents King George III, the new Lord of Man.

Holland and New England, is a fitting tribute to his wealth and importance, while the 'pomegranates' mounted on the gateposts have proved objects of curiosity to all who have seen them.

The Speaker of the House of Keys, Mr. George Moore of Ballamoar, Patrick.

STAMPING OUT THE SMUGGLING

The harsh hand of the English Government is being felt more and more keenly throughout the Island. The new 'General Surveyor' of Customs, Mr. Lutwidge, is making his presence felt in no uncertain manner. In the early summer of 1766 he and his men descended on the port of Ramsey with their blunderbusses, pistols and cutlasses. Houses were broken into, beds and sacks run through with swords, boats smashed and burned, all without consideration for the people. The bitterness and anger that such conduct arouses is hard to exaggerate and the determination to outwit the Customs Officers increases with each outrage. It is no coincidence that at Peel the acting Collector of Customs was told that if he attempted to seize any boat his payment would be a brace of pistol balls through his head! These English Officers not only have the right to search all suspected ships, but offences can, in certain cases, be tried in courts outside the Isle of Man. Furthermore, in this concerted attempt to put an end once and for all to the Running Trade, it is rumoured that the forts and batteries around the Island are to be restored and Peel Castle, which in its ruinous state has proved an ideal store for the smugglers, is to be carefully observed.

Whether these measures will prove effective is, of course, another matter. Manxmen have sharpened their wits and gained considerable experience over many years. Claret barrels can be hidden beneath a layer of white herring barrels, brandy with the red herring, tobacco with oak staves — all these dodges which have proved effective in the past could well be practised again. And no doubt the system of informants now firmly established will be extended. More seriously for our great merchants, if indeed sympathy can be felt for these wealthy men, there remains the problem of the vast quantities of spirits, wines and tobaccos stored in a great diversity of places in almost every port and village of the land. It is reported on very good authority that in the cellars of Peel there lie no less than 6,000 gallons of brandy, 4,000 gallons of rum, 17 hogshead of claret and 17 pipes of Portugal and Spanish wine. All are said to be the property of our distinguished Speaker of the House of Keys. The problem it appears is that, as all had been purchased before the 1st March 1765, they will not qualify for some sort of licence. Rumour has it that these goods will eventually be licensed by the Board of Customs to provide some compensation at least for the stock left on the hands of our merchants. Some have decided to cut their losses by selling at ridiculous prices and then leaving the Island.

It now seems highly likely that the Manx coinage, for long a symbol of our independence, will be replaced by the regal coinage of King George III. It will be recalled that James Stanley, tenth and last Earl of Derby, had been so impressed by the first Manx coins issued by Douglas merchant John Murrey as far back as 1668, that he decided to issue his own coinage which he was prepared to accept as rent. As the British Mint insisted that the coins bore the image of Queen Anne, the Earl set up his own mint at Castle Rushen. The coins were cast, not struck, in copper and limited to pennies and halfpennies, there being no demand for coins of higher values. These first coins were rather crude in quality by today's standards but caused interest by the design they bore which features the Derby crest adopted by the first Sir John Stanley, King of Man from 1405 to 1414. Sir John had married Isabel, the only child of Sir Thomas Lathom. The parents of Sir Thomas were childless and when out walking together they came across a baby boy lying in an eagle's nest. They took the boy back to Lathom House and adopted him as their son who became Sir Thomas, the father of Isabel. From that time onwards the Stanleys have used The Eagle and Child lying in a nest as the family's crest. On the coin the crest is positioned above a Cap of Maintenance and is surmounted by the motto *'Sans Changer.'* On the reverse the coins bear the Three Legs surrounded by the Manx motto *'Quocunque Gesseris Stabit'* ('Whichever way you throw me I stand') which also appeared on the Murrey pence.

The first of the Derby coins appeared in 1709 and it was not until 1733 that a further issue appeared. Even then there was a chronic shortage which allowed a considerable amount of counterfeiting to go on, especially from Irish quarters. Even today coins are rarely seen at markets and fairs where bartering is still the chief means of transacting business. This second Derby issue of copper coins was struck on blanks prepared in England but some, especially those in brass, were prepared at Castle Rushen where the coins were minted. Two English coiners were employed assisted by local smith George Wilks and his son John. Part of the issue comprises the attractive pennies and halfpennies struck in Bath metal, said to have been that of a number of brass cannon stored in Castle Rushen. The coins bear the Stanley crest and detail of the earlier Derby coins but the reverse side bears the initials I D (for James Derby) between the Three Legs and the spelling of Gesseris was corrected to Jeceris. A few silver proofs were also struck, one of which was sent as a gift to Bishop Wilson.

The Derby issue had to suffice until the first Atholl coinage appeared as recently as 1758, despite the rapid rise in trade and the continuance of much counterfeiting. James Murray, 2nd Duke of Atholl and successor to the Derby Lordship coined the Atholl copper pennies and halfpennies alike, except in size. They were minted by John Florry in Birmingham despite doubts expressed by some that this would encourage yet more forgery or even illicit use of the legal dies. The obverse side bears the monogram A D (Athol Dux) based on the date and surmounted by a ducal coronet. The reverse has retained the Three Legs and Motto. It is hoped that these features will be retained when the first of the new regal coins appear.

Derby coins, 1709

Derby coins, 1733

Atholl coins, 1758

HERE IS THE NEWS: 1777
VISIT OF JOHN WESLEY

John Wesley, the leader of the people calling themselves 'Methodists,' ended his visit to the Isle of Man today and said the support and encouragement he had received from the Manx people had led him to believe that the Island will be entered as a separate circuit at next year's Wesleyan Conference. He added that he hoped to return to the Island in the near future to see how well his work has made progress. We have this report:

'It now seems that Methodism has gained a strong foothold in the Island after many years of resistance and opposition from the established Church. And there is no doubt that it has been the preaching of John Wesley during his visit that has won over many new adherents. It is now nearly 20 years since the first Methodist preacher arrived in the Island. He was John Murlin, known as "The Weeping Prophet," who arrived at Ramsey and stayed a week. But he departed declaring that he believed he could do no good in what was a nest of smugglers. Two years ago the Methodist Church in Liverpool sent John Crook to Douglas to pursue the cause and although he had some success, he also encountered official opposition, and was even offered violence by a mob in Douglas set on him by the minister of St. Matthew's Church. There has since been a pastoral letter to the Clergy sent out by the Bishop of Sodor and Man condemning the Methodist preachers and their presence in the Island. But this does not appear to have convinced all the clergy — or Lieutenant Governor Richard Dawson. As a result John Wesley was afforded a genuine welcome when he arrived in Douglas by sailing ship from Whitehaven earlier this week. During his stay he preached throughout the Island, notably at Castletown where he spoke to a huge concourse of people outside Castle Rushen. At Peel he preached twice — once at five o'clock in the morning and even then he had a large and enthusiastic audience. Before leaving the Island this morning he said he had found the Manx people deeply serious but more lovingly simple-hearted than he had found anywhere else in his travels — which was no wonder, he added, because there were only six papists and no dissenters to be found in the Island. The text of the Lord Bishop's pastoral letter on Methodism has just been published in full and it is in severe terms. Bishop Richmond speaks of the "crude, pragmatic and inconsistent, if not profane and blasphemous, extempore effusions of these pretenders to the true religion." He says his Clergy should "use their utmost endeavours to dissuade their flock from following or being led and misguided by such incompetent teachers." But many clergy have said they will ignore his Lordship. A spokesman said "they regarded his views as violent and intolerant".'

CLASH BETWEEN THE DUKE AND KEYS MEMBERS

There has been a clash between the House of Keys and the fourth Duke of Atholl over his continuing place in Manx affairs. It was the third Duke who sold his family's sovereign rights as Lord of Man to the Crown of England in 1765. The present Duke, who succeeded him on his death three years ago, now alleges that the Keys have been obstructing him in his collection of the manorial dues in the Island which he says are still the right of his family to receive. The Duke has accused the Keys of being no more the representative of the Manx people than of the people of Peru.

EMIGRATION ON THE INCREASE

It has been estimated that well over a thousand people have now left the Island in search of work because of the depressed conditions in the Manx economy following the so-called Revestment of 12 years ago. Others are finding it difficult to live because prices are being forced to rise steeply. But there is encouraging news. There appears to be a major revival of the Manx fishing industry taking place, after many men had abandoned it to join the smuggling trade which resulted in Revestment. Exports of salted and pickled Manx herring are now going to Britain, France, Spain and Italy — and even to the Americas.

MILITIA TO BE REFORMED

Militia forces in the Island are to be put back on a proper footing and recruiting is expected to start shortly. A spokesman for the Regular Army garrison at Castle Rushen said the militia had fallen into such disarray that there were no longer watch-and-ward duties being carried out. There is also a lack of trained officers and of men capable of responding to military discipline. The spokesman said there was a need for an organised Manx military formation because of the present threat of war with France and Spain. It is proposed that the unit should be called the Royal Manx Fencibles.

SYSTEM OF YARDING TO GO

Finally, reform of the old and often controversial system of taking men and women into employment by the more prosperous in the Island — known as yarding — is contained in a new Act of Tynwald. This lays down that labourers and maid servants will no longer be obliged to enter employment only at certain times of the year — and at certain fixed rates of pay. The intention is to create a more open employment market in the Island. Critics of the yarding system say it is feudal and oppressive — and typical of the many outdated laws that still apply in the Isle of Man.

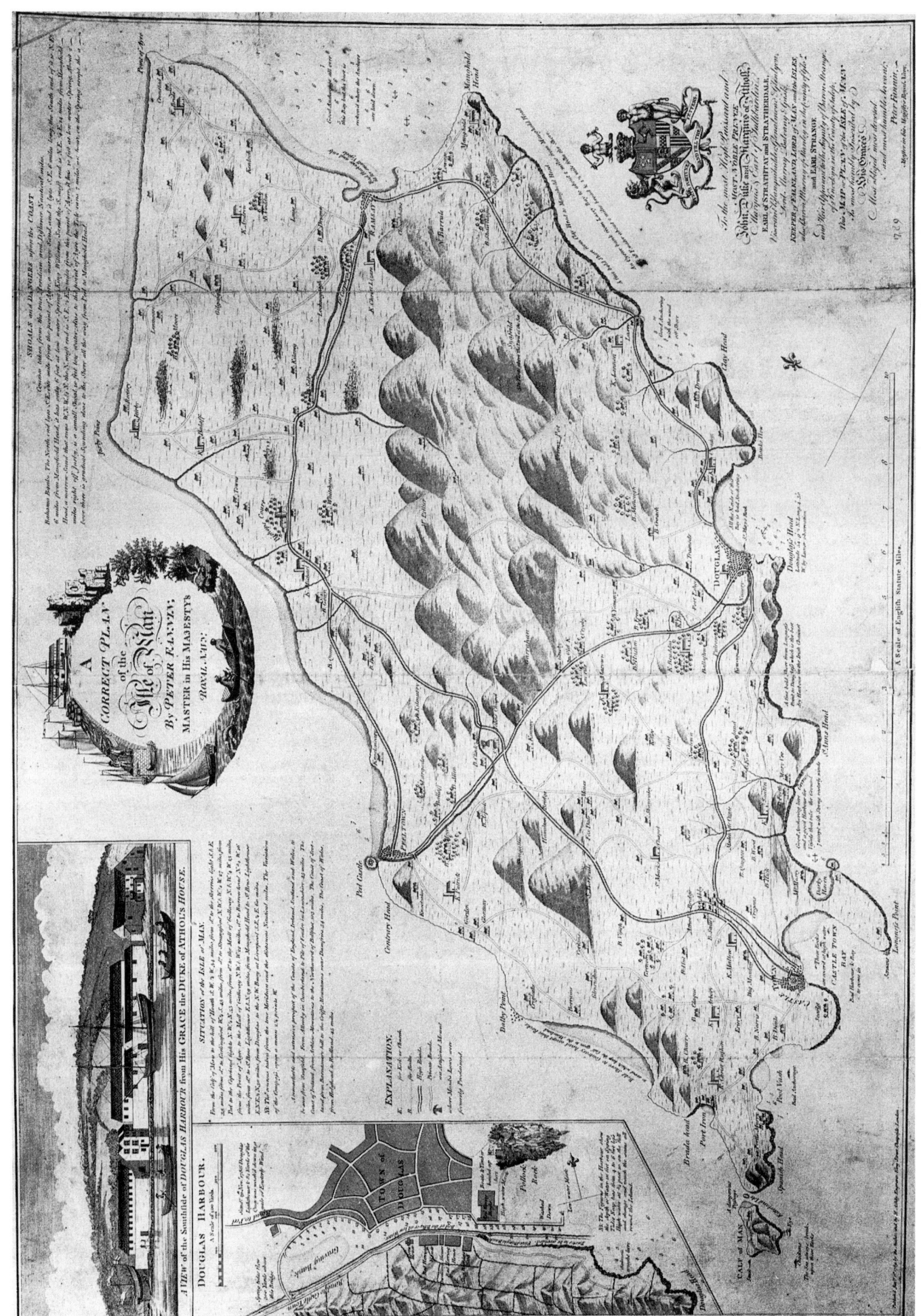

HIGHWAYS AND BRIDGES

Those Island residents who have endured the perils of the arduous sea journey on the packet to Whitehaven have returned with wondrous tales of the new turnpike roads now abounding throughout Lancashire and surrounding counties. The newly introduced mail coaches have speeded up the carriage of letters to such an extent that recent correspondence posted in London reached its destination in Castletown in only seven days. It is hoped that ere long such stage coaches will be speeding along the roads in this Isle, but our local intelligence indicates that the Highway Committee has much work to do before this can become a practical consideration.

Mixed reports are received from various parts of the Island as to the condition of the roads and bridges. It was only recently, in 1787, that the ravine at Ballure was bridged as a result of a petition from the inhabitants of Kirk Maughold and Ramsey who were having great difficulty in travelling to and from the parish church. Other bridges that have been completed or repaired during these past several years include the harbour bridges at Douglas and Ramsey; the bridge across the Sulby river on the ancient highway from the mountains towards Andreas; the new crossing at Ballaleece on the realigned road from St. John's chapel to Peeltown; and those at Ballacorlett and Ballig on the new road from Kirk Michael through Barregarrow, Cronk-y-Voddy, Cronkbane and Rhenass to where it joins the Douglas to Peeltown road at the farm of Mr. Craine near St. John's.

Although the main bridges mentioned in the Bridges Act passed over fifty years ago have now been erected, there are a number of fords on bye-roads which are proving very hazardous for travellers, particularly in the winter months, and the Committee is being urged to remedy this serious situation. The roads, too, are of varying quality and some of these are so narrow as to prevent two horses laden with creels from passing, let alone carts. Surely, this is a contravention of the succession of Highway Acts passed this century.

Those roads which are in a passable state are the new lines laid out by Mr. James Hamilton some twenty or thirty years ago. His policy was to leave alone the ancient twisting highways that had been used from time immemorial, and strike out across virgin countryside laying down new straight roads, quarrying material as he went along and utilising the gradients and hill passes to the maximum effect. Mr Hamilton was appointed as the first Supervisor General of Highways by the Highway Committee shortly after their formation following the Highway Act of 1753. His first role was to co-ordinate the work of the parish surveyors who previously had been functioning in a rather haphazard manner.

The parish surveyors' responsibility, since the 1712 Highway Act, had been to ensure that each quarterland holder, and those landowners with road frontage, expended three shillings and fourpence on repairs to the parish highways. If this was insufficient they then organised all the residents of the parish into completing the work, a most difficult task without central control, particularly for those parishes traversed by the main routes.

Mr. Hamilton was also charged with making new highways as directed by the Governor and the Highway Committee. The first such road was to be from Castletown to Douglas via Newtown to supersede the ancient highroad nearer the coast that was proving increasingly inadequate for the considerable traffic between the capital and the main port. Work on this road started at the bridge at Castletown and then went past the Creggans' farmhouse to Ballasalla. The roadworks then proceeded through Portobello and left the Malew Abbeylands near the new bridge at Ballaglonney where the Santon labour force took over from the Malew men. Progress over the Santon hills was slow although the most economical route was chosen; several years passed before the new road crossed into Braddan at Newtown from where a link was made with the ancient highway at Kewaigue leading past the Nunnery to Douglas harbour.

Mr. Hamilton next set to work to establish a new line of road from Castletown towards St. John's chapel. The first obstacle he reached was the Silverburn river where he built a magnificent bridge dedicated to the Duke of Atholl. From there the road was laid almost in a direct line across the shoulder of Barrule and down to Foxdale waterfall where Hamilton constructed a high level bridge which now bears his name. The road was completed to St. John's chapel and recently a link was laid past the farm of Mr. Craine and on towards Kirk Michael. It was on this road that the previously mentioned bridges at Ballig and Ballacorlett, near the 'rough road' or Bayr Garroo, were erected.

A distant view of the Nunnery mansion showing the Douglas Stone Bridge. It was erected in 1778 to the design of George Steuart, the Duke of Atholl's architect. Nearby can be seen shipping and the brewery at the top of Douglas harbour.

The highroad crosses the Glass river over the Quarterbridge and leads across the Claddagh to the Duke of Atholl's present Manx seat at Port-e-Chee House. In the centre of the picture can be seen Kirk Braddan Church nestling in the trees.

Other new roads that the Highway Committee have recently completed include an improved line from St. John's chapel to Peeltown and from Peeltown to Kirk Michael. This road has been continued on through Milntown to Ramsey and is proving most useful to travellers in the north. It is planned to embellish the new roads with milestones similar to the ones already placed on the Castletown to Douglas road.

The work of Mr. Hamilton has now been taken over by Surveyor General Mr. William Harpur and one of his first projects has been the construction of a new road northwards from Douglas to Laxey and on to Ramsey. The new route is more direct and, apart from the dip down to Laxey, has eliminated many of the precipitous inclines that proved most hazardous on the old track.

With many areas of the Island still devoid of highways there is much to be done. For example, the farmers south of Peeltown have been agitating for some time now for a route to the south to enable them to have access to the lime kilns.

A fine new map of the Isle of Man (shown on page 54) has recently been published by Mr. Peter Fannin and for the first time the roads of the Island have been shown. The map also includes the first published street plan of Douglas together with a view looking southwards across the harbour from the Duke of Atholl's town residence. Mr. Fannin is an eminent cartographer who sailed with Captain Cook on his second voyage of discovery after which he settled in Douglas where he runs a navigation school.

(With acknowledgement to Stuart Slack)

The hamlet of Laxey at the river-mouth which is crossed by a new bridge carrying the great road which leads from Douglas to Ramsey. On the river bank can be seen the 'bleaching fields' where the long lengths of linen cloth are laid out to dry.

HERE IS THE NEWS: 1790
MANX MARINERS INVOLVED IN SERIOUS MUTINY

The Admiralty in London confirmed today that there has been a serious mutiny aboard one of His Britannic Majesty's ships — and that a member of a well-known Isle of Man family is alleged to have been one of the ringleaders. The news follows the arrival at Portsmouth several days ago of the Captain of HMS 'Bounty', 36 year old Lieutenant William Bligh — who is himself related by marriage to a prominent family in the Island. We have this report:

'Lieutenant Bligh has given the Admiralty a full report of the dramatic events which have taken place since the Bounty sailed from Spithead nearly 27 months ago for the South Sea island of Tahiti. Her mission was to collect breadfruit plants in order that these might be conveyed to and grown in the colonies in the West Indies for the feeding of slaves. But it seems this peaceful mission had a violent and near fatal ending. Bounty reached her destination a year after setting out and stayed at Tahiti for three months taking on board more than 1000 breadfruit plants. She left the Island for Jamaica but, according to an Admiralty spokesman, it seems that many of the ship's company had fallen under the spell of the charms of life in an idyllic part of the world. On April 28th last year Lieutenant Bligh was seized while asleep by mutineers led by his second-in-command, Acting Lieutenant Fletcher Christian, member of the Christian family of Milntown, Lezayre, who belongs to a branch of the family in Cumberland. The Admiralty said another ringleader appears to have been Midshipman Peter Heywood, son of the late Deemster Heywood and member of another distinguished Isle of Man family. The Deemster was the Duke of Atholl's Seneschal. After the mutiny Lieutenant Bligh and 18 loyal officers and men were set adrift in an open 23 foot launch with, as sustenance, 150 pounds of bread, 32 pounds of pork, six quarts of rum, six bottles of wine and 28 gallons of water. In the ensuing 47 days they covered 3,618 nautical miles and endured terrible privations before making landfall at Timor in the Dutch East Indies on June 14th last year. The Admiralty says it was **Lieutenant Bligh's seamanship and leadership that brought them through, and he immediately started making his long journey back to England. Meanwhile nothing is known of Bounty and her 25 mutineers, but they are suspected to have stayed somewhere in the South Seas.**

Lieut. Bligh is married to the former Miss Elizabeth Betham, daughter of Dr. Richard Betham, Collector of Customs in the Isle of Man. They were wed at Onchan church in February 1781 while he was serving in Manx waters aboard HMS Ranger. Their daughter was baptized at St. Matthews, Douglas, three years later. Mrs. Bligh has had a letter from her husband in which he declares: 'I have now reason to curse the day I ever knew a Christian or a Heywood or indeed any Manxman.' But the mutineers will be brought to justice. The Admiralty says the frigate HMS Pandora is to be sent to the South Seas to search for them.'

ROYAL COMMISSION

The Duke of Atholl is to petition the King in Council for the appointment of a Royal Commission to inquire into his remaining rights and privileges in the Isle of Man. It was his father, the third Duke, who agreed to Revestment in 1765. But when the present Duke succeeded 16 years ago he began campaigning for more compensation from the British Government, and for the strengthening of his revenue rights as Lord of the Manor in the Island. This has already brought him into serious conflict with the House of Keys.

TRADE BADLY AFFECTED BY LICENCE SYSTEM

Traders in the Island are complaining that business is continuing to to suffer because of the trade restrictions imposed by the British Treasury. They point out that foreign ships are not allowed to transport goods to and from the Island, and what trade there is, is restricted to the mainland of Britain. They say the main drawback is the licence system operated by the Commissioners of Customs. Under this limited quantities of dutiable goods can be imported into the Island, by licence. But the Manx traders say the licences are monopolised by English traders outside the Isle of Man, often operating under fictitious names, and charging the Manx people excessively high prices.

CALL FOR VACCINATION AGAINST SMALLPOX

Doctors have warned that there is still a risk of outbreaks of smallpox in the Island, and there have been demands for the introduction of vaccination. The last epidemic was only 10 years ago and there have been two others in the last 35 years, causing considerable loss of life. Vaccination has been used in England since 1721 and its use has become particularly widespread in the last 40 or 50 years. There has been criticism that it carries health risks of its own. But there are moves to be made in Tynwald for its introduction into the Island.

NEED FOR MORE AND BETTER POLICE

Finally, the deterioration of law and order in the Island, especially at night, has led to members of the House of Keys calling for more adequate policing. Community leaders in Douglas say the present force of peace officers, which operates under the control of the High Bailiffs, consists of men who are too old and feeble, and too badly paid, to be effective. The situation is made worse because they are only on duty by day, allowing lawlessness to run riot in the streets after dark. The strength of the force is a Chief Constable and five constables at Douglas, a Chief Constable and one constable at each of Peel and Ramsey. A Chief Constable is paid £12 10 shillings a year and his men are paid £5.

THE PLIGHT OF THE HEYWOODS

The news of the serious mutiny on board HMS *Bounty* has come as a profound shock to the growing social circle in Douglas among whom Lieutenant Bligh, Acting Lieutenant Christian and Midshipman Peter Heywood are well known. It appears that Fletcher Christian was one of the ringleaders and that Peter Heywood also found himself among those who cast Lieutenant Bligh adrift. Whilst no news regarding the whereabouts of Fletcher Christian is available, Peter Heywood was brought back to England earlier this year as a prisoner along with other mutineers. The anguish of the Heywood family can be appreciated and the fact that Peter's father died just before news of the mutiny was received on the Island has not helped matters. The widowed Mrs. Heywood is receiving support from her daughter Hester (called Nessy by everyone who knows her) and everything possible is being done to support young Peter now held at Spithead on board HMS *Hector*.

The Heywoods, of course, have been a leading Manx family for nearly two centuries going back to the time when a nephew of Peter Heywood, who was responsible for the arrest of Guido Fawkes of the infamous Gunpowder Plot, came to the Island to settle. Since then members of the family have variously occupied high positions including Governor, Attorney-General, Speaker of the House of Keys, Captains of Militia, Deemster and Seneschal. The late Peter John Heywood and former Deemster took a great interest in all local affairs, including the Manx language. Two of his sisters married Midshipmen whom they met at a ball given by Captain Elliott to celebrate his defeat of Thurot. The ball was held on board HMS *Aelous* in Ramsey Bay in 1760. Both the Midshipmen have risen in the service, Hester (a popular family name) is the wife of Colonel James Holwell of the Royal Marines, and Mary is the wife of Commodore Thomas Pasley.

The Heywoods lived at the Nunnery for many years and it was, as Deemster, Peter John Heywood sold the estate to John Taubman of the Bowling Green, Castletown. That was in 1773 when the Deemster resigned his position and moved his family to Whitehaven. His wife was the former Elizabeth Spedding of the Parade, Douglas, the fashionable quarters on the North Quay near the entrance to the harbour. There are nine children and at the time of the move Peter was only one and Nessy four years older. In 1780 the family returned to Douglas following the father's appointment as Seneschal by the fourth Duke of Atholl. They took up residence at the Parade and amongst their neighbours were the newly-weds William Bligh and Elizabeth Betham.

The young Peter Heywood decided to make the sea his career and probably learnt much of the art of navigation from the famous cartographer Peter Fanning who had set up a School of Navigation in Douglas. The Taubmans, close friends of the Heywoods, were also friends of the Blighs before they left to set up home in London. It is believed that it

Portrait of Nessie Heywood

was the Taubmans who recommended that Peter Heywood should be included in the crew of the *Bounty* expedition to Tahiti. That was two years ago leading to the sorry state of affairs in which the unfortunate midshipman and his family now find themselves.

In Nessy, her young brother has a devoted sister who is doing all she can to support him and her widowed mother. She is a popular and vivacious young lady and is forever writing letters, usually in verse and of a trivial nature. But in these recent weeks of desperation she has written many letters of a different nature, not only to Peter, but to all those whom she thinks can help the cause of her brother. Among these are her uncles, Colonel Holwell and Commodore Pasley. It is the latter who is the most influential and is in constant touch with his friend Captain Montagu, in command of the *Hector* on which the prisoners are being held. He has also hired the brilliant naval lawyer Aaron Graham to act as Peter's counsel.

The mutineers were held for three months before the trial began on September 12th. It lasted for seven days but it was not until the 24th that the long awaited result reached the Island, delayed as a result of stormy weather. The news reached the Heywoods in a most bizarre manner. It was a young boy who ran in to report the story he had just heard from a man recently arrived in a fishing boat from Liverpool. The man had read the report of the trial in a newspaper but had not brought the paper with him. The news was that Peter Heywood had been found guilty and sentence of death pronounced upon him and some of the others on trial. However, a recommendation for the King's mercy was announced in respect of Peter and one other. This news was later confirmed by letter from Nessy's brother James.

Nessy has now left the Island to ensure that no stone is left unturned to ensure that the King's mercy is granted and her brother is set free. She left on October 1st by fishing boat to Liverpool. By all accounts she had a most wretched journey which lasted 49 hours in heavy seas and torrential rain. Being both cold and wet she could only sleep fitfully. Having met her brother James she travelled up to London and has sent an appeal to Earl Chatham, First Lord of the Admiralty. It is also believed that she is preparing a petition to King George himself. It is likely to be the end of the month before any final announcement is made though there are high hopes that the recommendation to mercy will result in an acquittal. In the meantime our thoughts and prayers are with Miss Heywood and her brother still held on HMS *Hector* at Spithead.

The Nunnery Mansion, former home of the Heywoods.

HERE IS THE NEWS: 1792
ROYAL PARDON FOR PETER HEYWOOD

Three of the men who took part in the mutiny on board HMS Bounty in the South Seas two and a half years ago have been hanged from the yardarm of a ship of the Royal Navy at Spithead. But they did not include Midshipman Peter Heywood from the Isle of Man, who has been granted a royal pardon, or Acting Lieutenant Fletcher Christian. We have this report:

'The men who died were Tom Ellison, who was sixteen at the time of the Mutiny in April 1789, John Millward and Tom Burkett. They met their deaths on board HMS *Brunswick* with boat crews from the rest of the fleet standing alongside and looking on. Millward was allowed to make a final address to the ship's company and he is said to have been nervous but strong and eloquent in confessing the errors of himself and his comrades. But, the full story of the mutiny on the *Bounty* still remains to be told. It was in March 1790 that news of it reached England with the ship's captain, Lieutenant William Bligh. The Admiralty immediately despatched the frigate HMS *Pandora*, under the command of Captain Edwards, to the scene of the mutiny in the South Seas. She reached the island of Tahiti in March last year and there found ten of the mutineers who were put in irons. Of the *Bounty* and the other mutineers, including Christian, there was no sign, but the arrested men did include Midshipman Peter Heywood, the son of the late Deemster Heywood. On her way back to England, however, *Pandora* was wrecked on coral reefs off Australia in August last year and four mutineers and 31 of her ship's company were lost. The surviving ten mutineers and 81 *Pandora* officers and men made their way in open boats over a period of 16 days to Timor — the place where Bligh and his men had made their landfall after the mutiny just 26 months before. Captain Edwards and his prisoners reached Spithead in June this year and three months later the court-martial was held under the presidency of Lord Hood. Six of the mutineers were found guilty but two were subsequently pardoned and one was discharged on appeal. The other three went to their deaths and the whereabouts of *Bounty* and the other mutineers is still a mystery. The pardoned men include Midshipman Heywood, who was only 15 when he set sail in *Bounty* nearly five years ago. His elder sister Nessy played a great part in saving his life, going to London personally to petition the King. It was decided by the court martial that Heywood had been loyal to Bligh but his mistake had been not joining his captain in the open boat. The Admiralty has since announced that Lord Hood himself is to take Mr. Heywood into his flagship HMS *Victory*, which means his career in the Royal Navy appears to be secure.'

DUKE OF ATHOLL APPOINTED GOVERNOR-GENERAL

It has been announced that the Duke of Atholl will become Governor-General of the Island from next year. This will invest him with all the civil patronage and also give him a veto on legislation. The move follows his dispute with the House of Keys and the Westminster Parliament over his powers in the Island now that his family are no longer the Lords of Man. His appointment as Governor is the outcome of a Royal Commission of Inquiry into the matter set up by the King last year. But the British Government is still refusing his pleas for an increase in the £70,000 paid by the Crown to his father, the third Duke, under the 1765 Revestment Act.

DOUGLAS TO HAVE NEW PIER

Meanwhile the Parliament at Westminster has voted £24,000 for improvements to Douglas Harbour. The intention is to build a new pier to give the harbour greater protection from the weather. This follows strong pressure on Britain by Tynwald following the gale which sank many boats of the Manx herring fleet in Douglas Bay five years ago, with great loss of life. The fleet was caught in the gale at night and was unable to find a safe haven in the harbour because the existing pier had itself been largely destroyed in a storm the year before.

GROWTH OF LOCAL INDUSTRY

A report issued today says industrialisation is increasing in the Island. A number of flax mills have started operations and are finding local markets for linen goods including sheets, towelling, sailcloth and sackcloth. The biggest of these is based at Tromode. There are also factories at Ballasalla engaged in cotton spinning — where the famous Spinning Jenny invented by James Hargreaves nearly 30 years ago saw first use in the Island. Unfortunately Customs officials in Liverpool are refusing to accept consignments of the company's cloth into England. They say importation of Manx goods in the raw state is illegal. A company spokesman said they were trying to resolve this difficulty.

ISLAND'S FIRST NEWSPAPER

Finally, publishing of the Isle of Man's first newspaper has been started. It is known as the Manks Mercury and Briscoe's Douglas Advertiser. A spokesman said today they believed they could expect good circulation because of the Island's rapidly increasing population. The latest census results show that there are now just under 28,000 people living in the Island altogether, most of them in the rural areas. The number of people living in the towns is only 7,200 — and most of them are in Douglas, which has now grown to be much larger than the capital, Castletown.

A TOUR THROUGH THE ISLE OF MAN

Judging by the recent publication in London of a guide book to the Isle of Man it seems likely that the Island is to be visited by a new tourist class of person in search of the unusual and the picturesque. It appears that this is the result of the Grand Tour no longer being available to complete a gentleman's education as a result of the French Revolution and events in Europe. Already they are touring Snowdonia, The Lake District and Scotland in increasing numbers. The author of the publication is a certain David Robertson Esq. who is no stranger to our shores having been stationed here as a customs officer under Dr. Betham. He returned in 1791 and made a complete tour of the Island. The author reveals himself as a republican and critises the Duke of Atholl and his demands as Governor of the Isle of Man. Indeed, the book is dedicated to John Christian Curwen M.P., who is a member both of the House of Keys and the House of Commons where he has spoken out against the role of the Atholls. It is believed attempts are being made to suppress the book. However, leaving aside the political contents, the copies available will no doubt cause considerable interest because of Mr. Robertson's comments on the Island and the Manx way of life. We leave readers to judge for themselves from these extracts:

'Douglas, from its trade and commerce is the most important town in the Island; and its inhabitants, from their intercourse with strangers, the most polished in their manners. Officers on half pay, and gentlemen of small fortunes resort hither; invited by the abundance of the necessaries, and the easy access to the luxuries, of life. They have given life and gaiety to the town; and have contributed to polish the manners of the natives. Convivial societies, assemblies, and card parties, are now frequent among the higher circles of Douglas. Whist is their favourite game and cards are introduced on every occasion, and generally accompanied with a plentitude of excellent wines . . .'

'Among the inferior classes gaming is far more pernicious and inebriation is here its constant attendant. The harmony of society is sometimes marred by mutual prejudices. In many of the natives, notwithstanding a show of politeness and hospitality, there is a secret aversion to strangers: and in several of the English an unreasonable contempt of the Manx . . .'

'It was here that the bold adventurer, following the establishment of the Excise in England, by illicit commerce acquiring affluence, erected a mansion, more flattering to his luxury and ambition; while his less fortunate neighbour contented himself with a residence, barely adequate to shelter himself from the severities of the weather. This will account for the present irregularities of the streets; and the surprise which a stranger feels, on viewing several of the best houses hemmed in by so many miserable clay-built cottages. Several of these, however, have lately been demolished: and a spirit of architectural elegance seems now rising in Douglas; to which the Manx have many inducements, particularly from their easy access to some fine quarries of lime, stone and marble . . .'

'There is a free-school at Douglas; but what perhaps will appear astonishing to an Englishman, there is not in the whole Island a single edifice devoted to the restoration of the sick or the relief of the poor: yet, in few places, is private charity more universally liberal . . .'

'On some rocks near the mouth of the harbour, is an ancient fort, formerly intended for defence, but now used as a temporary prison for criminals. In the centre of the town is a small chapel dedicated to St. Matthew and on an eminence, a little west from Douglas, rises St. George's chapel which is a modern edifice, at once spacious and elegant . . .'

'At a little distance from Douglas is situated, in a most delightful solitude, the Nunnery — a modern building with an air of elegance superior to any other in the Island. The gardens are spacious and luxuriant; and the surrounding fields, being highly cultivated, and finely interspersed with woods and waters, present an exquisite landscape. Captain Taubman, the worthy proprietor, enjoys the esteem of strangers for his politeness and generosity and the respect of the natives for his worth and benevolence . . .'

'The Manx are solicitous to pay every respect due to deceased friends. When an inhabitant dies, he is attended to the funeral by a great concourse of friends and neighbours. Before the corpse a funeral hymn is sung, which closes on leaving the town but is resumed on approaching the place of burial. The corpse is then interred according to the rites of the Church of England: the solemnity of which, at Kirk Braddan, is considerably heightened by the quiet and gloom of the surrounding scenery . . .'

'The next object which engaged our attention was a bevy of country lasses, going at the early hour to Douglas market. They were seated on small horses with panniers; one side of which were filled with the produce from their little farms, and the other generally balanced with pebbles. The rose of health was glowing on their cheek; and gladness smiled in every eye. Their deportment was modest and unaffected; and, as they advanced they wished us good morning. 'Happy souls!' I exclaimed . . .'

'After leaving Newtown we proceeded to Ballasalla, a neat village. Here is a cotton-work which is conducted on the same principles with those in Lancashire and gives employment to many poor families. But the village acquires a greater degree of importance from the residence of Deemster Thomas Moore, a man of considerable abilities and penetration. The Manx have a culpable propensity to trifling litigations — a rash word, a choleric action, or a wound which the hand of friendship might easily have healed, is by the malicious industry of those who batten on the follies and errors of mankind, swelled into an intolerable offence until the eloquence of the Manx bar begins to flow . . .'

'Castletown, though dignified with the residence of the Governor of the Isle, is in wealth and mercantile importance greatly inferior to Douglas. It is however an airy and pleasant town; and though considerably smaller surpasses the other in neatness; the houses being more uniformly elegant, and the streets more spacious and regular. In the centre of the town, Castle Rushen rears its gloomy and majestic brow, and here is held the courts of Chancery and Common Law: but these are now conducted on principles nearly similar to English courts of justice. Although any person may plead his own

Douglas Pier before it was severely damaged during a storm in 1786

cause, yet none but the natives are allowed to practise at the Manks bar. More universally important is that no native, without intending to leave his country, can be imprisoned for debt. While a loathsome and hideous prison is ever ready for the most trifling debts, on swearing that he has no maintenance, he is entitled to 3s. 6d. a week from his creditor: and this generosity of the law generally prevents any tedious imprisonment in the dungeon below. Near the Castle stands the House of Keys, a building certainly not corresponding with the dignity of the representatives of the country . . .'

'About a mile from Castletown there is a very fine quarry of black marble, which is much esteemed by the natives for chimney pieces, tombstones etc. Here, too, are quarries of limestone which are wrought at low water; and during the recess in the fishery, employ some boats for its conveyance to the more distant parts of the Island . . .'

'Doctor Langhorne has observed, 'The Isle of Man is the only place where there is any probability of seeing a fairy.' The existence of these imaginary beings is still most devoutly believed in this Island and they have invested them with unlimited influence over the fishery. They frequently supplicate their favour, or deprecate their wrath, by various offerings. Whilst rambling among the mountains during my previous visit I was benighted and sought shelter in a lonely cottage. The sole tenant of this clay-built hut was an aged peasant who received me with much hospitality. He trimmed his little fire of turf and gorse and 'beguiled the lingering hours' with stories of places still haunted by fairies — some playful and benignant and those who were sullen and vindictive. The former of these he had frequently seen on a fine summer evening, sitting on the margin of the brooks and waterfalls, half concealed among the bushes; or dancing on the tops of the neighbouring mountains. He described them as gay, beautiful and shy; for they never permitted him more than a transient glance of their charms. The more sullen ones lived apart from the others and were generally enveloped in the clouds or haunting the hideous precipices and caverns on the sea-shore. To them Manxmen imputed all their sufferings and he himself had often heard them, in a dark stormy night, yell, as in barbarous triumph, when the tempest was desolating the country, or dashing vessels to pieces on the neighbouring rocks . . .'

'From Fairy-Hill we proceeded through a mountainous part of the country, to the lead-mines at Foxdale; which are wrought, under a company in London, by a few miners from Derbyshire. The ore being rich and abundant, the mines afford an ample recompense to the work-men; and would prove highly lucrative to the proprietors, were they conducted with more vigour and attention . . .'

'Nearer Peel is the Tynwald-Hill, a Danish barrow of a conic shape and beautiful structure, which, considering its ancient dignity and importance, we regarded with some degree of enthusiastic reverence. The approach to the summit is up a spacious flight of grassy steps, fronting the ancient chapel of St. John's. The chapel is now desolate and ruinous; the roof is greatly shattered, and the walls are now a sheltering place to the sheep in the neighbourhood . . .'

'About noon we passed the pleasant villa of Sir George Moore; and soon arrived at Peel, which now ranks as the third town of the Island; though from its impregnable castle, it was anciently deemed the most important. Previous to 1765, Peel had a considerable traffic with the Irish and the Scots smugglers; but since then its trade has almost disappeared. The town is at present inert and solitary, and the houses in general have a poor and miserable aspect; yet, situated near the harbour, are some stately buildings, which may be considered the only relics of its former wealth and commerce. The inhabitants are for the most part indolent and poor; but being hardy, seem contented with their humble blessings . . .'

'Next morning we proceeded on our ambulatory excursion returning to St. John's and taking the road to Kirk Michael

Tynwald Hill and the ancient chapel of St. John's

through country enriched with villages and farms, extending many miles before us. At noon we reached Kirk Michael, an extensive village pleasantly situated near the sea, about half way from Peel and Ramsey . . . About a mile from Kirk Michael is the residence of the Bishop of Sodor and Man which was formerly a venerable edifice; but by the present bishop the ancient palace was demolished, and on the ruins a modern building erected; inferior in external magnificence, but more adapted to the refinements and luxury of modern times . . .'

'On leaving Bishops Court we had a delightful walk in the evening through a fine country to Ramsey, where we arrived to supper. What I observed of Peel may with little variation be extended to this town. Both places flourished by the gains of illicit commerce; and since then the inhabitants of both seem to have been affected with a sublime indifference towards opening new channels of trade and commerce. In one instance Ramsey has the advantage of Peel. The neighbouring country, being highly cultivated, produces a considerable quantity of grain, part of which is annually exported from the little harbour of Ramsey; but this may be considered as the traffic of the farmers rather than of the merchants in the town . . .'

'Kirk Maughold, notwithstanding its former celebrity, is now the most poor and lonely village in the Island. The church stands on a very lofty promontory, in the centre of a church-yard, containing not less than five acres. It is enclosed by a strong mound of earth, faced on the outward side with stone; and a great variety of ancient and modern gravestones are scattered over this spacious enclosure. Perhaps from pious veneration to the memory of St. Maughold, the natives, for several ages, used this consecrated spot as the chief place of interment in the Island . . .'

'On leaving Kirk Maughold we proceeded, through a very sterile part of the country, towards Douglas and reached the village of Laxey. The group of cottages lies in the bosom of a deep glen; and from its retired creek, is resorted to by the few smugglers who now visit the Island . . .'

'Amid the wild and picturesque scenes, in the vicinity of Laxey, we passed the greater part of the day; and in the evening proceeded to Kirk Onchan, a pleasant and airy village, where the aliens who die in Douglas are usually interred. We visited the church-yard, which contains some marble monuments of recent date; and about sunset arrived at Douglas, highly delighted with our excursion through the Island.'

(From A TOUR THROUGH THE ISLE OF MAN by David Robertson Esq. Printed for the author by E. Hodson, Bell-Yard, Temple-Bar, London)

PROSPECTS FOR THE NINETEENTH CENTURY

As we move to the end of the present century let us take stock of our situation and with renewed hopes and aspirations assess the future. The political situation remains unclear with the position and privileges of the Duke of Atholl still a bone of contention. In religious affairs Nonconformity is challenging even more strongly the supremacy of the Anglican Church. But the economic position is, without doubt, our greatest cause for concern. As was stated a hundred years ago trade is our main hope closely linked with our manufactories which are still extremely limited. Many have already left the Island in search of a better living; and who can blame them with landowners paying wages at present of only eight pence a day without keep or about £5 a year with keep. Women can only earn half this amount. Better wages can be earned in the mills and factories dotted about the Island but the numbers employed continue to be small.

For too long our traders have endured a variety of obstacles. The infamous Navigation Acts have prevented our Manx merchants competing on equal terms with their protected English counterparts; cargoes taken to the British Colonies have been seized regularly by English officials. Nor does the Revestment seem to have improved the position. The introduction of the iniquitous Licence System has limited the quantities of such articles as spirits, tea, tobacco, sugar, coffee and salt which can be imported and then only through English agents who have had the Manx merchants at their mercy. This has been adjudged as unfair by the Commissioners so Manx merchants can now import and a few of them are prospering though the prices have remained as high as before. The Quarantine Laws, important in that many of the countries our ships visited were plague ridden, have meant the sight of vessels lying at anchor for weeks in our bays while their cargoes rotted or missed the market. The frequency of wars and the activities of the Press Gangs have added to the normal hazards of the sea yet, despite these difficulties, our ships still travel the oceans of the world. Nevertheless something more is required to stabilise our economy and we must look in other directions.

The upheavals on the Continent are beginning to bring about certain changes. The restrictions imposed by the British Government since 1765 are being slowly eased. Farm animals (horses, cattle, sheep and swine) are now regularly exported as indeed are potatoes and butter. Coarse linen from our flax mills, especially in the form of sailcloth, is proving a profitable business while herrings, both the red (smoked) and white variety are still in big demand and continue to be the basis of our economy. Coal and salt are, of course, major imports while 'luxuries' such as tea, sugar and tobacco remain at exorbitant prices.

In England the increase in wealth from the development of the great manufacturing and heavy industries is obvious to all. Perhaps off-shoots of these new industries will spread to the Island. There is the example of the spinning works established at Ballasalla in the late '70s with the finished product being returned to Manchester. We have our flax mills, woollen mills and flour mills ready to respond to demands from overseas. Then there are the kelp traders, the net makers and the breweries. Shipbuilding is on the increase and the main ports on the Island boast at least one yard apiece, and such is the high reputation of Manx-built vessels there could indeed be more. The Island has no coal, it seems, or at least none has as yet been found. It does have other minerals and some have, as copper and lead at Mine Hough (Bradda) and iron at Maughold, been mined for centuries. Lead and copper ores are now being extracted in various parts of the Island and, with such metals being required in the new industries of Britain, it could well be that the next century will see considerable exploitation of our mineral wealth.

Certainly it is in everyone's interest to develop in every way possible all these industries to enable the Manx people to break away from what too long has been an almost total dependence upon the simple crofting way of life with its farming and fishing.

We also need better harbours which have been sadly neglected and are now in a ruinous state. Peel has benefited by the shelter provided by the causeway now connecting St. Patrick's Isle with the mainland. But it is particularly heartening to see the new pier taking shape at Douglas; perhaps this can be regarded as a portent of a better future for the Isle of Man.

This drawing, from Mr Peter Fanning's 'Correct Plan' of the Isle of Man, shows part of the South Quay, Douglas. It details ship building and a visiting merchant vessel. The dwelling house separates the long red herring houses, while a brew house can be seen on the right.

THE RED PIER

Great scenes of jubilation accompanied the official opening of the new pier for Douglas harbour. The ceremony was led by John, fourth Duke of Atholl who laid the foundation stone some eight years ago, in 1793, following his appointment as Governor-General. Just about all the town, and many from beyond, crowded the harbour to join in the celebrations and take a first walk on the pier. It is the first public building work on the Island for many years and has been paid for by the English Government out of accumulated revenue. The pier has been completed at a cost of £22,000 and is an admirable construction which replaces the earlier attempt of building a pier in 1760 which was wrecked in a severe storm. The architect for the new pier is Mr. George Steuart who, as his name suggests, is from Scotland and has long been under the patronage of the Dukes of Atholl. He has completed a wide variety of commissions and gained a high reputation. Mr Steuart is no stranger to the Island having paid visits from as early as 1779 when he was concerned with the vexed question of the gaol at Castle Rushen and the general state of public buildings. Details were discussed with Lieutenant-Governor Dawson but nothing happened as a result of no funds being available.

In 1790 the English Treasury sent an engineer to report on the condition of Manx harbours and authority was given to the Island's Commissioner of Harbours to proceed with the building of a new pier at Douglas, one reason being that it would provide safe harbourage for the revenue cutters operating in the Irish Sea. At first a Mr. Voss was chosen to design the pier, but it appears the Duke of Atholl favoured Mr. Steuart.

Much of the pier and its buildings have been completed in sandstone from Arran, Scotland, a freestone which is readily carved. Because of its reddish hue the pier is already being called The Red Pier. It is skilfully blended into the North Quay from which it extends a total length of 530 feet thus providing deep water berths at high tide which means passengers can land for longer periods without being rowed from anchorages in the bay. The pier is 40 feet wide but after 450 feet it suddenly expands to 50 feet and is raised 3 or 4 feet above the other. This part is circular in shape in the centre of which is a handsome lighthouse.

On entering the pier the first object of attraction is a small octagonal house, surmounted by a tower, designated the Watch House where the Customs House officers are to be found, especially during the arrival of the packet ship from Whitehaven. Passenger luggage is examined lest it should contain smuggled goods such as spirits, tea and tobacco. Douglas is, of course, the only point of arrival for the packet ships and a record is kept of all arrivals and departures. Adjoining the Watch House is a plain building in which the Deemster for the southern division holds his court, as also the High Bailiff and the district magistrates. (The northern Deemster has recently been provided with a court house of similar simple but pleasant proportions in Ramsey, the

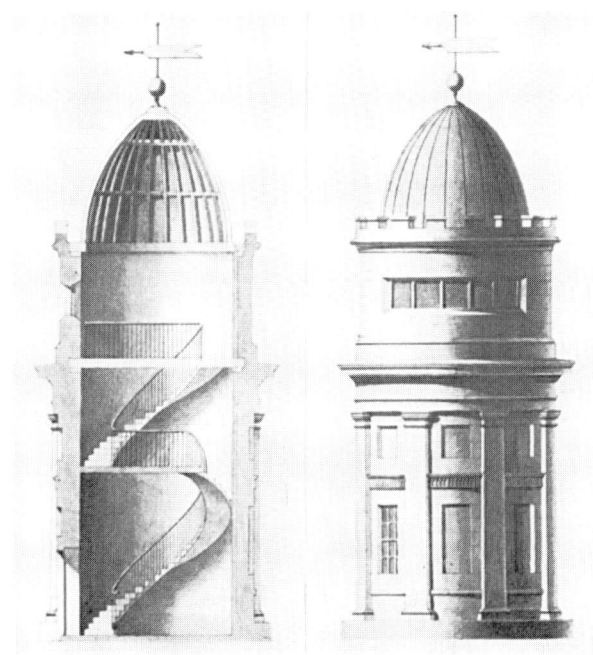

Details from the original elevations prepared by Mr George Steuart showing (above) the Lighthouse, whose canopy has since being modified, and (below) the Court House on the left and Customs House on the right.

architect again being Mr Steuart.) The court house also contains a temporary gaol before those convicted are transferred to the dungeons at Castle Rushen. Hitherto the old sixteenth century fort on Pollock Rock, and now in a very ruinous state, had been used to hold prisoners.

Undoubtedly, Mr. Steuart is deserving of high praise and the appearance of Douglas harbour has been greatly enhanced. Before the departure of the Duke in August of 1801 a tented dinner was held on land to the north of the town where, it is rumoured, the Duke intends to build himself a fine residence to replace the one he presently occupies during his visits at Port-e-Chee. Mr. Steuart is certain to be the architect.

The Red Pier is already proving popular as a promenade and in fine weather is crowded with the genteel so it is likely to prove the social centre of the town. News from the wars in Europe is eagerly awaited and fresh information from the passengers arriving quickly spreads throughout the town and beyond. The pier is neatly paved with flagstones and, in order to preserve its surface, people are being warned not to wear heavy footwear.

PRESS GANGS AT LARGE

There have been many examples recently of the Press Gangs of the Royal Navy operating in Manx waters. Every single bay round our coast has seen Press vessels cruising to and fro like sharks waiting to snap up our unsuspecting fishermen. Many are now so scared of putting to sea for fear they will not return. Everyone will recall only too clearly the arrival of H.M.S. *Adamant* in Douglas Bay only a few years ago when every vessel that could be reached was raided for men, and remember too that sad occasion when some forty men were seized in Port Erin Bay. Some managed to escape only by leaping overboard and hanging on to the anchor chains of their boats with their heads barely above water. It has become a familiar sight to see seamen fleeing in all directions from our harbours at the sound of the Press Gang's drum; even more familiar are the stories of our countrymen hiding in gorse ovens or cutting their way out to safety through the thatches of their cottages. To watch men running in panic from Douglas Harbour along the road to Braddan with armed sailors, and indeed soldiers in pursuit is not a pleasant spectacle. What is worse is the knowledge that when men, and even boys, are snatched by the Press Gangs no one, least of all their wives and families, knows really where they've been taken to or what exactly is happening to them. Many months can pass before a scribbled letter home can ease the worried minds. And not even that can ease the problem for the wives and mothers of finding food for themselves and their children. Jobs are hard to find and too many are forced through no fault of their own to rely on the cold and self-satisfied hand of charity.

From what can be gathered about His Majesty's Royal Navy our seamen, being experienced mariners, are highly prized, and many we know have distinguished themselves in the service. Manxmen have found other Manxmen in every sea and ocean of the world and no one would argue that in these perilous times, with our French enemies seeming to grow ever stronger, that the Royal Navy must be armed. Yet haphazard seizures cannot be the best way of achieving this. Merchant sailors diving overboard to escape the Press, as indeed happened some years ago to Hugh Crowe of Ramsey, cannot be accepted any longer. It would undoubtedly be better to expect the Fishing Fleets of Britain to provide a certain proportion willingly, say 1 in 7, and exempt the rest. Exemptions of the sort already in existence could be granted more readily and perhaps the Quota System introduced in England in the mid-nineties could be extended here.

Only by establishing some sort of organised system can our fishermen be given the confidence to make the herring catches so necessary to feed our people, and indeed swell the coffers of the Duke. Only by this can be avoided the dreadful

Perhaps a better alternative to the Press gang in these troublesome times is to accept the Royal bounty and enlist for naval service on the conditions detailed on the poster above.

calamities that befell the son of the Reverend Hugh Gell of St. Mark's some years ago. On being exchanged as a prisoner from France he managed to avoid the Press Gang in Plymouth by rowing ashore in the dead of night with three other Manxmen and then set off to walk to Liverpool. Reaching Runcorn, they were seized by another Press Gang but were able to free themselves after a vicious struggle. Fortunately, they were then able to find a boat in Liverpool so they could return safely home. It seems that only by battles like this the scandalous business can be avoided. We all know what happened at the Thorn Bush on the road to Peel, where the local men enticed the Press men and then set about beating them up! Such scenes should not be necessary and are certainly most undesirable.

IS THIS THE END OF DOUGLAS FORT?

The Fort, or Watch-House, has stood on the rocks to the north of the entrance to Douglas Harbour for many centuries though not as long ago as Roman times when, it is said, the brothers of Queen Boadicea sought sanctuary within its walls! In fact, the Fort was constructed about 1540 probably to the design of Stefan von Haschenberg who was in charge of military architecture for King Henry VIII. It is a contemporary of the Peel Battery on St. Patrick's Isle and the original of the Derby Fort on St. Michael's Isle, Derbyhaven. A similar fort can also be found at the entrance to Ramsey Harbour, both being used by the night watch in the days of Watch and Ward. The forts were activated by the Great Earl at the time of the Civil War. The Douglas Fort has periodically been repaired and re-equipped, and used by the Manx Militia. More recently it has become known as the 'Black Hole' and has served as the main cell for holding prisoners in Douglas. The dismal building is in a ruinous state and is not likely to survive much longer, now that the new Douglas Court House has a gaol to hold condemned prisoners awaiting transfer to the dungeons of Castle Rushen.

HERE IS THE NEWS: 1804
PRESTIGIOUS RESIDENCE FOR THE DUKE

Work is nearing completion on the Duke of Atholl's new residence in the Island, the Castle Mona, which stands in a commanding position on Douglas Bay about a mile outside the town. His Grace hopes it will be ready for occupation in August this year. We have this report:

'The work has been going on for the past few years and it is the biggest single building project to be undertaken in the Island in modern times. It was commissioned by the Duke following his appointment as Governor-General in 1793. As head of a prominent Scottish noble family he has resided mainly in Scotland since he succeeded to the title in 1774. But although his family no longer holds the Lorship of Man, he still exercises considerable manorial rights in the Island and as Governor-General he felt he should have a palace to go with the position. He decided against using the existing Governor's quarters in Castle Rushen, officially, because they have fallen into a ruinous state, but in reality because the English Government failed to support him in his bid to evict the Lt. Governor who was already living there. While Castle Mona has been under construction he has been residing on his estate at Port-e-Chee. The design work has been by the eminent Scottish architect George Steuart who built the Atholl family's London residence in Grosvenor Place. Mr. Steuart was originally commissioned to carry out a survey of public buildings in the Island, and he also designed the new Red Pier in Douglas harbour, which was completed three years ago. In the building of Castle Mona he has used stone from the quarries of the Isle of Arran. This was transported to Douglas by ships which sailed close into shore at high tide opposite the building site, and then tipped the huge blocks into the sea. At low tide the workmen recovered them and hauled them into position. A large lawn has been laid out in front of the main entrance and the approach to this from the south is by way of a half mile long curving driveway, which runs parallel to the sea from a pair of twin gatehouses. The interior of the building is particularly magnificent, unlike anything seen before in the Isle of Man. The fireplaces are imported — and the grand salon with its huge painted ceiling is acknowledged to be the finest of its kind. His Grace the Duke is planning to celebrate final completion with great conviviality.'

DEATH TO THE SMUGGLING

The British Authorities have launched a major effort to try and wipe out the last vestiges of the Manx smuggling trade, which led to the Revestment nearly 40 years ago. Under changes in the Revenue Laws all boats in the Manx herring fleet have to be registered so that their activities and movements can be better supervised. There has also been a big increase in the number of Customs officers based in the Island, and there are more armed Revenue cutters based in Manx waters. A British Treasury spokesman said the incidence of smuggling had been considerably reduced since the Revestment, but it was still giving some trouble.

ROYAL MANX FENCIBLES

The Royal Manx Fencibles have returned to the Isle of Man after their service in Ireland. They have been there since the Irish rebellion which broke out six years ago. Now that the war between Britain and France has broken out again it is expected that they will now be retained for service in the Isle of Man only. Their total strength is 800 men and they are reputed to be the most broad-shouldered troops in the British Army. When they parade shoulder to shoulder they cover more ground than any other regiment.

POOR STATE OF HIGHWAYS

The standard of highway repair in the Island has been criticised as indifferent, in spite of increased expenditure approved by Tynwald. A report to the Court says one of the reasons for the situation is neglect of their duties on the part of the parochial surveyors. The report adds that more public funds will have to be made available. It points out, however, that there have been considerable improvements in the last 40 years, with many highways reaching 18 feet in width. This has made it possible for wheeled carriages to be used in the Island for the first time.

CALL FOR MORE MANX BIBLES

The Society for Promoting Christian Knowledge has been asked to provide funds to assist in the printing and publication of the Manx language version of the Bible. The work of translation was carried out through a large part of the last century by the Clergy of the Island, strongly encouraged by the great Bishop Hildesley. But since his death in 1772 little has been done to make Manx Bibles, and also the Manx version of the Prayer Book, more readily available to the people of the Island. This is why the Society has been called in by members of the Clergy anxious to complete Bishop Hildesley's work.

LIFEBOAT FOR DOUGLAS

Finally — Douglas has taken delivery of one of the so-called lifeboats which are now to be found stationed around the coasts of the British Isles. The Duke of Atholl has paid for the 20 foot vessel, which is to be crewed by volunteers who will take it to sea to aid ships in distress in or near Douglas Bay. It has extra buoyancy because of the use of cork in the construction of the hull. The vessel will be kept in a state of readiness in a cove below Douglas Head. The Duke is a member of the Royal Humane Society and he has followed the example of other Society members around the country who have donated similar lifeboats to their communities.

Mr Meredith's detailed drawing of Douglas backed by the hills which are somewhat romantically exaggerated. On the left stands loftily the church of St. George, while the buildings of the North Quay lead to the the promenade of the Red Pier. In the foreground are some red herring houses. There is also a distant view of the driveway to the newly completed Castle Mona, beyond which are private villas.

THE MAGNIFICENT CASTLE MONA

The citizens of Douglas have for the past three years watched with great interest the construction of the magnificent residence of the fourth Duke of Atholl, some half a mile to the north of the town. Built on the edge of Douglas Bay, some say too near the tide line, it affords splendid views along the whole sea front. Of light coloured stone, shipped to Douglas beach from the quarries of Arran, the building is set in imposing grounds which are entered through twin lodges built where the Ballaquayle stream enters the sea. A sweeping driveway leads to the portals of what is becoming known as 'Castle Mona.' The completion of the Castle was marked with much conviviality which recalls the summer of 1801 when the Duke announced his plans at a tented dinner on the chosen site which was attended by numerous local gentry from all parts of the Island. A real party spirit was maintained throughout the day, the participants departing eventually for their homes, it is said, 'in festive mirth and harmony.'

The edifice is a fitting tribute to the architectural skills of George 'Athenian' Steuart, a man already noted for other fine structures both in Douglas and Ramsey. Alas, the great architect, now in his 74th year, no longer enjoys good health. When the Duke celebrated the completion of his Castle on 4th August, Mr Stewart was too infirm 'to partake the pleasures of the table' but he did make his appearance during the course of the evening, to the great joy of the Duke and the rest of the company. Some 52 of the quality attended an elegant reception and splendid banquet in the new house. There is to be an extensive planting programme which will, no doubt, add much to the distinction of the house and the reputation of the owner. It is reported that the cost of this splendid residence far exceeds the original estimate. Many will recall his attempts to claim the continuation of the ancient manorial rights which would have compelled his many tenants throughout the Island to provide labour and cartage free. He failed in his attempts and immediately, of course, labour costs became a considerable item. It is known, too, that from the outset the cost of materials — stone, wood, iron and so on — rose steadily during the building period. Indeed, the cost of the house is now reckoned to be no less than four times the original estimate of £8,000. It is, therefore, not surprising to hear that His Grace has approached Mr. Pitt at Westminster in the hope of gaining some remuneration; nor is it surprising to hear that the Duke has sold some of his Scottish acres to raise funds. Fortunately the difficulties attending the supply of freestone from Arran in the early years were overcome and the arguments over the number of tons sent to the Island, and the payments for them, were happily resolved so the building could be completed. No such arguments attended the supply of Leith Crown Glass for the windows.

No doubt, Castle Mona will prove a fitting residence for the Governor of the Isle of Man. Succeeding to the Atholl title on the death of his father in 1774, the fourth Duke has battled long and hard to improve to his advantage the terms of purchase of the Island by the British Government. At times this struggle has seemed to prejudice the interests of the Manx people; at others to support them. However, the Duke's appointment in 1793 as Governor-General with power to superintend the administration of the Island somewhat appeased his demands and was greeted with some enthusiasm by the people. It will be recalled that they took the horses from his carriage and pulled him to his residence at Port-e-Chee. As both he and they had been injured by the Revestment they seemed to regard him as a 'fellow-sufferer.' Everyone hopes that now his new residence is completed the Governor will be able to spend more time on the Island and not merely leave his duties to his Lieutenant-Governor and officials.

The Duke of Atholl's stately Castle Mona which now stands on the shore-line of Douglas Bay.

QUAYLE'S BANK, CASTLETOWN

Already proving popular with tradesmen and gentry is the Isle of Man Banking Company, more often referred to as 'Quayle's Bank' after its Managing Partner, Mr. George Quayle. It is offering the first banking service on the Island and began in May, 1802, operating from Bridge House built by George Quayle some years ago across the river from Castle Rushen. George Quayle is, of course, a member of the prominent Manx family whose origins date back centuries in the parish of Malew. He is the eldest son of John Quayle, former Clerk of the Rolls and the Duke of Atholl's Seneschal, or Steward, on the Island, and Margaret, daughter of Sir George Moore of Ballamooar Patrick. George Quayle was a member of the first regiment of the Royal Manx Fencibles in which he became a captain. Later, in the wars against France, he raised a corps of Manx Yeomanry which was disbanded at the Peace of Amiens in January, 1802. (The so-called Peace, as we all know, was soon broken and we are once again at war with the hated Napoleon). Mr. Quayle has been a member of the House of Keys since 1784 and is much travelled. It was while he was in London he met Major John Taubman, also returning from the wars. The Major is a son of John Taubman and Dorothy Christian of Milntown. He had been commander of the South Manx Volunteers before commanding regiments in the regular army. It was during the meeting in London that he and George Quayle decided to embark on their banking enterprise, something which the Major had previously attempted with a Mr. Kennish as partner.

The instigators were joined by two other founder members James Kelly and Mark Hildesley Quayle, younger brother of George. Mark has been Clerk of the Rolls since the death of his father in 1797 and so continues the family tradition of holding this high office since 1736. The partners set up the Isle of Man Banking Company with each providing 500 guineas. Bank notes of one and five guineas are now circulating (to be followed with copper pennies and halfpennies) and the Bank is inspiring much confidence from leading merchants who regard the notes as safe as those of the Bank of England. Mr. Quayle has indicated that he is prepared to dispose of the Barony of St. Trinian's in Marown should the Bank find itself in difficulties. The Bank operates from the south side of Bridge House and it is planned to open offices in the other towns. The strongrooms at Bridge House, with openings by secret doors from two floors of the house, and having an independent stairway, have been fitted with an intricate lock system which it is said will trap any unauthorised intruder. The whole building has been modified by the inventive George Quayle. Beyond the house is the extensive stables where Mr. Quayle keeps his carriage which is one of the first to be seen on the Island. It causes great interest when Mr. Quayle uses it for his visits to Douglas.

Mr. Quayle has many interests and is a member of the Ancient and Noble Order of Bucks, a branch of which was founded in Douglas in 1764. Founder member was Peter John Heywood who at that time was a young advocate before inheriting the Nunnery estate on the death of his father, Speaker Thomas Heywood. John became a Deemster and he was the father of Peter Heywood of the Bounty affair. Another leading founder of the Order was Hugh Cosnahan of Santon, one of the foremost Douglas merchants and a patriotic Manxman. He had dealings in many Continental ports, was a member of the House of Keys for 35 years and appeared before the House of Commons in defence of Manx trade. Other leading Bucks have come from the Leeces, Drinkwaters and Stowells, all with connections with the maritime trade. Thomas Stowell is remembered as the foremost lawyer of the day, publishing the first volume of the Manx Statutes in 1792.

Whilst intent on furthering Manx commerce, fishing and agriculture, the Bucks are also noted for their social activities. To entertain his fellow Bucks and friends, George Quayle has built in the yard of Bridge House a most odd little building containing a dining room fitted out in every respect like the stern of a privateersman with the west wall containing cabin windows and a small 'promenade' deck. Inside there is a cook's galley and extensive wine bins. Whilst a bachelor, the owner loves to entertain and the cabin is the scene of much conviviality. The cabin was built as part of the extensions to the boathouse to accommodate boats owned by George Quayle and his partners. The boathouse is connected by a short slipway leading from Castletown harbour. One of the boats which find shelter here is the '*Peggy*' which was built in Castletown in 1791. She is a schooner rigged clinkerbuilt yacht designed to take part in local trading, carrying goods of various kinds, together with mail and passengers, between Castletown and mainland ports. She is also used for pleasure and in 1796 was taken across to the Lake District and trailed overland to Lake Windermere where she successfully took part in the well-known Windermere regatta. As may be expected the '*Peggy*' is no ordinary boat and the ingenious George Quayle has equipped the boat with sliding keels which operate through slots in the bottom. This means she can operate in shallow and deep waters where the keels add stability in rough conditions. It is said that this contraption will become standard equipment in boats of '*Peggy's*' size. She is 26′ 5″ in overall length with a 7′ 8″ beam and an inside depth of 4 feet. Because of the unsettled conditions and the danger from French privateers, '*Peggy*' is armed with swivel guns and she makes a brave sight when tacking out of Castletown harbour.

George Quayle M.H.K.

The Peggy at sea

HERE IS THE NEWS: 1805 VICTORY AT TRAFALGAR

News has just reached the Isle of Man of a great victory by Admiral Lord Nelson over the French and Spanish fleets off Cape Trafalgar near the straits of Gibraltar, in which a Manxman serving on board the flagship *'HMS Victory'* played a vital role. Unfortunately we also have to record the fact that in his moment of triumph Nelson himself was killed. We have this report:

'What is to be known as the "Battle of Trafalgar" has brought distinction for 34 year old Lieutenant John Quilliam, who is the eldest son of Mr. John Quilliam formerly of Ballakelly, Marown. He serves as First Lieutenant on *Victory*, having been appointed personally by Lord Nelson. At a critical point in the battle — which occurred on October 21st — the ship's mizzen topmast was shot away and her steering seriously damaged. To keep her in action a juryrigged steering system had to be set up with tackles either side of the tiller worked by parties of seamen in the gunroom below decks. It was Quilliam who supervised this throughout the action and then went on to show even more spirit. After Nelson had succumbed to a ball wound inflicted by a French marksman, an officer made to haul down the Admiral's flag. But Quilliam ran it back up declaring: "This ship is still under Admiral Lord Nelson's command and every man will continue to do his duty." This is not the first time Quilliam has achieved distinction since he ran away to join the Navy while still in his teens. After serving before the mast for some time he was commissioned as Acting Lieutenant at the age of 27 by Admiral Lord Duncan during the Battle of Camperdown seven years ago. Two years later while serving in the frigate H.M.S. *Elhalion* he was present at the capture of the Spanish treasure ship *Thetis* — which earned him £5000 in prize money. Eighteen months after that while in the frigate H.M.S. *Amazon* at the Battle of Copenhagen he had to take command when all his senior officers were killed. His conduct brought him to the attention of Lord Nelson, and led to his appointment in *Victory* where incidentally he found other Manxmen in the ship's company. Quartermaster John Cowle of Bride transferred to the *Victory* by rowing boat in the midst of the battle. There is also a claim that John Lace, also of Bride, lost his arm to the same bullet that killed Lord Nelson. Lieutenant Quilliam was promoted to Commander immediately after the battle and his achievements are now expected to give him even further advancement in the Royal Navy.'

NEW APPOINTMENT FOR CAPTAIN BLIGH

There is also news of another Royal Navy man — Captain William Bligh of the infamous *Bounty* mutiny. His name has been put forward for the appointment of Governor of the Colony of New South Wales, which becomes vacant in three years time. He has held a number of sea commands since the mutiny sixteen years ago — and a ship he commanded was involved in the infamous Mutiny of the Nore in 1797. But he went on to fight at the Battles of Camperdown and Copenhagen — as did Lieutenant Quilliam. Captain Bligh was married in the Isle of Man and lived in Douglas for some time. He and his family later moved to London.

WESTMINSTER HOLDS OUR MONEY

Revenue is now exceeding expenditure in the Isle of Man, according to figures issued by the British Treasury. They show that £23,000 has accrued to the Island's account at the Treasury. But the Parliament at Westminster is being accused of refusing to allow the money to be spent in the Island itself, where our harbours and public buildings are falling into decay. A Commons committee set up to consider the surplus funds has decided that they should be absorbed into the Consolidated Fund, in spite of strong protests by Manxman Mr. John Christian Curwen who is Member of Parliament for Cumberland.

WOOLLEN MILLS FOR ISLAND

Plans have been announced for opening woollen mills in the Island. It is intended that a concern to be known as *Mwyllin Doay* (Union Mills) should start operations on a site two miles outside Douglas, on the road to Peel. The intention is to use the fleeces of Manx sheep as raw material and the move will be a big step forward in the growth of manufacturing industry in the Island. Paper mills, flour mills and tanneries have also opened up in the last few years. The Island's first newspaper, the 'Manks Mercury', has had a short-lived career however, having closed down after thirteen years of publication. But it has been replaced by a new paper, the 'Manks Advertiser'.

VACCINATION TO FIGHT SMALLPOX

Tynwald has agreed that vaccination should be introduced into the Isle of Man in the battle against smallpox. This follows a disastrous epidemic in the Island six years ago, the fourth in the second half of the last century. Vaccination has been in widespread use in England since 1740. But it has been subjected to criticism by many medical authorities, who say it can actually lead to the spread of smallpox. A spokesman for the Governor General said the situation in the Isle of Man would be closely monitored, and vaccination halted if necessary.

INCREASE IN POSTAGE RATES

Finally, postage rates in the Island are going up later this year. The cost of mail sent to England will be twopence per letter carried on the packet service operated by the Government between Douglas and Whitehaven. Internal rates are also going up, to a much greater degree. They will be fourpence an ounce for carriage up to fifteen miles, fivepence up to twenty miles and sixpence up to thirty miles. The Island's postal accounts show that it had receipts of £347 and expenditure of only £179.

THE ROYAL MANX FENCIBLES

When news was received from France that Napoleon Bonaparte had crowned himself 'Emperor of the French' at the end of 1804 the spectre of a French invasion was raised again. Memories were still strong of the failed rebellion of the United Irishmen led by Wolfe Tone in 1798 and supported by French troops. For centuries our defences were entrusted to the Lord's Garrisons and our own Militia whose numbers, 18 Companies from the Parishes and 4 from the towns, were provided by the obligation of all Manxmen to military service. They met for an annual camp at St. John's Chapel near Tynwald Hill, and on occasions were supported by a Horse Militia of some 68 men. Since the Revestment, however, it is fair to say that the Militia had fallen into almost complete disuse, although some troops were called out in 1793 to garrison Castle Rushen. For many years this country had been at war and the need for a more professional defence force had been apparent. In 1765 the Lord's garrisons were replaced by units from English Regiments of the line. However, the demands on the regular Army, first of the American and then the French Revolutionary and Napoleonic Wars, meant that we have been entrusted largely with our own defence. More recently several 'Volunteer' Corps have sprung into existence but it will be recalled that since 1779 the Island has had its very own professional troops. The Royal Manx Fencibles, resplendent in their red uniforms with blue facings, have become a popular and respected body of men throughout the Island. The first three companies, some 345 men, received the same pay and allowances as the British regulars. Sergeants earned one shilling a day, privates eight pence a day. They have occupied the barracks in the absence of the regulars but it was understood they were required to serve only in the Island. This condition did not, it would seem, apply to the Second Royal Manx Fencibles who were formed in 1793 and disbanded in 1802 after having served both in Ireland and England. Such had been the success of the Fencible troops in the support of the authorities, especially in the rebellion in Ireland, that it was no surprise that with the ending of the Peace of Amiens in 1803 and the new activities of Bonaparte that Lord Henry Murray, brother of the Duke, our Governor General and Commander in Chief, decided to raise a new body of men to be known as the Third Corps The Royal Manx Fencibles. There were three companies, each of 84 men, and they were intended exclusively for Home Defence. Each approved recruit, it will be remembered, received the princely sum of three guineas on enlistment. Only men under the age of 40 and over 5' 3" in height were recruited, although growing lads were exempt from the latter requirement. As the Continental War increased in intensity, especially in the Spanish Peninsula where the young British General Arthur Wellesley, later Wellington, was rapidly making a name for himself, it was decided to increase the establishment and by 1809 there were ten companies. It has not been easy to find the men in view of the determined activities of the Press Gangs who have taken many of our young men from our towns and villages. In 1806 Lord James Murray, the second son of the Duke of Atholl and nephew of Lord Henry Murray, succeeded his uncle as Lieutenant Colonel of the Corps. He was gazetted Colonel in 1809. Douglas has been the Headquarters for the Third Corps with companies detached in Castletown, Ramsey and Peel. The usual place for the Douglas detachment to parade except for guard mounting was the Camp Field but occasionally drills have been held on the Red Pier with an issue of ten rounds of ball shot to be fired out to sea. With the French not appearing the Fencibles were employed in apprehending smugglers who have used our shores from time to time. In 1807 parties of a corporal and four privates were detached from Douglas Headquarters for such duties at Laxey. Similar parties were detached from Ramsey to cover Cornaa and Bride; from Peel to cover Kirk Michael and Dalby and from Castletown to cover Port Erin and Derbyhaven. At the end of the decade, with the Royal Navy in undisputed command of the sea following Trafalgar, the need for the Fencibles has declined and the companies have been reduced to the original three. News has now come through that the Corps will be completely disbanded on 24th March 1811. Critics have claimed that little attention has been paid to real military training and too much time has been devoted to the details and trappings of the uniforms, splendid as they may be. Nevertheless, the men deserve much praise for their smart appearance and discipline, something expressed by the Duke of Atholl himself following an inspection. Nor can it be denied that The Royal Manx Fencibles have played an honourable part in the Island's military history and they have served the Island well at a most dangerous time in our history. It is our fervent hope that the armies of Europe will unite and put an end to the upstart Bonaparte once and for all.

Typical uniforms of the Royal Manx Fencibles in 1793. From left to right Light Infantry Company, Battalion Company, Grenadier Company, Battalion Company.

HERE IS THE NEWS: 1817
DEATH OF WILLIAM BLIGH

A report has reached the Isle of Man that Rear Admiral William Bligh, one of the central figures in the world-famous mutiny aboard 'HMS Bounty' 28 years ago has died of cancer at the age of 63. His wife, the former Miss Elizabeth Betham of Douglas, whom he married in Onchan parish church eight years before the mutiny, died at their home in London five years ago. We have this report:

'Admiral Bligh had a long and happy family life but his professional career was filled with controversy, even after the crew of the Bounty mutinied under his command in the South Seas. Only eight years later another ship he commanded was involved in the general Mutiny at the Nore. Then, after fighting in the Battles of Camperdown and Copenhagen, he was involved in more controversy nine years ago when he was serving as Governor General of New South Wales. After two years of his governorship his military and civil officers, alleging that he had used his powers tyranically, rose against him and put him out of office — although it was later claimed that the revolt was really inspired by the firm way in which he attempted to defeat official corruption in the colony. After his return to England he was never employed at sea again and retired to Farningham in Kent. His death coincides with the publication of an Admiralty report which clears up the last mysteries of the Bounty. After the mutiny she vanished into the South Seas with Acting Lieutenant Fletcher Christian and eleven mutineers on board. In 1809 an American ship under the command of Captain Mayhew Folger called in at a hitherto unknown volcanic island known as Pitcairn, to find the last surviving mutineer, John Adams, living there. He told the story of how most of the others, including Christian, had died in fighting with the natives round about 1793. Bounty herself had been burned and sunk shortly after arrival at Pitcairn in January 1790. Adams expressed his relief at Bligh's survival, and presented Folger with Bounty's chronometer. The war of 1812 between Britain and America prevented the latter reporting his remarkable discovery to the Admiralty, but several years ago it all came to light when two Royal Navy frigates chanced to visit Pitcairn. Their captains decided that Adams should be allowed to live out his life there in peace. And so the full story of the Mutiny on the Bounty has finally been told.'

CONFLICT BETWEEN DUKE AND KEYS

There is increasing conflict in the relationship between the Duke of Atholl and the House of Keys. The House has complained that since his appointment as Governor General 24 years ago he has spent most of his time on his estates in Scotland. Members say his last visit to the Island was two years ago and since the completion of his £40,000 ducal palace, the Castle Mona, in 1804 he has been in residence there only three times. Meanwhile, they add, the highest paid offices in the Island have gone to Scotsmen who are either connected with or dependent upon the Atholl family.

DROP IN WAGE LEVELS

Wage levels in the Island are falling drastically according to a recent Treasury report. The main reasons are depression in the Manx farming industry — and the large number of Manx soldiers and sailors who have returned to the Island in search of work following the peace of 1815. The report also points out that prices are going up at the same time — particularly for bread following bad harvests in the last three years. It says there are now scores of beggars to be seen in the streets and crime, especially sheep stealing, is on the increase. The report warns that the unrest in the civil population could erupt into violence.

DOUGLAS EXPANDING

House building in Douglas is on the increase and it is expected to be stepped up further when the new stone bridge over the harbour is completed next year, opening up new areas to urbanisation. This is in spite of a fall in the town's population in the last three years. This was mainly caused by Tynwald's decision to remove the immunity from prosecution enjoyed by foreign debtors who had fled to the Island. The loss is being made up by the migration of half-pay Army and Navy officers who are finding the Manx cost of living lower than England's. Town developers say the standard of housing is improving, and that consideration should be given soon to introducing some form of street lighting.

CALL FOR LIFEBOATS

There is concern over the lack of adequate lifeboat services in the Island. This follows the loss of the Douglas lifeboat several years ago when it was swept out to sea from the cove below Douglas Head where it was kept. It had been presented by the Duke of Atholl in 1803. Attention to the difficulties its loss could cause has been drawn by Lieutenant Colonel Sir William Hillary, Baronet, who set up residence in Douglas nine years ago. He has suggested that a lifeboat service for the British Isles should be set up on a national basis. But he admits there are improvements in the Island in other directions — including the lighthouses built last year at the Point of Ayre and the Calf of Man.

QUILLIAM BACK IN KEYS

Finally, the Island's hero of the Battle of Trafalgar, Captain John Quilliam, has been elected to the House of Keys. It has also been announced that he is to marry Miss Margaret Stevenson, daughter of Mr. Richard Stevenson, of Balladoole, Arbory. Captain Quilliam served in Lord Nelson's flagship 'Victory' at Trafalgar, returning to the Isle of Man for a brief period in 1807 when he was elected to the Keys a first time. But he was recalled to war service and in 1813 commanded 'HMS Crescent' on the Newfoundland station when she captured the American privateer 'Elbridge Gerry', of 14 guns. Captain Quilliam's personal fortune, gained by way of prize money, has made him a substantial landowner and businessman in the Island.

THE STATE OF OUR FARMS

The state of Manx agriculture has long been a cause for concern amongst the more thoughtful members of our Island community but its present condition can arouse no feeling other than that of utmost distress. And yet this century opened with such hopes of progress! John Christian Curwen, M.P. for Carlisle and a good friend to the Isle of Man, succeeded in 1806 in establishing a Manx branch of the Workington Agricultural Society and at last an organised attempt to drag Manx agricultural practices into modern times succeeded in getting under way.

Until these developments occurred it is reasonable to comment that what in the United Kingdom has come to be known as the 'Agricultural Revolution' was in danger of passing the Manx by. Until very recently many of our small crofters and labourers lived in huts with sod walls seven feet high, clay floors and a hole in the straw thatched roof. Their food was a mixture of meal porridge, potatoes, fish and, occasionally, a little meat. The major landowners, the quarterland farmers, whose standard of living was immeasurably higher, displayed for the most part little interest in improving their acres, while on the many small upland crofts lazy beds were, and in some cases still are, the order of the day. Even their ploughs, it is claimed, went no deeper than three inches. Their wages were scarcely enough to keep body and soul together. A married worker had to supplement his earnings by the labour of his wife and children as soon as they were old enough to work, while a single man might earn as little as £6. 6 shillings per annum with keep. Work was never done. Going from dark to dark in winter a man obeying his employer's edict would have his horse hooked to the plough in the field so early that it would be too dark still to see where to begin his furrow. Even the fishing, so necessary to give something extra to their diet, tended to contribute to the inefficiency of farming because most of the men were away for three months or so. Such was the widespread distress that many, if they could, left the Island which was described officially as 'descending into that miserable state of containing a few great landowners and their miserable dependents.'

However, the increase in demand during the late war, the missionary zeal of John Christian Curwen, even the arrival on the Island of English farmers, did result in considerable improvement upon that deplorable state of affairs. Turnips and clover introduced sporadically in the last quarter of the century have become extensive. Crop rotation has rapidly become common practice. Corn drills have appeared, swing ploughs are now regularly seen, while in the 1790's horse-operated threshing mills, many from Scotland, have been a welcome addition to the scene. Wheat, barley and oats have all benefited greatly from these new successful techniques.

THE AGRICULTURAL SOCIETY

Formed in 1806 the Society has done much to encourage farming improvements and visits by the major landowners to agricultural shows in Cumbria has led to the introduction of the latest ideas. Annual premiums have been awarded for such things as the best managed farm, stock of cattle, stallions for agriculture and the saddle, best crops of clover and flax, skill in ploughing, most land sufficiently limed and special awards for servants of both sexes in husbandry with unblemished characters and continuous service.

The Society held its first meetings at St. John's but, owing to the impassable state of the roads, a site at the end of the recently built Athol Street in Douglas was chosen for 1812. However support has continued to dwindle and the Society has now been disbanded. The chief supporters were the richer gentry, lesser farmers becoming suspicious that involvement might lead to some sort of taxation on their land and livestock.

The general prosperity of the country has been reflected in the sight of stone built cottages gradually replacing the old earthen dwellings. Perhaps the main area in which progress still needs to be made is in transport. Manx roads, such as they are, are thick with mud in winter and with dust in summer while sledges still outnumber carts.

Today, unfortunately, such progress and prosperity has come to a sad and sorry end. When the war ended in 1815 agricultural prices collapsed, wages were slashed, small farmers went bankrupt and poverty and despair once again stalked the countryside. This deep distress has been made worse by the fact that the returning soldiers and sailors have increased the competition for jobs and so wages have been depressed even more. At the end of the war £20 p.a. was a common wage for farm workers. It is already down to £14 p.a. and is going down further, while in the parishes the beggars are becoming numerous once more. The decision by the Duke and Bishop to increase rents has become a major source of discontent and judicious observers are already foretelling either a great wave of emigration or, failing that safety valve, widespread rioting and civil disorder if things do not improve.

UPPER BALLACHRINK, MALEW, is a typical quarterland farm representing the more prosperous members of the Island's rural communities upon whom the labourers are heavily dependent. Held by the Harrisons 'of the hill' for over two centuries, the present farmhouse dates from the end of the last century. Like most buildings of its type it is built of local stone with a slated roof, the walls being rough cast and whitewashed. It has two full storeys with an attic storey, a central hall and staircase and a stone-flagged dairy at the back with sloping roof and forming an integral part of the house. Many similar houses can be found on the quarterland farms throughout the Island.

HERE IS THE NEWS: 1822
FISHERMEN DROWNED IN RESCUE ATTEMPT

Three Castletown fishermen were drowned last night while trying to rescue members of the crew of a Royal Navy brig-of-war, '*H.M.S. Racehorse*', which had been driven on to the rocks of Langness. Six members of the crew of '*Racehorse*' also lost their lives in the stormy seas. We have this report:

'15th December 1822. The *Racehorse*, a two-decker of 18 guns, left Holyhead just over a week ago and was on her way to Douglas to take in tow the Royal Navy cutter *Vigilant* which was wrecked on Conister on October 6th this year. With 112 officers and men on board, the *Racehorse* sighted the Calf of Man light at four o'clock yesterday afternoon. Her pilot and master then set a north-easterly course to clear Langness, but in the December darkness and a heavy swell they lost direction and, seeing a light on shore, believed they were off Douglas pier. But the error was realised as the tide began driving them inshore and the commanding officer, Captain W. B. Suckling, who is believed to be a nephew of the late Lord Nelson, ordered the ship's cutter and galley to be launched to try and bring help. In the darkness they rowed all the way round Langness to Fort Island and it was nearly midnight before their crews reached Castletown. Meanwhile *Racehorse* started firing her guns and setting off rockets to raise the alarm on shore. She was driven hard on to the rocks and began to take in water. Fishermen in Castletown had by now realised what had happened and tried to launch their boats into the strong surf in the bay. But only one was able to make its way through the breakers, after which its gallant crew made five trips to and from the wreck of the *Racehorse* to bring the Navy men ashore. She was on her last trip, with Captain Suckling and First Lieutenant Falkner among those on board, when she was completely swamped by the waves. Three fishermen and five crewmen were lost. The loss of a cabin boy at the wreck itself brought the night's total death toll to nine. This morning daylight showed that the *Racehorse* had been pounded by the waves, causing her to break up and sink. The survivors reached land with only the clothes they stood up in.

The officers were lodged for the night at the George Inn, Castletown, and the men at the barracks.

Captain Suckling, a veteran of Trafalgar, was said today to have conducted himself throughout the dramatic events with cool courage. But he will have to face a court-martial for the loss of his ship. Meanwhile there is concern for the welfare of the families of the three fishermen who died. Lieutenant Colonel Sir William Hillary, of Douglas, who is in the forefront of moves to set up a national lifeboat service in Britain, said this morning the men's wives and children deserved pensions from the Admiralty. He said he would be enlisting the support of Captain Suckling in asking for this to be done.'

KEYS OPPOSE CHEAP FOREIGN GRAIN

The Duke of Atholl has persuaded Tynwald to petition the Crown for restoration of cheap foreign grain imports to the Isle of Man. His intention is to bring down the high price of bread and flour which led to the violent rioting at Peel and Douglas in September and October this year. The Duke's action is being opposed by the Keys, who want the embargo on imports to be retained. The riot ringleaders are now detained in Castle Rushen. The 29th Regiment of Foot, which was drafted into the Island to maintain law and order, is shortly to return to England.

POTATO TITHE TO CONTINUE

Meanwhile there is growing unrest over the insistence of Bishop Murray in continuing to collect the tithe on potatoes, turnips and green crops. Farmers say that if the tithe on crops is not abolished there is a likelihood of disturbances in the Island similar to this year's corn riots. Last year the Exchequer Court at Castletown upheld the Bishop's right to collect the tithes. Now the farmers are preparing to take their case to the Privy Council in London. It is estimated that the Church share of the annual crop under the tithe would amount to about £1,800.

REGULAR STEAMSHIP SERVICE?

Business leaders in the Island are considering ways and means of establishing a regular steamship service between the Island and Liverpool — to encourage summer visitors to come to Manx shores. They estimate that if this trade could be developed it would provide a useful source of new revenue for the Manx economy. They say the annual return could be equal to that of a good herring fishery. A growing number of summer visitors are already being seen in the Island. In the last three years steamers have been calling at irregular intervals and now a regular Douglas-Liverpool connection is suggested. It is pointed out that the mail packet service to the mainland has already been transferred this year from Whitehaven to Liverpool.

NEW SPEAKER OF THE HOUSE OF KEYS

The man who was Governor of St. Helena when the Emperor Napoleon was sent there in exile seven years ago is to be Speaker of the House of Keys from next year. He is 63 year old Colonel Mark Wilks, whose father was Vicar of Kirk Michael and later Rector of Ballaugh, and who is a godson of the late Bishop Hildesley. Colonel Wilks served in the Indian Army before transferring to the Civil Service. He was appointed Governor of St. Helena in 1813 and is reputed to have developed an excellent relationship with the Emperor. The Duke of Wellington is on record as saying that Wilks should never have been removed, as he was in 1816. Since returning to the Island he has lived on his estate at Kirby and taken a seat in the Keys. His wife is daughter of the late Speaker Taubman.

TRIUMPH FOR SIR WILLIAM HILLARY

The wreck of His Majesty's Brig-o-war 'Racehorse' on Langness Point and the fearful loss of life once again focussed attention on the urgency of providing purpose-built lifeboats and some sort of security for those who are prepared to risk their lives for the sake of their fellow mariners. Christmas, 1822, was not a happy time in Castletown with three well-known fishermen lost in the rescue attempt. Robert Quayle left a widow and eight children, the youngest of which was only four. Thomas Hall left a widow and two daughters while Norris Bridson, although a bachelor, had taken on the responsibility of maintaining a sister and her two sons. Being Christmas, the Governor's Appeal was well supported and it was possible to begin weekly payments of 3s 6d. to the widows and 2s. 0d. to the sister. But charity was not the answer as far as Sir William Hillary was concerned. He sent letters to the Admiralty in London and on Christmas Eve he received news from the Lord Commissioners that, in view of the 'courageous endeavours' of the rescuers, they were awarding life pensions to the bereaved families. Further, for those who assisted in the saving of the 'Vigilante', some weeks before, a small sum of money was being provided.

Sir William Hillary, since becoming resident on the Island some years ago, has become a notable figure around Douglas harbour. His origins were humble, having been born into a farming family of Quaker connections in Wensleydale, Yorkshire. His parents provided him with a good education to which he added the social graces. Through the contacts he made he was appointed equerry to Prince Augustus Frederick, the young son of George III. They spent much time sailing in the Mediterranean until Napoleon appeared. Back in England he married a wealthy heiress whose estate was in Essex. With invasion threatened from France he formed a large yeomanry army of cavalry and infantry for which he was created a Baronet. Unfortunately, his efforts exhausted the estate of his wife from whom he became estranged. Somewhat impoverished, he chose the Isle of Man for his new home and, in 1808, found accommodation in a recently-completed house on Prospect Hill. He had acquired a love of the sea and from here he has a magnificent view of Douglas Bay and all its activities.

In the early hours of Monday, October 6th, 1822, Sir William was awakened by the sound of cannonade being fired in the bay. From his window he could see flashes coming from St. Mary's rock. It was the Royal Navy cutter 'Vigilante' sending distress signals. Sir William rushed out into the stormy night and joined the crowd assembling on the Red Pier. Action was needed and it was Sir William who called for volunteers to man some rowing boats moored in the harbour and normally used for pleasure. Volunteers were slow but Sir William persisted and eventually the little boats headed out into the treacherous sea. The crews strove with might and main to reach the stricken 'Vigilante'. Her captain had ordered all heavy objects, including the cannon, to be thrown overboard to lighten the ship and he waited to see if there was any response to his distress signals. Then he saw the boats battling towards him. Lines were thrown and the rowing boats turned and the crews strained to free the 'Vigilante'. Slowly she was dragged clear of the rocks and was found not to be holed so she was able to be dragged nearer the pier from where lines were fired by rocket to be attached to the ship. Many willing hands hauled her to safety while Sir William and his companions collapsed with exhaustion. Ten weeks later came the wreck of the 'Racehorse' with tragic consequences. That Christmas Sir William pondered on what could be done not just around our coast but also around the British Isles where, annually, many lives were being lost despite valiant rescue attempts. Nothing but a properly organised lifeboat service would suffice. He reasoned that such a service should finance the building of specially designed rescue boats, organise and train the crews, and give a guarantee of support in the event of lifeboat men losing their lives. In 1823 he published, at his own expense, his ideas and looked towards the Admiralty to give a lead. He was to be bitterly disappointed but his perseverance brought a response from the Lloyd's insurance men in London. They would subscribe £50 towards the cost of providing a lifeboat for Douglas. More donations have been received and the boat is now being built in Sunderland.

This was a beginning but by no means what Sir William was striving for. Earlier this year he returned to London to continue his cause. A chance meeting with Mr George Hibbert, Chairman of the West Indies Merchants and a keen supporter of Sir William's ideas, led to a breakthrough. He was introduced, through Mr Hibbert, to Liberal M.P. Thomas Wilson. The latter's advice was that the appeal should be directed at the wealthy members of society with a view to creating a philanthropic organisation. It was agreed by the three that they should meet again at the Tavern in Bishopsgate Street and, in the meantime, each would try to enlist support. When they met again at the Tavern on February 12th the three were elated to find a large gathering of enthusiastic supporters. Terms of reference for the new institution were agreed and a public meeting was arranged to which the nobility, gentry, merchants and traders would be invited. This meeting, which will go down in history, was held on March 4th, 1824. Eminent people of all kinds attended and the Archbishop of Canterbury took the chair. A series of resolutions, based on Sir William's ideas, was quickly passed and the new body gave itself the name: THE NATIONAL INSTITUTION FOR THE PRESERVATION OF LIFE FROM SHIPWRECK.

Donations have been pouring in and there are plans to provide lifeboat stations at strategic points around the British coast, each under the control of a District Association. In honour of Sir William's efforts the first of the new lifeboats, to be built by Pellow Plenty of Newbury, is to be stationed at Douglas. Of sturdy construction the boats will be 24 feet long and will be propelled by banks of oars. Sir William has accepted the new boat which he considers ideal for rescues in Douglas Bay while the larger Sunderland boat will be used over longer distances around our coast. Sir William hopes to follow this with lifeboat stations at Castletown and Ramsey so that the Isle of Man will become a District Association affiliated to the National Institute. The achievements of Sir William brought much acclamation and we on the Isle of Man can be justly proud of his triumph.

An early type of lifeboat such as the one provided by the Duke of Atholl at the beginning of the century, but allowed to decay in Douglas harbour. The new lifeboats to be provided by the National Institution will be of improved design making more use of air-tight cases as an aid to buoyancy.

THE RECENT RIOTS AND CIVIL DISORDERS

The Isle of Man has witnessed over the past few years the most serious outbreaks of disorder, indeed of outright rioting, for several centuries. The grievances, whether they be considered real or imaginary, of the common people seemed to be directed in a worrying fashion against the pillars of established Society. While many might argue that it is the Duke of Atholl and his interests that are the real objects of the opposition, it cannot be denied that there is a clear possibility that such antipathy could easily be redirected even more strongly than in the past to the Manx landowning classes.

At the start of the decade in 1821 the Town of Peel witnessed a most serious disturbance caused by the high cost of flour and bread. The oats and barley crops had failed; the great landowners, who supported the English Corn Laws of 1815, were seen to have prevented the import of cheap foreign wheat that would have eased the situation; and the angry inhabitants of Peel rioted. They attacked the shops of the flour dealers, forced them on their knees, even stole their goods. As news of the rioting spread, the Yeoman Cavalry were sent to restore order, but only six of them unfortunately were found to be available. On their arrival one of them was posted as sentry in the Churchyard in the Market Place to prevent the mob ringing the Church bell to summon more rioters. Sadly he was pelted with stones, disarmed and had his sabre broken. Meanwhile the Commander, Captain Gawne, acting in his capacity as Deemster, had succeeded in seizing a few rioters and was proceeding to the Court House. In court the ring leader, Thomas Shimmin, promptly knocked down a Crown witness, attacked the Constables and the Coroner of Glenfaba, punched the Deemster and, so it is claimed, bit the High Bailiff on the leg. The uproar inside was matched by the growing riot outside. Shimmin escaped, the Deemster and his Constables were beaten back into the Court House when they pursued him, and the Deemster's horse was driven into the sea.

The rioting found its counterpart in Douglas but happily in both towns order was restored in a couple of days. This pleasing result came about, it must be said, not because the Deemsters were able to re-impose discipline, but because the Lieutenant Governor (General Cornelius George Smelt) acted with great speed and wisdom in forbidding any further export of Manx grain. Bread and flour prices went down rapidly and the unrest vanished into thin air.

However, the events left a legacy of bitterness. All attempts to recruit Special Constables in the west of the Island failed miserably while the determination of the landowners to export Manx grain and at the same time prevent the import of foreign corn has not been forgotten. Comments such as 'A winter eating barley bread will bring them (the lower classes) to their senses' might have incalculable consequences yet.

The general unease and resentment resulted more recently in 1825, in an outright rebellion against what was seen as the unjust actions of the Bishop and his supporters. Although the Fish Tithe had ceased, the Church has always levied a tithe on corn. However recent agricultural improvements have meant that the acreage down to corn has decreased while the cultivation of green crops, turnips and potatoes has increased. In October, 1826, Bishop Murray had announced from the pulpits of all the Parish Churches his new tithe on the green crops. Immediately the countryside was in uproar. In Arbory the Collectors were attacked; a mob marched on Castletown; at Knockaloe, near Peel, rioters burnt down 17 stacks in a farmer's haggard — he was the Bishop's Proctor — and then threatened to march on Bishopscourt. Bishop Murray and his family, escorted by 23 armed men, fled and took refuge in the Castle Mona. The Yeomanry Cavalry, who should have helped to maintain order, were branded as sympathisers to the rioters. Fortunately the Bishop rapidly came to his senses. He renounced his intention to collect the Green Tithe and immediately the disturbances ceased.

It is significant that such was the sympathy for the rioters throughout the Island as a whole that when the ringleaders were finally apprehended and tried recently, the Jury steadfastly refused to consider the death penalty and instead sentenced only two of the leaders to transportation to Botany Bay.

On reviewing the whole situation there can be little doubt that those sections of the population, commonly known as the lower classes, are becoming less inclined to accept the impositions of their rulers with the same docility as in the past. The spirit of the times shown in contemporary events both on the Continent and in Britain indicates that from now on the responsible authorities will need to be far more sensitive to the aspirations of the people if the stability of the social order is to be preserved.

From John Corrin's plan of Peel, showing the Court House by the harbour.

A MANX SKETCH BOOK, 1825

Mr. T. Ashe, a resident of Douglas since childhood, has published a most interesting bound volume entitled 'A Manx Sketch Book.' It is proving of interest to visitors and locals alike, especially to those who rarely, if ever, visit other parts of their Island home. Most of the highly-detailed sketches are the work of Lady Sarah Murray, wife of our Lord Bishop. Each sketch is faced with a page of description written by the author. The well-executed plates are the work of W. Day, Lithographer, of London. The printing of the text and binding has been undertaken by Mr. J. Penrice of the Manx Rising Sun Office, North Quay, Douglas.

We here reproduce some of the plates, with extracts from the text, which it is felt will prove most illuminating to present and future generations.

CASTLE RUSHEN (on stone by L. Hague) *'Castletown is an airy pleasant place, 10 miles from Douglas, 16 from Peel and 26 from Ramsey. It is divided by a small creek, which opens into a rocky but beautiful bay. In the centre of the town stands Castle Rushen which still braves the injuries of time and is a formidable object. A draw-bridge and stone-bridge cross the river and formerly there was a handsome piazza in the market-place, with a cross in the middle. The Castle now has a suite of excellent apartments, occupied by the Lieutenant Governor, nor can there be a safer or more commodious prison for public defaulters. Mr. Fitzsimmons, the jailer, bears a very high character for humanity as well as vigilance; and from being the very worst prison in His Majesty's dominions, it may now be considered as one of the best.'*

THE NUNNERY (Miss Goldie) *'The delightful Seat of Lieutenant General Goldie embellishes Douglas very much. It is in the immediate vicinity of the Town and was long celebrated as the favourite Residence of that hospitable and amiable character, the late Major Taubman. The saloon and other apartments are fine and well finished; but a new Mansion, in the Gothic taste, and situated on a higher ground, is in course of erection, and when complete, the old admired house is to be levelled to the earth. The Nunnery is universally admired for its beautiful prospect: From its windows upstairs, are picturesque views of great beauty; near the front of the House runs a clear river, wandering serpentine through the vale, till it meets the harbour — over it is a handsome bridge, and near it a corn-mill, fertile meadows, and many other objects of picturesque beauty.'*

KIRBY (Artist not named) *'This Mansion, which is a Seat belonging to Colonel Wilks, is situate about two miles to the north west of Douglas, and commands a delightful prospect of variegated landscape, with a boundary line at once gracefully and boldly indented. The House is one of the largest structures in the Island, and the chief beauty of the Peel road. The apartments are admirable for convenience, and the drawing and banqueting rooms approach the magnificent nearly as much as those of Castle Mona, on the Strand. Situated near the Nunnery, and close to Braddan Church, it forms a favourite walk for company. The most distinguished beauty connected with Kirby, is its plantations and woods which embellish the parish church, rural cottages, green meadows and arable grounds, all of which makes the Seat of Kirby a model.'*

LAXEY GLEN (Lady S. Murray) *'The group of Cottages expressed in the annexed plate lies in the bosom of Laxey Glen; and from its retired creek was resorted to by the few Smugglers who till lately visited the Island. On the East it opens into a fine Bay; and on the South, West and North, is surrounded by steep and lonely mountains which, with the deep vales between, afford some of the most romantic scenery. Laxey Glen is about 6 miles from Douglas on the road to Ramsey. It is the most direct route to Snaefell: as it enjoys unparalleled prospects most Visitors to Laxey determine to ascend it, though with much difficulty and fatigue. The wood of the Glen, though for the most part of nature's planting appears managed with exquisite taste, and on the heights are situated the Lead Mines: they are now in active operation, and contribute to the amusement of the Visitor.'*

SULBY GLEN (Lady S. Murray) *'This region, on the borders of the road from Kirk Michael and Ramsey, is the most enchanting spot on the Island, and a singularly rich one. It is, as its name expresses, a Glen, with deep woody banks, terminated by a river running over the rocks, and forcing a rapid way to the sea at Ramsey. The scenery here is highly diversified. The ground is well covered with trees and shrubs, apparently all planted. The valley winds considerably, and, in many places, by excluding foreign objects, renders the scenery more romantic. At the bottom of the Glen is a bridge, and on the summit of the highest ground from which the Glen descends is a Cottage, grandly situated with trees about it. Swelling grounds, cultivated hills, naked rocks, variegated groves and falling waters, present themselves to view in stages rising above each other, till mountains clustering together in the back-ground shut up the scene.'*

BISHOPSCOURT (Lady S. Murray) *'About a mile from Kirk Michael stands the Episcopal residence, called Bishop's Court. It is pleasantly situated, shaded by a grove of trees, and watered by a beautiful stream which passes through a delightful shrubbery and flower garden. The present Bishop, the Hon. and Right Rev. George Murray, has modernised the house, and expended large sums of money to render it comfortable. Though not very commanding in appearance, it possesses every desirable appendage; the gardens and walks manifest infinite taste, and the detached offices are at once extensive and convenient. There is a small Chapel annexed to the house. It has also been rebuilt, or modernised, in a style not less appropriate and admirable than that of the dwelling-house and other structures.'*

PEEL CASTLE (Lady S. Murray) *'Peel-Town, about ten miles from Douglas, is chiefly remarkable for the ruins of its Castle, Church and Cathedral which stand on a small rocky Island joined to the mainland, several years ago, by a strong stone wall to secure the Harbour. Since 1765, the Officers of the Crown have taken possession of this Island. It is now occupied by the High Bailiff of Peel who uses it as a sheep walk and annually pays a lamb, or some small consideration, to the Governor by way of acknowledgement. No doubt, from the vast remains of Religious and Military structures etc., scattered over the whole of this rocky Isle, it may be reasonably concluded that Peel Castle once afforded protection to all that was great and venerable in the Isle of Man. Were it profusely decorated with the ornament of the evergreen ivy no ruin in England could equal it in interest and sublimity.'*

DALBY BAY (Lady S. Murray) *'The group of cottages seen in the plate is the Village of Dalby situated between Port Erin and Peel Castle. It is too secluded to participate much of the benefit of enlightened science or improved customs. The inhabitants have little connection with the more polished Towns of the Island except for litigatory purposes, or in subservience to the profits from the fisheries — the fish taken from Dalby Bay are superior to all others in flavour and plumpness. The people are but very few degrees removed from the aboriginal colonists of the Celtic tribes when first drawn or driven towards the Island. The state and appearance of Dalby has, in fact, undergone no material change. The buildings, called cottages, are little better than hovels, or the kraels of savages, and all the features of society are blended under the law of a similar wildness and ignorance.'*

KIRK BRADDAN CHURCH *(by Rev. Thomas Howard) This drawing by the Vicar of Braddan shows the bridge built in 1793 to cross the River Dhoo. Behind the church can be seen the obelisk to the memory of a son of the Duke of Atholl, commander of the Manx Fencibles.'*

DOUGLAS FROM THE NUNNERY HOWE (by Jacob Strutt) *This fine oil-painting is by the highly renowned English landscape and portrait artist. The view of Douglas in the early 1830s shows St. George's's Church on the left, the church being originally built on the fields above the town but now being approached by the new buildings. The north side of Athol Street is nearing completion and the unusual viewpoint gives an unrestricted view along the broad street. Most of the best furnished houses contain at least one of Strutt's paintings while his principle patron, Sir William Hillary, has almost a gallery of them.'*

DEATH OF TRAFALGAR HERO

'**By the example of Duncan and Nelson he learned to conquer. By his own merit he rose to command: above all this he was an honest man, the noblest work of God.**' These words have been inscribed on the memorial of Captain Quilliam RN which has been erected by his wife in Arbory parish churchyard. Captain Quilliam died on 10th October 1829, and the inscription states in the simplest of ways the great respect and affection in which he is held by his fellow Manxmen and women. Above all, he will be remembered as the Lieutenant whose action at Trafalgar enabled Lord Nelson's flagship, the *'Victory'*, to continue in the battle following severe damage to her wheel. Quilliam rigged tackles to either side of the tiller so the ship could be controlled in the gunroom. Initially he supervised its use so giving rise to the much-quoted story 'that he steered the *Victory* into the Battle of Trafalgar.' A farmer's son from Ballakelly in Marown, the only parish not to border the sea, John Quilliam decided that farming was not for him and ran off to sea and joined the Royal Navy. He served before the mast and worked his way up to Commissioned rank through his own endeavours, no mean achievement. On his first ship, the *Lion*, he took part in a two year trip to China with the Embassy party led by Earl McCartney which met with the mandarins in Shanghai and Peking. The captain of the *Lion*, Erasmus Gower, was knighted for his services and Quilliam was again to serve under him in later years. Also aboard the *Lion* was John Barrow as secretary to McCartney but now, and for the last 25 years Secretary to the Admiralty and one of the most important people in the Naval Administration. Quilliam went on to serve at the Battles of Camperdown and Copenhagen but his fortune was assured by the capture of the Spanish treasure ship *Thetis* when he was serving on *Ethalion*. His share of the prize money amounted to £5,000. The fateful Battle of Trafalgar on October 21st, 1805, and the death of Nelson are now part of British History and Quilliam's reward for his conduct was to be promoted Post Captain and given his own command. This was in December 1805, and the following year he returned to the Island. He was one of 70 passengers who arrived at the Red Pier on board the *Duke of Atholl*, a well known Liverpool trader. In 1807 he became a Member of the House of Keys but it was to be but for a brief period for in the following year he was recalled for naval duties. He had various commands including trips to the Arctic. On one of these he had as his newly commissioned Lieutenant, William Parry, who has since made a great name for himself as an Arctic explorer. Quilliam's last command was *H.M.S. Crescent* and when cruising on the Newfoundland station captured an American privateer of 14 guns and 66 men.

With the war against Napoleon over Quilliam returned home and in 1817 became a Keys member once again. Later that year he married Margaret Christian Stevenson, second daughter of Richard Stevenson, the head of the well-known family who had owned their estate of Balladoole in Kirk Arbory since the middle ages. After their marriage they lived in the parish at Ballakeighan although they had a second house on the Parade in Castletown, where they resided in wintertime. This house is fitted with some fine mahogany doors made from wood imported from Spain by the Captain.

Captain Quilliam put his experience and energy to good use in Manx affairs for the next decade. He was one of those who challenged the Duke of Atholl concerning his methods of governing the Island. He will be particularly remembered for the part he played in revitalising the Herring Fishery which had fallen on evil days. Quilliam took a leading part in

Detail from 'The Death of Nelson' by Benjamin West. Among the sympathisers can be seen 1st Lieut John Quilliam who is standing on the far right of the group.

the Tynwald inquiry of 1827 which led to a new type of fishing boat being introduced in place of the old cutter-rigged vessels. These have been in service for many years and larger ones of up to 60 tons are ocean-going, trading red and salted herring to Liverpool and Mediterranean ports, returning to Southampton with oranges and onions.

The new boats, modelled on a Cornish design, were smaller and handier, their nets longer and deeper and the gear so much improved that fewer men were required as crew. To set an example, Quilliam had his own boat, an undecked fishing smack built in Ramsey in 1806, altered with half-decking and a single mast lugger-rigged. During more recent years the Dandy Smack or 'Lugger' has been evolved by adding a mizen mast on which is set a small lugsail. They have a crew of seven including a boy learning the craft and are now the mainstay of the Manx herring fleet, bringing fresh hope to this vital trade. Captain Quilliam also put forward projects for a breakwater at Derbyhaven and for a canal linking Derbyhaven Bay with Castletown Bay to facilitate the progress of the many Dublin brigs which are often marooned by easterly winds on their way to Douglas. At the moment there is no sign of either of these projects being brought to fruition.

The Captain had not enjoyed the best of health in recent years and has lately been staying at the White House, Kirk Michael, the home of General Goldie, Speaker of the House of Keys. His passing will be mourned by many but his uncompromising firmness of character and his views in promoting the welfare and interests of his native country will long be remembered. And the part he played during the mayhem on board the stricken *'Victory'* will be not be forgotten in the annals of naval history. He was, indeed, a great Manxman.

EMIGRATION: SEEKING A NEW LIFE

Perhaps the most striking feature of the Manx countryside at present is the number of deserted cottages (*tholtans*) that are to be seen especially in the northern and western parishes. The days when the hillsides in the evening gleamed with dozens of lights from the cottage windows seem to have gone. Soon the thatches or slates will be off the roofs and gorse will invade the once busy kitchens. It seems that all those who could beg, borrow or steal the passage money have gone and the Northern parishes, especially, have suffered great losses. Yet, sad though such sights may be, it cannot be denied that those who tore up their roots and emigrated to new lands seem to have justified their decision. Indeed such have been the hardships of the poorer classes of late, such the number of beggars, that many would declare that anything was bound to be better than the life they left.

The voyage, it is true to say, is an arduous one which, if the winds are unfavourable, can last several weeks in cramped and uncomfortable conditions. The fare a few years ago of £3 or £4 per adult, half for children, must have seemed a high price to pay for enduring the great dangers of the mighty oceans. No doubt there are wonderful sights to be seen — letters home report mountains of ice floating in the sea, great fish as big as any sailing vessel and so on. But there is much despair and often tragedy too. Both adults and children have died on the passage to the Americas, and on the less attractive voyage to Australia yellow fever is a regular fellow passenger. Even making landfall doesn't end the dangers. New York is apparently riddled with cholera and best left swiftly behind while Thomas Kelly, writing from Ohio to John Cowley in Laxey a year or so ago, refers to the disease striking even in Cleveland, where apparently a good many Manx people had already died.

It appears that most of the Manx head for an area called Ohio largely because of the glowing account of the region given to Manx audiences some years ago by the brother of the Rev J. E. Harrison, the Vicar of Jurby. Having reached New York the emigrants strike off up the Hudson River to a town called Albany and then Lake Erie and the Erie Canal, finally arriving at Buffalo. From there they make their way to the Cleveland area where those with some money may buy land and those without may find work. But most it would seem find happiness or, at least, contentment.

Letters sent home have proved most interesting. Many refer very precisely to the type of tools and implements to bring, even the type of seed to carry. Others, less practically perhaps, speak of the free society they find there, the lack of class distinction, the opportunities available for all. 'Ho, my boys, this is the place!' or 'The girls here do not work on dunghills like slaves as they do back on the Island. There is no begging, no men in rags, no striving for work as there is plenty for all.' Or, 'Here they scorn to be called master or mistress . . . . a poor man or woman is as much thought of as the richest . . . . you do not have to put your hand to your hat and humble yourself to the dust when you speak to a gentleman here like you do back home.'

Such sentiments, added to the fact that land is in an abundant and cheap supply, are no doubt greatly appealing to many Manxmen and women, especially the young ones. To our compatriots of the Methodist persuasion the reports that no one has to pay tithes to an Established Church is most surely a great attraction. Indeed, men like Patrick Cannell who it is reported preached on every single day of his voyage out in 1827 must find the religious freedom exhilarating. Those reports, written often with urgency and undoubted truthfulness, have a far greater impact than some of the more fanciful news that 'bread grew on trees and ginger root was the worst root here.'

Few will question that America for many years to come will act as a magnet to many Manx people. Experience has shown that once the contact has been established, the relatives settled, then others will follow. The availability of reasonably priced land, the abundance of employment, the social equality that certainly exists there, are too attractive to lose their appeal. For the time being, however, it seems that the initial rush is over. Many, many hundreds have left the Island and that in itself has done much to ease the social situation. The hope now is that after the turmoil and upset of the last few years, the Island will be more peaceful for a while at least. The deserted tholtans in our countryside can act both as a memorial and as a signal to those who might wish to follow in the footsteps of the emigrants.

FOR NEW YORK.

SUCH Persons as are desirous to Emigrate to the States of AMERICA are informed, that a large size Ship is daily expected to arrive at Douglas, from whence she will sail for New York, in a few days.

An opportunity such as the present may not soon occur, as Families and Individuals will save all the trouble and expence of proceeding by way of Liverpool.

Passage to New York..........£4 10s.
Children at a less price in proportion to their age.
Apply to   THOS. M'MEIKEN.
Packet Office, Douglas, 9 June, 1828.
A ship bound to Quebec will also call at Douglas, if a sufficient number of Passengers offer.

FOR NEW YORK.

TO Sail on the 1st of May, a beautiful SHIP, just finished building, at Douglas, of the burthen of 500 Tons, upwards of 6 feet between the upper and lower Decks, to be launched on Saturday, 4th April, will prove a most desirable Conveyance for Passengers, and will positively sail from DOUGLAS direct to NEW YORK, on the first day of May.

PASSAGE to be................£4. 10s.
Children at lower Rates, proportionate to their age.
Apply to THOS. M,MEIKEN.
Douglas, 30th March, 1829.

HERE IS THE NEWS: 1830
THE WRECK OF THE 'ST. GEORGE'

The Douglas lifeboat under the command of Sir William Hillary today braved a fierce gale to rescue the 22 people on board the Royal Mail packet 'St. George', which was driven hard aground on St. Mary's Rock at five o'clock this morning by powerful south-easterly winds. But 60 year old Sir William one of the founders of the Royal National Lifeboat Institution, has suffered extensive injuries, and the 'St. George' has broken up and sunk. We have this report:

'November 20th, 1830. The "St. George", commanded by Lieutenant Tudor R.N., had made passage from Liverpool during the night and anchored outside Douglas harbour to await daylight. The Isle of Man Steam Packet Company vessel "Mona's Isle" also arrived from Liverpool but because of threatening weather her captain decided to stand well out to sea. In the early hours of this morning the wind swung round to the south-east and built up to gale force, making the "St. George" drag her chain cable. She had kept up steam through the night and the crew were at their stations, but nothing could be done to stop the steamer going aground between the St. Mary's and Pollock Rocks. She began to fill with water and settled with her head towards the land with huge waves breaking over her. Sir William saw her distress rockets from his residence on Prospect Hill and immediately took the lifeboat to sea with Lieutenant Robert Robinson R.N., "St. George's" Steam Ship Company agent Mr. William Corlett, coxswain Isaac Vondy and 14 volunteer crewmen. In spite of the high seas they managed to get alongside the "St. George", between the ship and the rocks. But in doing so the lifeboat lost its rudder and six of its ten oars, and the two craft became locked together by fallen rigging. Sir William, who is unable to swim, was washed overboard with Mr. Corlett and two of his crew, and they were all hauled on to the wave-swept deck of the "St. George". Sir William was unconscious with six broken ribs. The crews of both vessels assembled on the "St. George" to make plans and began to cut away the fallen rigging. This took two hours of hard work in the storm but eventually everyone leapt aboard the lifeboat and, bailing water all the time, pulled themselves free. Fortunately, they were driven to the sheltered side of St. Mary's Rock with only a comparatively easy quarter mile pull to shore. They reached land with, miraculously, no loss of life. The "St. George" has been competing vigorously for the last three months with the Steam Packet's "Mona's Isle" for the mastery of the Liverpool-Douglas station. She has never been able to match "Mona's Isle" for speed and her loss appears to leave her Liverpool owners unable to carry on competition with the Steam Packet, which was formed in Douglas last year. A Steam Packet spokesman said the "Mona's Isle" was saved today by standing out to sea instead of anchoring inshore. He said it looked as though the Liverpool route might now be secured for what is a Manx owned and operated company.'

END OF THE ATHOLL CONNECTION

The death of the fourth Duke of Atholl brings to an end the Island's connection with the Murray family which goes back nearly a century to 1736. A settlement has been reached between the British Treasury and the Atholl family on the price to be paid for the latter's remaining manorial rights in the Island. It has been worked out at £417,144 — a sum which has already been condemned as exorbitant in the House of Commons. However, the British Treasury is likely to benefit handsomely from the collection of the Island's revenues and from their interest in the Crown lands and royalties from the mines. The fourth Duke, who died earlier this year, was still Governor General, if in name only. He had not visited the Island for four years. Now the Manx administration is entirely in the hands of Crown officials.

END OF CROP TITHE

Legislation is being drawn up to provide for a mutually agreed settlement of the long standing dispute over the collection of the crop tithe by the Manx Church. The intention is to prevent a repeat of the so-called Tithe Riots in the Island five years ago during which a mob of 5,000 men carrying bludgeons and pitchforks marched on Bishopscourt and forced Bishop Murray, for fear of his life, to abandon that year's tithe. Bishop Murray left the Island two years later and his successor, Bishop Ward, has been warned by the Clergy that the tithe should not be sought with any vigour in future for fear of causing disaffection among the people and more public disturbances.

KING WILLIAM'S COLLEGE

Work is progressing rapidly on the building of King William's College at Castletown, the foundation stone of which was laid earlier this year, on 23rd April, by the Governor, Colonel Cornelius Smelt. It is hoped that the first pupils can be admitted in about three years' time. It is now 142 years since Bishop Isaac Barrow, who was apalled by the standard of education he found in the Island on his arrival, established the Trust under which the school is now being built. The design work of the new building has been entrusted to the Douglas firm of architects, Hansom and Welch.

LAST OF THE 'BOUNTY' MUTINEERS

Finally, news has reached the Isle of Man that the last of the 'Bounty' mutineers, John Adams, died last year on the South Sea island of Pitcairn. All the other mutineers, including Lieutenant Fletcher Christian, had died or been killed by the time Royal Navy frigates found Adams living on Pitcairn 15 years ago. It was decided that he should be allowed to live out his life there. Meanwhile the only known survivor of the mutiny, which happened 41 years ago, is seriously ill and not expected to survive at his London home. Captain Peter Heywood, son of the late Deemster Heywood, was a 15 year old midshipman when he left the Island to sail with 'Bounty' on her fateful voyage. He has lived in seclusion, suffering from ill-health arising from the mutiny, for the last twelve years.

HONOURS FOR SIR WILLIAM

News of the dramatic rescue of all on board the *'St. George'* by the Douglas lifeboat has spread far and wide. It has also inspired an oil painting which vividly portrays the event and a close inspection reveals many details such as the following: Sir William Hillary in beaver hat in the stern of the lifeboat directing the rescue; the bright red costumes of the lifeboat men; the excited crowd on the Red Pier and, in the distance, the Steam Packet's *'Mona's Isle'* battling her way to safety in the south-easterly gale. Following High Bailiff Quirk's report to the Royal National Lifeboat Institute (now with the patronage of King George IV) Sir William has been awarded a second Gold Medallion which is unprecedented. Lieutenant Robert Robinson has also been voted a Gold Medallion with Silver Medallions to Mr. Corlett of the *'St. George's'* Company and lifeboat coxswain Isaac Vondy who, like Sir William is a veteran crew member. Twenty guineas have been given for distribution among the crew.

Sir William, now over 60, has recovered from his injuries being nursed by his second wife, Emma, the youngest sister of Caesar Tobin of Middle Farm. Their father, Patrick Tobin, was a periwig maker in Dublin but while still a young man moved to the Isle of Man. He made a fortune through privateering and as a local merchant while speculating in land and property. Emma was the youngest of fourteen children and when her father died in 1794 most of the estate went to her brothers John and Caesar.

From his Prospect Hill home Sir William has put forward many ideas, the most ambitious being the construction of a harbour asylum with breakwaters being built out from Douglas Head and from St. Mary's Rock. The cost no doubt will prove prohibitive but, more practicable, is Sir William's idea of some sort of sanctuary or shelter on St. Mary's Rock to enable those cast upon it to be saved from being swept away by the waves. The Island's Attorney General, John Quane, is the owner of the rock and he has agreed to bequeath it to the Isle of Man Branch of the Royal National Institute. There is much enthusiasm for the idea and the Harbour Commissioners have started the appeal with a donation of £75. Mr John Welch has been commissioned to design the construction and he has suggested a miniature but sturdy medieval-style castle.

Sir William is involved in many business interests and was a founder member of the Lonan Mining Association which shows every sign of striking it rich with the discovery of new veins of copper, lead and silver. He uses his new-found wealth in good causes and he has been able to satisfy his passion for art by assembling the finest collection of oil paintings on the Island. He is also interested in the welfare of the poorer townsfolk and has suggested that a House of Industry, a sort of almshouse, be built for their benefit.

The last weeks of 1831 have seen Sir William become the proud owner and occupier of the Fort Anne mansion on Douglas Head. It is said he has paid an exorbitant price for it having paid £600 down with a mortgage of £900 at five per cent. Nevertheless, Sir William is delighted to have realised a long cherished ambition. The fine castellated mansion was built towards the end of last century by an eccentric Irish gentleman of somewhat dubious character, by the name of Buck Whaley. He is said to have married a wife of considerable fortune who enjoyed the interest of a large estate provided she continued to live on Irish soil. To secure his wife's interests he sent for a schooner-load of Irish soil which he spread over the foundations and the whole area of the house! Sir William has embarked on extensive plans for the place having secured the surrounding land for privacy and for a private beach. The inside of the house is to be redecorated and provision has been made for an art gallery. It is hoped this great character and benefactor will enjoy a long and happy retirement in his new home.

Sir William Hillary Bt.

HERE IS THE NEWS: 1832
A TOWER OF REFUGE FOR MARINERS

Work has started on building a safe refuge for mariners whose vessels are wrecked on St. Mary's Rock in Douglas Bay. It will be a solid stone castellated structure on the rock itself which will provide shelter and also food and water for shipwrecked men until they can be brought ashore in safety — and it is to be called the Tower of Refuge. We have this report:

'The tower, the foundation stone of which was laid on April 23rd this year, is the idea of Sir William Hillary, of Fort Anne, Douglas, who was one of those who founded the Royal National Lifeboat Institution eight years ago. The building work is expected to be completed before the end of this year, in advance of the worst of next winter's gales. Sir William has long been convinced that such a shelter should be built in view of the number of vessels that have been wrecked on St. Mary's Rock, including the Royal Mail Packet "St. George" two years ago. He led the raising of the money by public subscription to pay for it, realising a total of £254.12 shillings. The list is led by the Isle of Man Harbour Commissioners, who contributed £75, the Steam Packet Company and the Laxey and Foxdale mining companies, followed by many family names of distinction in the Island, including the Tobins, the Bacons, the Cosnahans, the Drinkwaters, the Forbes, the Genestes, the Harrises, the Heywoods and the Spittalls, as well as the Quayles of Bridge House, Castletown. There was also a contribution from Mr. John Quane, of Ballapaddag in Braddan, whose family have owned St. Mary's Rock for many years. Sir William and his family gave £8 and will also meet the £73 6 shillings due to the builders and the architects of what is going to be a substantial structure designed to brave the elements for a great many years. The architect is Mr. John Welch. The Tower of Refuge will be a great contribution to maritime safety in Douglas, along with the plans to build a new lighthouse this year on Douglas Head. The Harbour Commissioners believe the next step should be the building of a breakwater to provide more shelter for Douglas harbour from the southeast. This matter is to be taken up with the British Treasury.'

GAS LIGHT COMPANY TO BE FORMED

The introduction of gas lighting into the streets of Douglas is under consideration. Plans are being made for the formation of a Douglas Gas Light Company for the purpose of 'supplying gas or inflammable air by the use of coal or oil'. Legislation is being drafted and the company will be launched in three years' time. Experiments in the making of gas are already taking place in Douglas. What street lighting there is at the moment is provided by only a few oil lamps. It is intended that the first gas lamps will appear in Athol Street.

WATER SUPPLIES TO BE CONTROLLED

Legislation is being drafted for controlling water supplies in Douglas as a sanitation and public health measure. The Douglas Waterworks Bill will authorise a company to collect and purify rainwater and organise its distribution by way of a network of pipes. Doctors have long warned that the open drainage system of the town and elsewhere is responsible for the recurring epidemics of cholera, smallpox and typhus which have caused serious loss of life in the Island for centuries. It is also proposed that Boards of Health should be appointed to make health a matter of official responsibility.

CASTLE MONA HOTEL

Work on converting the prestigious Castle Mona into a hotel has now been completed. Castle Mona was built 28 years ago as the palace of the fourth Duke of Atholl at a cost believed to be over £30,000. Occupying a central position in Douglas Bay it will provide first class accommodation for the increasing number of visitors coming to the Island, now estimated to be as high as 30,000 a year. The Duke was last in residence in 1826 and when he died two years ago he was still nominally the Governor General of the Island.

KING WILLIAM'S COLLEGE NEARS COMPLETION

It has been announced that King William's College at Castletown, which is now nearing completion, will open its doors to its first pupils on 1st August next year. It is expected that about a hundred boys will be enrolled for its first term. The principal is to be the Reverend Edward Wilson M.A., a fellow of St. John's College, Cambridge. The opening of the College chapel is scheduled for 1st September. The foundation stone of the building was laid in April 1830 amid scenes of great celebration in which more than 5,000 people took part. The architect is Mr. John Welch — the designer of the Tower of Refuge.

ORGAN TO BE REPAIRED

Finally, the great organ of St. George's Church in Douglas, the instrument from which Handel conducted the first performance of 'The Messiah', is to undergo major repairs next year. After 55 years in St. George's it has become increasingly dilapidated. Now a second manual and a new set of pipes for the pedals are to be added. Handel conducted The Messiah from the organ when he was in Dublin in 1742. The instrument was sold to the trustees of St. George's in 1778 for £100 Irish when the church was under construction. It was the first organ to be installed in a Manx church.

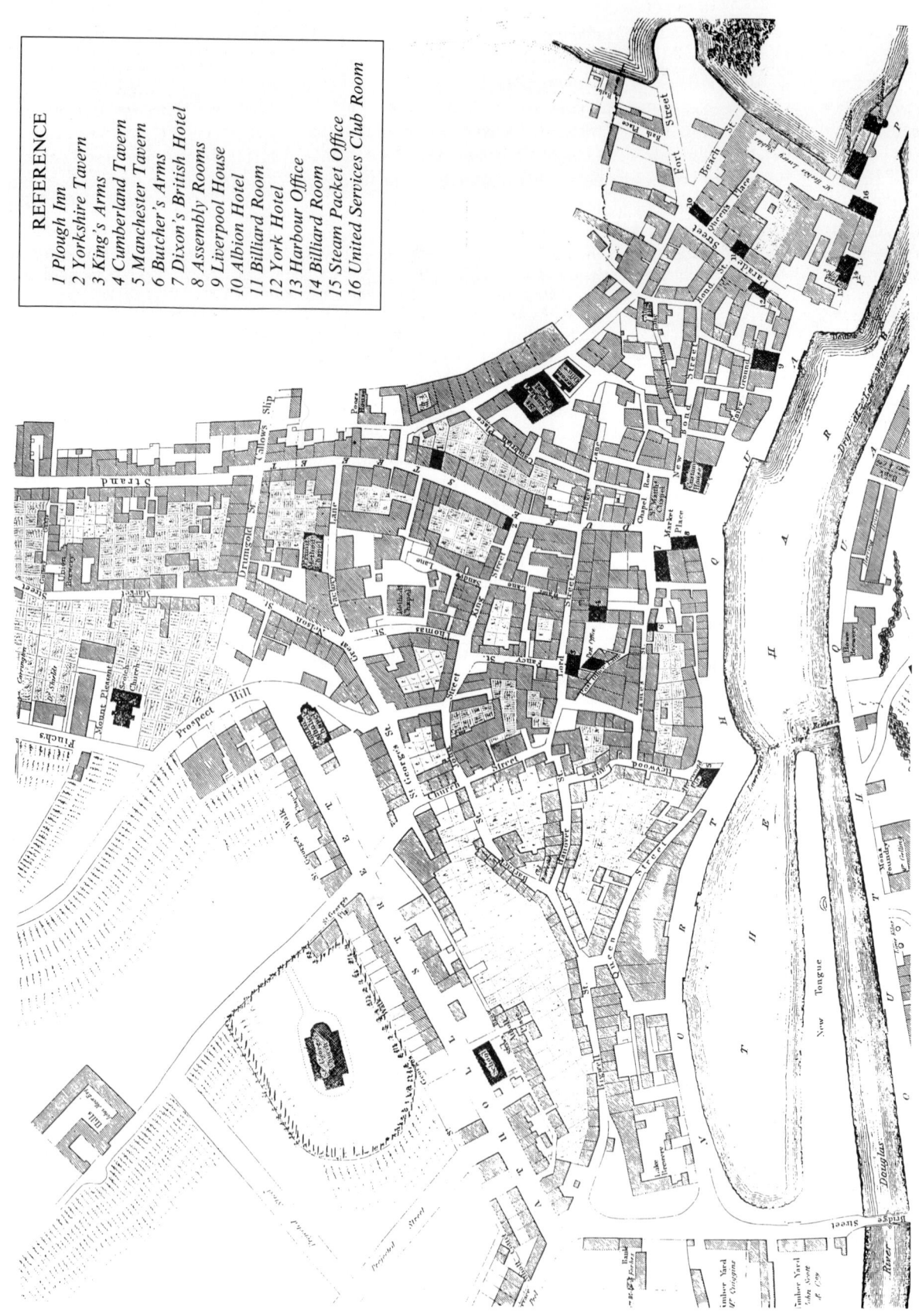

1832: A YEAR TO REMEMBER

At the end of the year a new sound rang out over Douglas calling the people to the Watchnight Service. It was the sound of the bell in the lofty steeple of St. Barnabas' Church, newly consecrated by that great church builder, Bishop Ward. Now the poor and underprivileged have a church to call their own, in contrast to St. George's where most of the pews are rented and reserved for those who can afford them. It has been a cause of great concern that an estimated 4,000 people of Douglas were necessarily excluded from Divine Worship because of lack of room. During the past two years the funds were produced, the land made available between Fort Street and Cambrian Place despite some difficulties, the plans drawn up by Messrs Hansom and Welch, architects, and the newly created parish entrusted to the Reverend William Carpenter who has already won the hearts of his parishioners. Of the 1,200 seats all those under the gallery are to be free — a remarkable and quite unprecedented arrangement, much appreciated by the townsfolk who are just recovering from the unhappy outbreak of cholera.

The year has seen many developments, by far the most significant being those at Castle Mona, the entire estate of 179 acres having been purchased last year by a local consortium of Messrs. John Hutchinson, Thomas Hutchinson, Caesar Bacon and John Wulff. Work began immediately on converting the late Duke's residence into a hotel, the work being to the directions of Messrs. Hansom and Welch the Architects. The Grand Saloon is now the Dining Room and, upstairs, the bedrooms have been fitted to sumptuous standards. By far the biggest problem has been the drainage system. The sewage was disposed of through pipes encased in timber leading to a cesspool beneath the cellar. These casings provided an ideal home for rats who had riddled them with holes from which noxious smells have permeated the building making it necessary to keep the windows more or less permanently open. An attempt to fill the holes with a mixture of crushed glass and cement had an even worse effect but the problem has now been overcome, fortunately, by by-passing the cesspool and leading the sewage directly into the sea.

Much of the estate has been laid out in building plots for mansions of a moderate but elegant scale. The Castle Mona grounds are said to be vying with the Nunnery Estate as the favourite resort of courting couples. The kitchen gardens at the head of the glen overlooking the hotel have been retained to supply produce but they have been traversed by a series of arches carrying a roadway to be part of the new town development of Woodville. Further to the north of the estate and bordering the sea have been built many beautiful villas, known as The Crescent. A family hotel is also flourishing. Beyond the foot of Burnt Mill Hill is Strathallan Crescent with a string of picturesque cottages which are let during the summer to genteel families who come to enjoy the bathing. The Crescent terminates with Castle Pollock.

Mr. Mallet of the London Coffee House is the new manager of the Castle Mona Hotel which opened its doors on April 23rd being Easter Monday and St. George's Day. The occasion was celebrated by a Dinner in the Grand Saloon, illuminated by the magnificent chandelier, to which 80 of the leading gentlemen on the Island were invited. It was the social event of the year and the Manx Sun reported: 'We doubt if there is another island in the British Empire that has a hotel which can compete with this hotel as an establishment for the public accommodation.' Major talking point was the subject of Douglas becoming a premier watering resort for the new wealthy classes of the industrial North of England.

That same afternoon the foundation stone of the castellated construction on St. Mary's, or Conister Rock was laid. Now completed, its design has brought forth much favourable comment, the compact and sturdy structure consisting of two small frontal towers backed by a larger round tower surmounted by a small square tower, resembling a miniature medieval castle. It is to be known as the Tower of Refuge and it is universally agreed that it enhances the beauty of Douglas Bay.

Another development has been the construction of a lighthouse on the low promontory of Douglas Head. Unlike the lights built in 1818 on the Calf of Man and at the Point of Ayre by the Scottish Northern Lights Board, the new lighthouse is the responsibility of the local Harbour Commissioners. Some years ago a tower, identical to the one on Langness which was built at the same time, was constructed as a landmark to prevent confusion with Clay Head and Santon Head. The tower will remain, as will the light on the Red Pier, but the new lighthouse will be an additional navigational aid to the growing number of ships arriving at Douglas. The light is lit by seven or eight candles which, with a tin reflector, can be seen up to fifteen miles out to sea.

THE STREETS OF DOUGLAS

The steeple of St. Barnabas, 140 feet high, now dominates the skyline and looks down upon the maze of streets and alleys of Douglas, a relic of the smuggling days of last century. A plan of the town, which is the work of Mr. Wood, has just been completed and is shown on the opposite page. It can be seen that the harbour extends the whole length of the town from east to west, the best shops facing the North Quay which forms the base of the triangular shape of the town. Midway along the North Quay is the Market Place, a focal point, though it provides shelter for neither man nor beast. It is the site of the Customs Office and other public buildings including the Magistrate's Office, the Harbour Office and the Assembly Rooms. From outside Dixon's British Hotel coaches depart for other parts of the Island. Yet reaching the Market Place from within the town is most difficult having to negotiate a labyrinth of disjoining lanes and alleys. Here most of the town's population (6,786 according to last year's census) live in 794 houses of all shapes and sizes between the harbour, the shore and Athol Street where the more affluent live in Georgian splendour.

The main street through the town is Duke Street which begins at St. Matthew's Church. Duke Street contains the shops which supply the necessities of life, there being many grocers, drapers and druggists — all shops being open from seven in the morning to nine or ten at night. Duke Street leads to the bottom of Drumgold Street and the top of Callow Slip which leads to the shore. A narrow twist in the road at this junction leads into Strand Street with its line of small houses and thatched cottages, those on the right backing on to the foreshore and protected by a low stone wall. At the bottom of Well Road Hill, north of the area shown on the map, a change is made into Castle Street which brings the town to an end at Senna Road.

Duke Street is also connected with the pier and entrance to the harbour by way of Fort Street which backs on to the shore, the street deriving its name from the ancient fort, recently demolished, which stood on Pollock Rock. Here are the shipbuilding yards of Messrs. Aitken and Windram, and the Douglas Baths. Further along, on the left, is the entrance to St. Barnabas' Church.

A MATTER OF LIFE OR DEATH

Whether rich or poor we live in constant fear of diseases such as measles, whooping cough, typhoid fever or, the biggest killer of all, smallpox. Our children are most at risk and at least one in three die before they reach the age of 15. We must now add the dreaded cholera to the list. Those who can read have followed in the newspapers the spread of the disease from Asia to Europe and then from England to the Isle of Man. Nothing, it appears, can prevent its onslaught. During the long hot summer of 1832 the toll of deaths rose steadily with 83 victims buried in Kirk Braddan churchyard and 34 in St. George's churchyard. The High Bailiff, responsible for the administration of Douglas, set up a Cholera Hospital on the outskirts of the town in charge of the Health Board. Apart from this, cannon were fired in the town and barrels of tar burnt in the most affected parts. It was but a desperate attempt to stem the outbreak. The disease attacks the body with a purging of the bowel and repeated bouts of vomiting with hands and arms turning blue through lack of circulation. Half die while the others start a long period of recovery. The following summer saw another epidemic resulting in 86 more bodies being buried at St. George's. Eye-witnesses tell of the appalling sight of graves being dug by the light of lanterns suspended from the trees and bodies being heaped in one upon the other. The names are not recorded on stone, the grave with a cross marked CHOLERA.

Over 200 cholera deaths have occurred while the survivors have been nursed back to health through the care and love of those who risked their lives. One name that has shone out above all others is that of Nellie Brennan. Left an orphan at the age of 16 she survived through taking in mangling and through her strong Christian faith — a woman of indomitable spirit. Even before the recent sad events she has been noted as one who is dedicated to the sick, never hesitating to visit homes which are often ones of overcrowding, filth and squalor. Here she washes bodies, cleans the clothes and prepares food which is all part of her care. She paid daily vists to the Cholera Hospital and won the hearts and respect of doctors and of the poor and not so poor.

How Nellie Brennan survived is a miracle considering how she completely exhausted herself. Perhaps her belief in strong personal cleanliness, which she also insists upon in others, has something to do with it. Or she may have escaped drinking and washing in contaminated water which is regarded as the main cause of the disease spreading. The town wells are always liable to dry up in summer so carts bring in water from the surrounding districts which are regarded as safe. But these can also dry up and it is known that water has been taken from the Douglas river. This river water, like that of the town wells, is always liable to become contaminated because of the disposal of sewage through the many cesspools. Our streets still leave much to be desired as regards cleanliness, being cluttered with garbage to which must be added the horse manure. Most of the streets have now been paved with stones from the shore but the stench from the open gutters is most noticeable; so too are the all too numerous rats while pigs roam at large in the streets. Walking the streets requires much care, especially at night with just a few oil lamps placed at corners.

'This disease baffles all medical skill. Many in good health in the morning were interred in the evening, and hundreds of the population of the Island became its victims.' St. George's churchyard.

There is much to be done in the way of sanitation and street cleanliness but the worst aspect of the matter seems to be a complete apathy by all but a few. The High Bailiff, though empowered by Tynwald, has seen fit not to act despite the calls for improving the streets, providing more lamps and providing police to bring discipline. The first to suffer, as usual, are the poor and destitute of which there are all too many. Attempts to improve their lot, such as by levying a Poor Rate, meet with scant regard. True, there is a growing number of charities which are taking over from the churches. The societies do tremendous good in providing soup kitchens and clothing. But more drastic remedies are still required.

Tynwald has at last been moved by bringing in the Douglas Waterworks Act of 1834. This has authorised a company to collect water and distribute it through pipes to all households in the town. Fresh water will also be available for the watering of ships in the harbour. Work is now well underway and the dam of the Burnt Mill at the northern end of the bay is the source of the water with provision for a second dam on the stream which runs through the Bemahague estate.

As regards nursing the sick, it is Nellie Brennan who continues to do her good works in support of the doctors. In 1834 she was appointed laundress to the new Castle Mona Hotel but she found she was too far removed from those she was helping so moved back into the town. She gets much support from the better-off who admire her strength and courage. The House of Industry, created in 1837, has proved a boon to many and now there is welcome news that a Dispensary is to be opened in Strand Street in 1839. Medicines, free of charge, are to be available to the poor. Dr J.H.F. Spencer of Prospect Hill has been appointed surgeon on a salary of £50 per year. The Matron is to be paid £10 per annum with house, gas and coal. There are two beds attached for the benefit of patients. It has also been learnt that Miss Nellie Brennan has agreed to take on the Matronship and, though unable to read or write, there is no-one in the town of Douglas better able to carry out her duties. She has the admiration of the doctors, the undying gratitude of many, and the best wishes of us all.

Cholera grave, Kirk Braddan churchyard

THE ROYAL MAIL

Since the year 1840 the Island has seen a veritable explosion in the amount of mail passing through and around its ports and villages. The Horse Posts leaving Douglas at 6 a.m., three days a week, have become welcome and habitual sights throughout the Island, so much so in fact that they are almost taken for granted. The ease and cheapness of rapid communication is now a commonplace part of our lives.

Yet this has not always been so. Indeed, it is only in the last few years that any form of written communication was other than haphazard, erratic, costly and frequently doomed to failure. Many will recall the early days of the century when the English Post Office, which was authorised to convey mail to and from the Isle of Man, contracted it out to a syndicate operating out of Whitehaven. The ships of the syndicate were, it is alleged, often less than seaworthy, the masters and crew poorly paid. The result was that the original one sailing a week in each direction became more honoured in the breach than in the observance. Even when the mail did arrive, and only the wealthy could afford the postage, it was up to each individual to make his own arrangements to have the mail delivered to his home or place of business.

The ever expanding commercial community, as can be imagined, found this a totally unsatisfactory arrangement. When the new paddle steamers replaced the old sailing ships, and even when the old Whitehaven syndicate was replaced in 1822 by one operating from Liverpool, the complaints continued. The winter months with their storms and delayed sailings caused absolute havoc with the regularity of the service. It will be remembered with some amusement today that the Douglas Post Office, despite its rather unsalubrious position near the Quay and Market Place, became, at times, a riotous place of assembly. Many businessmen sent their staff to collect the mail and the resulting pushing and jostling for places often resulted in the constables having to be called to restore order.

By the end of the 1820's it seemed clear to the business community, indeed to the population as a whole, that the only way to secure a reliable service was to have, as it was put at the time, 'a Manx company with a Manx steamer and Manx crew.' In 1830 this happy state came about with the Mona's Isle Company, formed by a local syndicate, ordering the first of its steamers, the *'Mona's Isle'*. The new ship was placed in the hands of William Gill from Glen Auldyn, near Ramsey. He had gone to sea as a lad and rose to command sailing ships like the *'Duchess of Atholl'* and the *'Douglas'* which traded between Douglas and Liverpool. He was renowned for his seamanship and knew the treacherous sands of the Mersey like the back of his hand. Now in command of the *'Mona's Isle'* he charted the standard route through the sands, now known as the Victoria Channel. The dramatic events of mid-August of that year will be remembered vividly. The *'Mona's Isle'* took on the *'Sophia Jane'* of the Liverpool St. George Company on the sail to and from Liverpool and beat her handsomely. A month later she took on the flagship of the Liverpool Company, the *'St. George'*, and beat her, too. The disastrous wreck of the *'St. George'* on Conister Rock confirmed the downfall of the Liverpool Company and, a year later, the Mona's Isle Company, which changed its name to the The Isle of Man Steam Packet Company in 1832, was awarded the mail contract and an enormous sense of triumph swept the Island. Two mails a week in summer, one in winter, sub-Post Offices at Castletown, Peel and Ramsey, opened up a new era. It remained, however, a costly business. Postage was charged on distance — four pence from Douglas to Peel, five pence to Ramsey. Many anomalies existed, of course, not least those leading to the scandalous abuse of the regulations by the publishers of journals and newspapers here. But 1840 marked another dramatic change. The introduction of the Penny Post altered the popular appreciation of the Royal Mail for once and for all. The result was an immediate expansion in the volume of mail between the Island and the United Kingdom. The Post Office in Thomas Street is said to be taking some £3,000 per annum in Post Office dues. Even the houses in the towns have had to be numbered, a new departure indeed.

There can be no doubt that in the near future, as the prosperity and population of the Island increase, the frequency and regularity of the mail is certain to increase as a result. Soon the Lords Commissioners of the Admiralty must surely cease their opposition to the suggested three packets a week from Liverpool instead of the present two. Perhaps one day a daily postal service might actually come about; or is this just wishful thinking? Below are given details of ships of the Isle of Man Steam Packet Company which is steadily expanding as more and more visitors arrive on our shores.

The 'Mona's Isle', a wooden paddle-steamer built in 1830 by John Wood and Co. of Glasgow.

'Mona' was built in 1831 in Glasgow and hurriedly ordered for the winter service to relieve the more valuable 'Mona's Isle'.

'Queen of the Isle', like the Mona was built by Robert Napier in Glasgow in 1834.

'King Orry' is the only ship to be built in Douglas for the Company, and is likely to be its last wooden vessel.

'Ben-my-Chree'. Iron paddle-steamer built by Napier's in 1845.

'Tynwald'. Iron paddle-steamer built in Glasgow and entered service in 1846.

AN ARCHITECT'S GUIDE

Another in the long line of guide books to the Isle of Man published over the last 30 years has recently appeared in the shops. It purports to have been written by 'A Stranger' and to be a 'A Six Days' Tour'. Perhaps the date of the Preface — 1st April, 1836 — is significant. The book, which is dedicated to Sir William Hillary Bart., is, on good authority, supposed to have been written by John Welch whose building and architectural activities are well known on the Island and some indeed are fulsomely described in the book.

Mr Welch is now 26 and has been on the Island some six years. He came to assist his brother Mr Edward Welch, partner of Joseph Aloysius Hansom in the well known architectural firm of Hansom and Welch. Messrs. Hansom and Welch had been responsible for many important buildings in North Wales and the North of England, including several churches and Beaumaris gaol, before being invited to design King William's College here in the Isle of Man. Whilst Mr Edward Welch made a number of visits to the Island, it does not appear that Mr Hansom ever set foot on our shores. Messrs Hansom and Welch won the design for the new Birmingham Town Hall but their bond in respect of the builder has recently forced both partners into bankruptcy and Mr John Welch very nearly so as witnessed by the recent sale of his books and other effects. Mr Hansom has recently taken out a patent in respect of a new design of a horse-drawn passenger vehicle which will bear his name. Whilst it is hoped that this may restore his fortune it is to be feared that, whilst it may achieve some small degree of fame, the fortune will not be forthcoming! At much the same time as starting the designs for King William's College, Messrs Hansom and Welch undertook the design of St. Barnabas' Church in Douglas. Other churches designed by them or by Messrs Welch, i.e. the brothers Edward and John Welch working in partnership, or by Mr John Welch are: Ballaugh New Church; Onchan; Michael; Lezayre and St. Luke's Baldwin. This last is a multi-purpose building, part church, part hall and part school, this being the idea of Bishop Ward. If funds permit, it is proposed to build at least two more such churches, the most likely sites being Dalby — which Mr Welch in his book describes as being 'the fag end of a God forgotten world' — and Sulby.

Mr Edward Welch had left the Island before the building of King William's College was complete and John Welch tells us in the book that he changed the design of the great tower. The design was certainly changed for the original drawings published by the architects show a tower very similar to that actually built at Ballaugh New Church.

Mr Welch has been involved in a number of buildings including the replacement George Hotel at Castletown, a proposed hotel adjoining the Court House at Douglas Harbour, a house for Mr James Newton on Douglas Head, another on the outskirts of Douglas above the road to Peel and even a proposed new house on the Calf of Man.

Mr Welch has been involved in at least two public schemes with Sir William Hillary, to whom you will recall he has dedicated the book. In one case he prepared the necessary drawings and supervised the work from a design prepared by Sir William for a memorial to Governor Smelt which is as yet unfinished at Castletown. The other project was the building of the Tower of Refuge, the foundation stone of which was laid on St. George's Day, 1832, the same day that Castle Mona was opened as a hotel. Mr Welch had been involved in the conversion of the Castle Mona to its present use and our 'stranger' of the guide book claims to have been recommended to stay there!

The book describes the *'droves of raw Lancashire men and women .... seen simultaneously dipping together, like devotees along the banks of the Ganges .... for the space of two miles along the shore, the principal recreation seeming to be — splashing each other'*. The author recommends that the gentlemen, as well as the ladies should wear bathing dresses, indeed that they should be of separate colours and that the whole should be supervised by a Bathing-Bailiff or Admiral of the Beach. He goes on to suggest that : *'There are two or three elderly gentlemen resident in the town who have been what is called rather gay in early life, and whose candle is now well nigh burnt out, to whom this office might be very judiciously entrusted'*.

That he himself does not fall into this category is apparent when he confesses to having hired a boat to survey the scene through a small telescope especially near Pollock Castle where he says : *'I could perceive some fair nymphs courting the lucid tide, like fawns, almost afraid of their own reflection in the water'*. Other adventures and misadventures of the visitors to, and natives of our Island are described in mischievous detail along with the scenery and establishments of the place. He describes the unbattlemented turrets of the Nunnery — the work of John Pinch, architect of Bristol — as having *'no further finished appearance than a man without a head.'*

The only Bishop Ward church not designed by the Welch 'connection' — New Lonan — is totally ignored. This church was designed by local-born architect John Taggart who carried out some work at Kirby and at Castle Rushen, as well as the National School which was the first building to be completed, in 1810, in Athol Street, Douglas. John Taggart will perhaps be best remembered for his many heavily built warehouses on the quaysides of the Island.

The House of Keys building and the new Chapel of St. Mary — both in Castletown — are also ignored save only for the acknowledgement of their existence. Both these buildings were designed by Thomas Brine who came to the Island over twenty years ago as Clerk of Works to the Barracks' Office and who stayed to design many of our more recent public buildings, and to design or alter houses for many of our notables.

Of the other and more recent architects and their buildings — Long, Kelly and Robinson — there is no mention at all, but no doubt other guides in future years may tell a different story of our Island and its buildings.

'Surveyor'

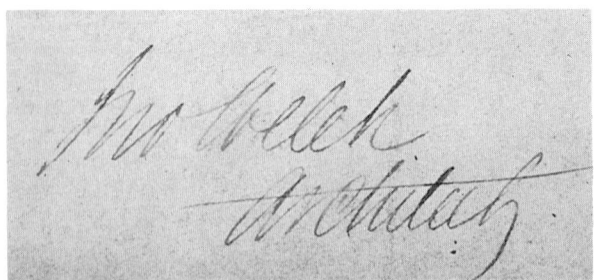

Original design for King William's College

King William's College as built in 1832 with revised tower by John Welch.

'Hansom cab' outside Birmingham Town Hall.

St Barnabas' Church, Douglas, 1832

St. Mary's, New Ballaugh Church, 1832

Kirk Christ Church, Lezayre, 1835

Kirk Michael Church, 1833

St. Mary's Chapel, Castletown, 1824

St. Luke's Chapel, Baldwin, 1836

New Kirk Lonan Church, 1831

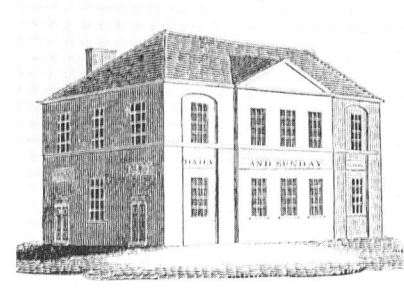
National School, Athol Street, Douglas, 1810

Castle Mona Hotel conversion, 1832

'Thornton,' overlooking the Peel road

John Newton's residence (Harold Tower) on Douglas Head

The Tower of Refuge, 1832

DEMANDS FOR POLITICAL REFORMS

Few will mourn the passing of the Tithe in 1839 — that most pernicious and detested of taxes in this Island. Generations of Manx folk hated the annual tribute of corn, of animals, of fish paid grudgingly to the Established Church; and with the rapid growth of Wesleyanism, and more recently Primitive Methodism, over the past half century or so that hatred deepened. Of recent years the Island has witnessed the undignified flight of Lord Bishop Murray and his family from Bishopscourt to Castle Mona pursued, it is claimed, by an angry mob; the main towns have been rocked by riots; the clergymen themselves have in correspondence with his Lordship denounced coercive measures to collect the Tithe. They determined that such a course of action would inflict a wound on the Church that 'the lapse of a century would scarcely heal.' Now that the Tithe has gone, the clergy will be compensated in cash collected by an agent. None, least of all our parsons we suspect, will regret it.

It must also be said that during the past ten years or so the Island has witnessed infinitely more political agitation than in the past ten centuries. Two major crises in Anglo-Manx financial relations have produced not only virtually unanimous nationalist opposition to the intentions of the English Parliament but also a powerful and well-supported movement to bring about the abolition of the self-elected House of Keys and its replacement by a democratically elected body. It now behoves all of a serious disposition to consider the origins and justice of these events and perhaps even their possible development in the future.

There is little doubt that the foundation of the *'Mona's Herald'* in 1833 by Robert Fargher, as an organ of 'political reform, nonconformity and temperance' was a vital step. For the first time those sections of the Manx population disenchanted with the self-elected Keys and the dominance of the landowners have been given a vehicle in which to express their views. As the economy of the Island has changed with the increasing importance of summer visitors and the rise of the business classes it was almost inevitable that challenges to the existing order of things would develop here as it has done in Britain.

It will be remembered clearly that a little over ten years ago, in 1835, the British Government tried to assimilate Manx customs duties to the level of those in the United Kingdom. This produced immediate opposition and many felt that a reformed House of Keys would be able to press our case more urgently, especially to a House of Commons which had reformed itself by the celebrated Bill of 1832. The outcome of these events was that the Island found itself split between the conservative group and the radical reformers who succeeded in producing a petition with over 3,000 signatures calling for an elected Keys. Harsh words were said on both sides and vituperation was the order of the day. Equally harsh was the firm but diplomatic 'No' to the petition from the Lieutenant Governor, Colonel John Ready. The hopes of the reformers were dashed and, although the attempts to alter the financial arrangements were abandoned, hints that the Island could be annexed by Westminster were enough to make even the most fiery Manxman tread most warily. Fears of political annexation had been paramount in raising support locally for Bishop Ward when, in 1836, he led the fight to prevent the Diocese of Sodor and Man from being annexed to the Diocese of Carlisle.

Two years ago a very similar set of circumstances developed. Once again an attempt was made to alter our financial arrangements although this time, admittedly, Westminster did have the courtesy to consult us first. The British Government did not, it should be noted, offer to return to the Manx people a single penny of the surplus revenue they have being collecting from our customs and excise for many years! These events once again produced a feeling that a reformed Keys could better stand up for the Island. Another petition was produced, this time with over 5,000 signatures. And another rebuff was given. Once again the suggestion that if reform was wanted, the idea of representation of the Isle of Man in Parliament was enough to stop the Reformers in their tracks.

Yet this cannot be right. Our population is increasing rapidly, our towns are growing apace, our business classes are becoming more and more important in our communities. Our old way of government with its concentration of political power in the hands of a very small self-elected group of people is at odds with the movement of our times. If the English Parliament reformed itself then there are surely no grounds for refusing similar changes here.

Thomas Fargher, co-founder of the Mona's Herald, *who is fearless in his demands for political reform.*

HERE IS THE NEWS: 1847
THE VISIT OF HER MAJESTY QUEEN VICTORIA AND PRINCE ALBERT

The Isle of Man was honoured this morning, 20th September, with a visit by the Queen and Prince Albert — the first ever made by a reigning monarch. It lasted only a matter of hours, but it is expected to remain forever in the memories of people in Ramsey and the North who celebrated the great occasion. We have this report:

'It had been known in the Island that the Royal Squadron, including the royal yacht *"Victoria and Albert"*, was cruising off Scotland and was close to Manx waters. But it was only at half past eight this morning, when the six steamships rounded the Point of Ayre and dropped anchor in Ramsey Bay, that the hopes of a Royal landing on Manx soil were fulfilled. News of the squadron's arrival was communicated immediately to the High Bailiff, Mr. Frederick Tellett, who was at breakfast in his Ramsey residence. He immediately sent a message to the Lord Bishop at Bishopscourt and to Government House in Castletown. The Lord Bishop arrived in his carriage at Ramsey after covering the ten miles in 35 minutes. Meanwhile Mr. Tellett went on board the Royal Yacht to present a loyal address to Her Majesty through Lord Palmerston, Secretary of State. Later the Bishop, the Archdeacon and Deemster Christian were granted an audience on the quarterdeck, while boats put off from the shore crowded with local people. Some included bandsmen who played traditional Manx airs for the entertainment of the Royal family. Meanwhile hundreds of people were pouring into Ramsey as word spread and at 11 o'clock Prince Albert came ashore with his suite and proceeded to climb Lhergy Frissell to admire the view — the Prince leaping hedges and ditches with great agility. Crowds followed him to the town and then back down to Ramsey beach where the royal barge was waiting to pick him up. The crowd sang "For he's a jolly good fellow" as His Royal **Highness was rowed back to the yacht. The Queen was looking on from the deck and appeared gratified and delighted by the scenes. With His Highness back on board the Squadron got up steam — and they were actually sailing away when the Governor arrived in all haste in his carriage and four, the message of the royal arrival having reached him too late. But for the people of Ramsey it was still an occasion for great celebrations, with bonfires and the discharge of cannon, which went on into the night, long after the Queen had departed.'**

BOOST FOR SHIPBUILDING

A decision by the British Government not to increase the duty on foreign timber imports has given a boost to the shipbuilding industry in the Island. The move will keep production costs down for the yards at present operating in Douglas, Ramsey and Peel. There are also to be requests now for the duty to be removed altogether. Barques of up to 500 tons are being built in Douglas. The speciality at Peel is schooners in the 100 to 200 tons range which are built for speed. They are in high demand by companies engaged in the fast shipment of fresh fruit.

CONTROL ON NEWSPAPER PUBLISHERS

Action has been taken to impose control over disreputable elements in the newspaper publishing industry in the Island. Under a new Act of Tynwald all printers must now register themselves and their titles. It was a decision of the Westminster Parliament 13 years ago that gave the Isle of Man and the Channel Islands the right to send newspapers free of charge to all parts of the Empire. This has resulted in large numbers of printing establishments being set up, some by unscrupulous operators who are bringing the Island's name into disrepute. Now there are demands at Westminster for the full postage rates to be imposed on newspapers which are sent from Douglas for circulation in Britain and Ireland.

POSTAL SERVICE ON THE INCREASE

Meanwhile Manx postal services are expanding, in spite of repeated refusals by the Lords Commissioners of the Admiralty to allow three mail packets a week instead of two on the Douglas-Liverpool route. In spite of the restriction the Douglas head post office in Thomas Street is taking more than £3000 a year in postage dues. The introduction five years ago of uniformed postmen in the Island to deliver letters to addressees — instead of the latter having to pick them up from the post office — has encouraged a big increase in business. The Island's postal service is now celebrating its 80th year of operation.

KING WILLIAM'S COLLEGE RESTORED

Work has been completed on the rebuilding of King William's College at Castletown following the fire which destroyed the west wing three years ago. The extent of the damage has been assessed at £4000. This has been a problem for the college trustees whose insurance for the buildings amounted to only £2000. Special fund raising efforts are being made to make up the difference. There was no loss of life in the fire, all masters and boys being evacuated as the flames spread in the early hours of the morning. Local people tried to no avail to extinguish the flames with buckets of water and when the fire engine arrived from Douglas several hours later the west wing had been completely destroyed.

SHIPBUILDING

During the first half of this century it has become the custom to build quite sizeable ships wherever convenient, even if some have required a complicated overland journey for the launch. There has been a revival and shipbuilding is prospering because of duty on imported timber being lower than in the United Kingdom. Attempts to raise the duty have been strenuously and, so far, successfully resisted. The result has been that the number of shipyards in ports around the Island has increased in number. The Bath Yard in Douglas was re-established in 1826 when the *Columbine* of 200 tons was launched, the largest vessel to be built on the Island at that time. This was surpassed in 1835 when the *Orleana* of 650 tons was launched from the same yard. She was built as the first packet ship to be used on the Liverpool–South Australia emigrant route. It is believed that several emigrants from the Island have travelled aboard the *Orleana*.

In charge of the Bath Ship Building Yard is Mr. Winram and a notable success came with the building in 1841 of the *King Orry* for the Isle of Man Steam Packet Company. The Yard employs over 80 men. Other yards are those of Williamson's on the Tongue and Robert Oates at the Lake at the top of the harbour. Quilliam and Company of Castletown Road have been specialising in vessels such as the *Yarra-Yarra*, one of seven built for the run to Australia where gold has been discovered.

In 1832 a shipyard was established in Ramsey by J. Taggart and Co. but it has now been taken over by a Newcastle firm. Despite much scepticism in the town they are planning to build 50 new cottages for the workmen and have added a new patent slip to the yard. They plan to build ships of wood or iron of up to 2,000 tons burden.

Peel now has two shipyards one of which is Grave's on the right bank of the harbour. Above the bridge is Watson's shipyard which has a water-powered saw. The problem of launching on the Neb above the bridge is that the river has to be deepened and considerable ballasting used. Children look forward to a launch as they are used as 'ballast' which can be moved about quickly to adjust the trim of the hull.

Castletown and Port St. Mary also have flourishing shipbuilders, mainly members of the Qualtrough family. Like Peel, Port St. Mary specialises in fishing boats for the local fisheries. It is claimed that fishing smacks can be built in 28 days while Peel has become deservedly famous for the fast 100 to 200 ton schooners which are not only used for exporting herring and mackerel to many ports in Europe and the Mediterranean, but are regularly employed by the Liverpool merchants in the fruit trade, in which speed from the producer countries is absolutely essential. Peel boats, such as the *Nora* make the round trip to Norway in three to four weeks, bringing wood back to supply the shipyards.

In support of shipbuilding, there are also many employed in the making of sails, ropes and nets. Quiggin's ropewalk in Douglas was established in 1821 while others can now be found at Peel, Ramsey, Castletown and Port St. Mary. The making of sailcloth is one of the specialities of Moore's flax-spinning, bleaching and sail-cloth manufactory at Tromode. Skilled manual workers are required and some have come from Ireland where they were employed in the linen industry. There are now about 80 employed at the Tromode Mills and they are accommodated in the tied cottages of Cronkbourne Village. Together the Moores have created a small industrial estate, unique on the Island, where the workers are well cared for and have amenities provided such as a cricket pitch and a reading room. In return, Mr. Moore expects the highest standards from his work people and has recently issued Rules and Regulations for maintaining proper order in his establishment, as can be seen from the extracts noted below.

RULES AND REGULATIONS

All persons employed in this concern are expected to attend on the Public Worship of Almighty God at least once on every Sabbath Day, and the Parents are earnestly requested to take their children along with them.

The hours of working are from 6 o'clock in the morning until 7 o'clock in the evening, (except on Saturdays when the Works stop at 5) allowing there-out each day 35 minutes for breakfast, and 45 minutes for dinner.

All the workpeople to be at their work by the time the bell ceases. Fines for being late are $\frac{1}{2}$d. for up to five minutes, 1d for up to 15 minutes and $1\frac{1}{2}$d. if 30 minutes late. Boys and girls earning less than 4 shillings weekly to be fined half the same for offences against these rules.

For trespassing on the grounds of the Works, bathing in the river or reservoir, or playing any game or games on the Sabbath will be fined 1d. or not more than 6d.

All hands in the Spinning Mill are allowed to go to the Water Closet five times daily; if they exceed 3 minutes each time fine is $\frac{1}{2}$d. The Foreman to decide time.

Any Person going out of the Mill or to the Water Closet without pass or permission from the Foreman fine is $\frac{1}{2}$d; for losing the pass, 1d. Any Person or Persons employed at the Works guilty of theft forfeit all wages due, and are discharged forthwith.

For profane swearing, using indecent or abusive language, lifting hands to strike or striking each other, not less than 2d. or more than 1 shilling.

For smoking or drinking spirits or fermented liquors at the Works, fine is 6d.

Persons practising that obnoxious habit of chewing tobacco in the Shops are to provide themselves with spitoons, the sand of which to be replaced daily. For neglecting this or spitting tobacco juice on the floor, for each offence, the fine is $\frac{1}{2}$d.

Neglecting to clean the Road and Gutter weekly, opposite the door of their Cottages, the fine is 3d.

For leaving a gas light burning unnecessarily, or neglecting to extinguish the light on leaving the premises, fine is 6d.

The fines will be deducted from the Wages and applied to the relief of the indigent workpeople when ill, and fines for all offences, such as the breaking of windows, by children, not employed at the Works, will be deducted from the Wages of their parents.

All Hands employed at these Works are expected to be Members of the Sick Fund Society for supplying medical aid.
W. F. Moore
1st January, 1850.

Shipbuilding on the foreshore at Castletown. The large building, right of centre, is Bowling Green House, at one time home of the Heywood family. Behind it can be seen Government House (Lorne House) and its long line of outbuildings.

HERE IS THE NEWS: 1852
THE BRIG "*LILY*" WRECKED ON KITTERLAND

Twenty-nine men were killed today (St. Stephen's Day) in a huge explosion which tore apart the wreck of the Liverpool brig "*Lily*" which went aground on Kitterland, in the Calf Sound, yesterday. The shock waves of the tremendous blast were felt as far away as Douglas and debris was hurled over a huge area, with two of the ship's guns reported to have fallen to earth at Scarlett. We have this report:

'There were 60 tons of gunpowder as well as 100 tons of general cargo in the hold of the "*Lily*" and this accounts for the scale and force of the explosion. The men who died were literally blown to pieces, along with the ship, and rescuers have found human remains scattered in all directions. The "*Lily*" was bound from Liverpool to the coast of Africa when gale force winds tore away her sails and combined with fierce tides to force her into the narrow passage of the Sound. She struck on Kitterland where five of her ship's company of 13, including the captain, were drowned. The rest were saved but the second mate's leg was so badly injured he had to submit to amputation. This morning, with a big improvement in the weather, the Lloyds sub-agent in Port St. Mary, Mr. Enos Lace, took a party of men onto the wreck to try and secure her cargo. They were accompanied by police officers led by Chief Constable Mr. John Craige. It was while they were at the wreck, at 7.45 a.m., that the explosion occurred, with devastating effect. People 20 miles away thought it was an earthquake and ran terrified into the streets. A huge column of smoke could be seen over the Calf for miles around. One survivor was a young Port St. Mary man, James Kelly. Rescuers found him badly injured lying on rocks some distance away, face downwards in a pool. He has as yet been able to say little about the event but there is now a theory that other men had made an unlawful landing earlier in the morning to plunder the cargo, and that whatever they had used to illuminate the hold had still been burning. Of the men who died 25 were from Port St. Mary, two from the Howe and two from Castletown. The oldest, William Kermode, was 55, and the youngest, John Hudgeon, 21. The dead men leave behind 22 widows and 74 fatherless children.'

KEYS DEPUTATION TO VISIT LONDON

As demand in the Isle of Man grows for the House of Keys to become a democratically-elected body it has been announced that a Keys deputation is going to the Treasury in London for talks next year. The talks will centre on Manx demands for more control over the Island's financial affairs. But it is thought that the British Government will bring counter-pressure to bear on the Keys to consider becoming elective. The system of self-election in the Keys has operated for centuries. Critics say members are always recruited from the same influential families and that the House sits in private, passing laws without public knowledge.

MORE EMIGRATION

Large numbers of young Manxmen have left the Island in the last five years for America and Australia. They have gone to seek their fortunes in the gold fields. There was a big strike in California in 1848 and another one in Australia two years later. Officials say the men's migration has depleted the population of rural areas in the Island, causing a serious labour shortage in farming. The root causes of the drift of young men from the Island have been unemployment, depressed economic conditions and the lack of food to keep body and soul together.

DECLINE IN CHURCH ATTENDANCE

The Lord Bishop has spoken out strongly against what he calls a widespread spirit of indifference in the Island to Church doctrines and discipline. His Lordship also referred to diminishing congregations and reduced numbers of communicants. His criticism follows that of Bishop Short about ten years ago when he said the Island's 17 parish churches were consistently empty of people on a Sunday, and the tone of morality among the population generally was low. Some church leaders believe the continuing resentment of the people stems from the tithe, even though the method of collection has now been substantially reformed.

BID TO IMPROVE EDUCATION

Legislation has been drafted for submission to Tynwald to make better provision for the education of Manx children. This will enable parochial vestries in the Island to levy rates to be used for the support of schools, and it provides for the appointment of management committees. There will also be borrowing powers to enable new school building to take place. The move follows a strongly-worded report to the Committee of the Council of Education by the Reverend Henry Moseley which said that educational services in the Island are well below the standards in England.

FIRST LUNATIC ASYLUM

Finally, a sum of more than £1,500 has been raised by public subscription for building the Island's first lunatic asylum. This follows a public meeting in Douglas at which it was agreed to accept an offer by the British Government to put up half the money for the project if the Island provides the rest. The offer was made earlier this year in a letter from the Home Secretary to the Governor, the Honourable Charles Hope. The building of an asylum is intended to end the long-standing practice in the Island of keeping lunatics tied to stakes in outhouses and stables, clad in rags and feeding on refuse – or of allowing them to wander the countryside uncared for by the community.

THE DISASTER AT THE CALF OF MAN

Further details have now come to hand concerning the fearful calamity which occurred in the south of the Island over the Christmas period causing deep distress to very many families and spreading gloom over the whole neighbourhood. The violent gales, approaching hurricane force, blew from the south and west from Friday night to Monday afternoon, causing great damage by sea and land. Many vessels have been seen dismasted and in distress drifting off the coast.

At twelve o'clock on Christmas Eve the "*Lily*", a vessel of 100 tons register, was bound from Liverpool to Ambrazo on the coast of Africa, and thence with slaves to America. On board was a general cargo consisting chiefly of bales of cloth, cottons, rum, cannon, firearms and upwards of 40 tons of gunpowder. She was guided past the Chickens Rock with the help of the Calf lights but during the night she was crippled by the fierce winds and was carried by the tide from the westward into the Sound of the Calf of Man, the breadth of which is about 500 yards and where the current at times runs at a rate of up to nine knots. The lighthouse keepers rushed to give guidance and shouted for the anchor to be dropped. With the masts broken the anchor fouled the stays of the jib and the helpless ship swung round on striking a rock and was dashed up on Kitterland. The carpenter had already been killed but seven of the crew were able to scramble onto the rock using one of the masts as a bridge. The master, the cabin boy of 13 and, it is believed, three others were carried away in the surf and drowned. Those left on the rock were rescued by a boat belonging to a local farmer; two were found to be seriously injured and one has since had a leg amputated.

It was Christmas Day and in the course of the afternoon the vessel was handed over to the care of Lloyd's agent at Port St. Mary and he subsequently took possession of her. He was assisted by the Chief Constable of Castletown and one of his subordinates, and by the constable of Port St. Mary and several others, who were stationed on the vessel as well as on Kitterland and the mainland to guard the wreck, and land the stores when the weather and tide should permit. It appears that during the night several shots were fired to deter people from venturing near, some parties having made attempts to plunder the wreck.

At five minutes to eight on the morning of Tuesday, St. Stephen's Day, the inhabitants of the whole of the south of the Island were alarmed at the fearful explosion and beheld a vast column of fire and smoke ascending to a great height above the Calf of Man. Cottages and houses were shaken as if by an earthquake, even beyond Douglas some 18 miles distant. Miners at work down the Ballacorkish lead mine at Colby felt the shock so great that they hastened to the surface in fear; their candles were extinguished, and one man was knocked down by the shock. As far as is known only three survived the explosion to give any record of the horrific event. Twenty-nine men, including the Chief Constable, are known to have been literally blown to pieces. The rocks in the vicinity are strewn with heads, arms, legs and trunks of what a few moments before had been living human beings. The vessel itself at once disappeared and its contents were scattered over a wide area. Of the men missing, twenty have left widows with families, two were widowers, and seven were single men. So terrible a scene has never before been witnessed on this Island and it has been graphically portrayed in the Illustrated London News.

The story of James Kelly of Port St. Mary is that when they first approached the wreck they imagined they smelled smoke – it was about half past six – and this soon proved to be a fact. As they knew the powder was in the fore and aftermost parts of the vessel, and the smoke about midships, they did not apprehend danger, although several proposed to leave the wreck. However some began to clear the cabin and sail case, and others to try to discover the cause of the smoke by cutting a hole in the deck, by which it is thought a current of air was created. This caused the fire to ignite which then led to the exploding of the powder. The origin of the fire remains a mystery. The chief mate stated that about sixty tons of gunpowder were shipped at Liverpool, but it is thought that about twenty tons were washed away, quantities of quarter-casks coming ashore at Port Erin. The Lieutenant Governor The Hon. Charles Hope has launched an appeal for the widows and children, and an appeal has been made to England for aid. A memorial to those who perished in the disaster is to be situated in Rushen churchyard.

GOLD FEVER!

For the last few years or so the Island has seen a wave of emigration similar to the exodus from the parishes that occurred in the 1820's. There is perhaps a difference in character. This time the whole enterprise has been fuelled by the lure of gold, rather than by the hope, some would say certainty, of finding cheap land. The discovery of the precious metal in 1848 in California, and in 1851 in Australia, has tempted many hundreds of our young men to seek their fortunes on the other side of the world. Once again our parishes, especially in the north, have suffered a corresponding decline in their populations.

The journey to either El Dorado is long, arduous and full of danger. California means a journey of some 3,000 miles overland through deserts, over mountains, past bloodthirsty Red Indians or a terrifying sea voyage around Cape Horn with its mountainous seas to the port of San Francisco. In one sense the route to Australia is better known. For many years it has been to unfortunate felons quite literally a lifetime away. Many on the Island will recall that some years ago a William Quayle was sentenced to seven years transportation to New South Wales for stealing a tablecloth. Now, however the rigours of the journey are better known. Journeys of over 90, indeed over 100 days are common. Hunger and disease are ever present for passengers crowded on the ships. Yellow fever and plague strike their victims down with frightening regularity and the children are often amongst the first to die. Nor do some of the other passengers help. John Sayle wrote that he had seen Irishmen have their filthy clothes taken off them by order of the surgeon.

Yet the rewards, it is said, are great. Or they are great for the lucky few and perhaps substantial for many more. Recent correspondence received on the Island from some who left to seek their fortune bear this out. The same John Sayle writing home from the Bendigo gold diggings in January of this year (1853) states that he had made more money in the last six months than in a great many years back home on the Island. Mind you, he went on to say that you had to use the pick and spade pretty freely. However, he did say that most of the Manx he knew out there were doing pretty well and many were establishing a fine reputation as miners, rivalling even the Cornishmen.

There can be no doubt that it was the sense of adventure and the prospect of making a fortune in double quick time that has fired the imagination of the 37 Manxmen, all but two of whom are from the west of the Island, who sailed from Peel on January 26th of this year in the "*Vixen*". Peel was full on that historic day. The schools were closed and Peel Hill was lined with spectators as, at three o'clock in the afternoon, the two-masted schooner made her way down the harbour with the heroes on board. Thomas Cubbon of Glen Maye is Captain, Thos. Corlett of Dalby is First Mate and Navigator, and John Gordon of Peel is Second Mate. The "*Vixen*" is a Peel ship of 160 tons burden, built at the Grave's Yard on the quay in 1851 at a cost of £2,000. She spent a year coasting and in the Mediterranean trade before she was picked up by the men. She is a well-tried and trusted ship, speedy and seaworthy. Those who had been present at her launching remember that she had been christened by the now customary breaking of a bottle of wine on her stem. And then she had a second christening of the kind the Vikings used when launching a war galley – that of reddening the keel with the blood of a human victim. That was in October last year when poor old Tommy Buttons, as Tom Welsh the pedlar was called, paid a visit to the "*Vixen*" one pitch dark night and fell overboard. Next morning he was found in the harbour with the keel of the ship lying across his back. But tragedy was forgotten as the cheers rang around the harbour and the booming voice of Mr. Kerruish the harbourmaster could be heard giving instructions. The "*Vixen*" soon stood out into the bay and with a lucky wind blowing down the channel from the north-east soon rounded Horse Point and headed south-west. It must be said there were many sad faces, perhaps some even envious ones, as the "*Vixen*" disappeared from view. But the saddest sound came from some lads who had run round the Hill and blew a mournful note from a gigantic buckey shell. By all accounts she is well provisioned with over 5,000 pounds of meat salted away with plenty of oatmeal to make porridge as a welcome change. They have guns and pistols with ammunition to defend themselves should the need arise. Also on board are carts and harness for the trek to the gold mines. And so the adventurers left with the good wishes of the whole Island. No doubt it will be many months before news is received from Australia, over 15,000 miles away by sea. Let us hope it is good news.

There was a public holiday on 26th January, 1853, so the citizens of Peel could wish the "Vixen" and her crew farewell for her voyage to Australia. Here she is passing the harbour light and a crowded quayside, having being towed out of the harbour before lowering her sails.

THE HOLMES BANK AFFAIR

On November 12th of this year, 1853, casual observers were no doubt mystified by the sight of Mr. Robert Boardman boarding the Liverpool boat in charge of a large iron box which needed four men to carry it. Others, more worldly-wise, could be forgiven for thinking that his departure had something to do with the death, just five days before, of his employer, the late Mr. James Holmes of the Holmes Bank. He was aged 75. In the iron box were the contents of the bank's safe – gold and Bank of England notes amounting to thousands of pounds. News of the death of the old man, the sole proprietor of the bank, together with the subsequent closure of the bank on the South Quay, Douglas, led to near panic as traders refused to handle the Holmes banknotes, causing a run on other banks to change them. Fortunately the Island's main bank, the Bank of Mona, reached an agreement with the Manx Legislature whereby they were permitted to issue on a one-for-one basis their own notes in exchange for Holmes' notes. On the appointed day £11,000 worth of notes were taken up, well beyond the stipulated limit of £8,000. By this means the overall loss to the general public has been minimised though the loss to depositors is likely to be much more serious and will take many years to sort out. It is said that creditors number over 500 and their deposits, totalling over £200,000, will have to await the outcome of a lengthy period of time for the liquidation of the bank's assets.

The news has come as a shock as the Holmes Bank, which also traded as the Douglas and Isle of Man Bank, has enjoyed public confidence for many years. The Bank was founded in 1815 by Mr Henry Holmes Sr. of Liverpool in partnership with his three sons, James, John and Henry Jr. The bank was one of the first five banks to obtain licences to issue bank notes after the passing of the Banker's Notes Act of 1817. James was already resident on the Island representing the family interests and was one of the privileged guests of the Duke of Atholl at the Dinner celebrating the completion of the Castle Mona in 1804. Subsequently, the Duke borrowed money from the Holmes Bank to finance property speculations on the Island.

As was often the case, the Holmes were merchants as well as bankers. John rose to be Mayor of Liverpool. They were boat owners, red herring curers, and timber merchants. James also looked after the considerable property holdings on the Island with houses and warehouses in Douglas. There were also Herring Houses at Douglas, Peel, Port St. Mary and Derbyhaven, and Mills at Port St. Mary and Lhane Moar. The properties also included twelve farms throughout the Island from Jurby and Andreas to Rushen. Also, the hotel and most of Port St. Mary village, with the exception of one house, was purchased by James Holmes at the sale of Crown property.

Such was the confidence inspired that horse dealers from Cumberland, while buying in the south of the Island, are known to have been obliged to return to Douglas and obtain Holmes' notes in exchange for their golden sovereigns and Bank of Englands. It was the Holmes Bank that was chosen to implement the changes in Manx currency following the Act of Tynwald of 1839. The trouble began with the new coins which showed Queen Victoria's head and the Three Legs. Up to then Manx coins circulated at 14 pennies Manx to the shilling British. Many will remember that if you took 12 Manx pennies to Liverpool or Whitehaven you could exchange them for a shilling and, returning to the Island, convert them back to 14 pennies. This encouraged the export of Manx copper pennies leaving the Island with a mixture of tokens and even metal buttons to be used as coins! Hence the Act of Tynwald of 1839 and Her Majesty, by Order in Council, authorising The Royal Mint to produce £1,000 of coins in pence, halfpence and farthings. These are dated 1839 and have the Queen's head on one side and the Three Legs and motto on the other side. When converting from 14 Manx to the new 12 British pence a small profit could be made.

The change to the new coinage was to be made at the Holmes Bank by September 12th, 1840. But considerable unrest resulted when goods costing a penny a piece remained at that price so that only 12 could be obtained instead of 14. Such was the hostility shown by the poorer classes that a riot took place in Douglas and other parts of the Island. The windows and doors of the legislators, and of shopkeepers favourable to the change, were demolished; the Riot Act was read and the military called out. Peace was only restored after a company of soldiers arrived from Liverpool. Since then the new copper has circulated freely and has brought great benefit to trade and commerce.

More latterly Mr. James Holmes had declined in health and was totally blind, relying on Mr. Boardman to assist in carrying on the bank's business. Someone who called to see Mr. Holmes in 1850 at his residence on the South Quay wrote: "January 17th, called to see Mr. Holmes and sat with him some time – poor man, his appearance is quite shocking, his clothes are all worn and dirty and have become too tight or small for him, his hands are black with dirt as a chimney sweep's, and his whole person is equally so. He is so blind he only knows me by my voice."

Strange to say, the older and feebler Mr. Holmes became, the wealthier everyone believed him to be. Matters have not been helped by the death of his brother John just a few days previous, James being left as his executor. Mr. Samuel Harris, Sumner General of the Island, has been called in to supervise the liquidation of the assets of the Holmes Bank but as this will be complicated and lengthy creditors may have to wait many years before a final settlement is made. It is hoped that this unfortunate experience will lead to better regulation and inspection of banking services in the years to come.

The "Vixen" – LATEST NEWS

News has been received in Peel that the "Vixen" reached Australia after a voyage of 92 days and dropped anchor at Melbourne, Victoria, on May 3rd. Despite being becalmed for about three weeks she, nevertheless, averaged 170 miles per day, a truly remarkable performance for a vessel of her dimensions. She passed various ships on the way including the "Prince Arthur", a fast emigrant ship, which left Liverpool, with five Peel men among the passengers, on January 24th but arrived four days after the "Vixen".

There seem to be quite a few Manx people out there and they gave a hearty welcome to the "Vixen" when they saw she was flying the Manx flag! The men remained on board for some time before heading for the gold fields, splitting into small groups. Captain Cubbon intends to stay with the "Vixen" on coastal trading before returning to home waters.

HERE IS THE NEWS: 1854
LAXEY WHEEL CHRISTENED IN HONOUR OF LADY ISABELLA

There were scenes of great celebration at Laxey today when a giant water wheel which is the biggest in Europe and perhaps the world was officially set in motion by the Governor, the Hon. Charles Hope. The wheel has been designed and built for the Great Laxey Mining Company and will be used to keep the extensive mine workings in the village pumped dry of water. We have this report:

'Wednesday, 24th September, 1854. There was fine late summer weather for this morning's occasion and nearly 4,000 people from all over the Island were gathered in Glen Mooar, Laxey. In addition to the Governor and Lady Hope the Company invited the Lord Bishop, members of the Legislature, Government officials and the gentry. The principal guests started arriving from 11 a.m. with the Governor due at 12 noon. At the same time nearly 600 work people in their holiday attire, led by the Chairman of the Directors of the Laxey Mining Company, Mr. George W. Dumbell, and the mines agent Captain Richard Rowe, marched in procession from the washing floors up the glen to the wheel. There the assembly watched the Governor turn on the water which set the mighty wheel in motion after which it was christened "Lady Isabella" with a bottle of champagne by Mrs. Dumbell in honour of the Governor's wife. The moment was greeted by the firing of cannon and the unfurling of a flag on top of the wheel structure. After this the official party ascended the spiral staircase to the viewing platform, remarking that there was not the least tremor from the wheel beneath their feet. Meanwhile, tables laden with beef, potatoes and ale, with ginger beer and milk for the totalists, had been laid out in the open for the workpeople. There was a blessing by Bishop Powys and the people gave three cheers for the Governor and Captain Rowe. Afterwards there were games for them while the principal guests retired to a wooden pavilion for a sumptuous repast. During the speechmaking afterwards Captain Rowe said but for Mr. Dumbell and the Company, the glen of Laxey would be silent and 600 miners and their families would be seeking employment elsewhere, perhaps in Australia. The use of the new wheel, which is capable of pumping 250 gallons of water a minute from the mine workings, is expected to increase output. The total credit for the design of the colossus goes to a 37 year old Manx engineer, Mr. Robert Casement, a native of Lezayre. The company has presented him with a cheque for £50 in recognition of his efforts.'

THE SMUGGLING FINALLY DISAPPEARS

The last vestiges of the old smuggling trade in the Isle of Man have finally been wiped out after well over a century. Treasury officials said this was a direct result of last year's British Government decision to bring Manx duties on spirits and tobacco up to English levels. It was the sheer size of the smuggling trade that led to the Revestment of 1765 but the Mischief Act never succeeded in eradicating it as long as there was an imbalance of duties in the Island, which continued until last year. Officials said with no profit to be taken there was no point in the so-called running trade continuing.

DECLINE IN DRUNKENNESS

It is also claimed that the increase in local spirit duty has resulted in a sharp decrease in drunkenness in the Island. At the same time the duty on tea has been reduced considerably, bringing about a marked change in social habits. Tynwald now plans to introduce a Taverns Act in three years time to effect further control. The cost of licence fees and recognisances paid by public house landlords will be greatly increased and Sunday opening will be banned. The number of public houses in the Island is already falling – from 460 twelve years ago to just under 300 nowadays.

BREAKWATER FOR DOUGLAS HARBOUR

Plans are being drawn up by Admiralty engineer, Mr. James Walker, for building a breakwater to protect Douglas harbour from south-easterly gales. His idea is to build it out for a distance of 200 yards from the two-gun defensive battery on Douglas Head. The cost is estimated at £32,000. His recommendations will be in a report to the Admiralty which should be completed next year. Mr. Walker also wants the 53-year-old Red Pier in Douglas to be extended and he has ideas for also building protective breakwaters at Ramsey, Peel, Port Erin and Castletown to put right the neglect of Manx harbour works that has been allowed to happen in the last century.

TOWN COMMISSIONERS FOR DOUGLAS

Tynwald has announced steps leading towards the election of town commissioners to take over municipal control in the town of Douglas. This follows demands by townspeople for civic improvements befitting the principal town and port of the Isle of Man. It is hoped that legislation will soon be implemented for the election of nine commissioners with extensive powers of action. There are now about 1,700 houses in the town and the commissioners will have power to impose rates on property up to a maximum of two shillings in the pound.

Richard Rowe
Captain of the Mines

Robert Casement
Creator of the Wheel

PUTTING LAXEY ON THE MAP

Following the recent developments in Laxey, the village will never be the same again. The magnificent wheel of 72 feet diameter, the largest of its kind ever built, turns majestically at the head of Glen Mooar to power the pumps that are said to be able to drain water from the workings at the rate of 250 gallons a minute from a depth of 200 fathoms. The depth of the workings are constantly being increased as new veins of lead (rich in silver), zinc blende and copper are being discovered. There is an air of prosperity about the place and the mine company shares, bought for £100 in 1848, are yielding rich dividends with over £1,200 being paid on each share during the past six years. There is plenty of employment and miners come from Baldwin and Sulby to earn a wage rather than toil on their meagre crofts. To cope with the increased output of ore there are calls for a new pier in the harbour to replace the old one, long since destroyed. This would greatly facilitate the loading of the sacks on to the succession of schooners which at present have to be brought up on to Laxey beach.

Laxey can also boast a New Road which was officially opened in April. When it was first mooted in 1851 there was a strong plea to have the road climb from the foot of Snaefell and over the rough land to Ramsey, this being considered as shorter and quicker to reach Ramsey. However, the Committee of Highways decided the lower coastal route would serve the community better. They are to be congratulated on their work not only in Laxey but in other parts of the Island. The New Road leaves the old road at Pinfold Hill and follows the line of the valley round to the top of Minorca where it crosses the old road leading to Ballaragh. This means that coaches on the Douglas to Ramsey service no longer have to use the tortuous and dangerous drop down to the harbour. Two bridges have had to be built, one with four arches of considerable height over the Glen Roy river and one with a single arch and embankment to take the road over the Laxey river. This viaduct is contiguous with the washing floors of the Great Laxey Mining Company. During the construction of the road a man was unfortunately killed on the section between the two bridges. When cutting into the high bank at this point a quantity of gravel fell and John Cleator, 41, was knocked to the ground and fell upon a sharp stone which caused his instant death.

First to pass over the New Road was Mr. Hayes' four-horse coach, the North Star, which runs a service between Douglas Market Place and Ramsey, leaving each place on alternate days. This means that travellers will now have a much better view of the Glen to which can be added the Great Wheel. Mr. Hayes has announced his intention of introducing a daily service next year using the North Star or the Royal Mail. They will leave the Market Place, Ramsey at 10 o'clock, returning from Douglas Market Place at 3 o'clock, changing horses at Laxey, going and returning. Already Mr. James Kewley has placed his van on the Laxey road starting from his own house in Drumgold Street at 12 o'clock and returning from Ramsey at the same hour on alternate days. He guarantees punctual delivery of all letters and parcels. Changes to the insular mail service have taken place whereby the mail cart will no longer use the shore road. Letters down to the village will be conveyed by foot messenger. This new arrangement has met with disapproval by some. It is good to note that steps have been taken to help the poor in the district. A week after the Wheel Turning Ceremony permission was obtained to use the tent erected for the miners' feast so that a Tea Festival could be held. Many of the miners, farmers and others with their wives attended. A public meeting was held with Captain Rowe as Chairman. Singing by the United Choirs of the Wesleyan and Primitive Methodist chapels enlivened the proceedings after which a total of £20 was collected to start a fund to help the poor, especially those who are sick or unable to work through accident. No doubt miners' families will benefit as there are frequent accidents below ground. A serious accident occurred in July when Robert Thompson was at his place of work loading up the kibbles (buckets) with ore to be hauled to the surface. A large piece fell from the kibble which split his head open and fractured his skull, causing his death. He leaves a wife and child; many attended his funeral at Lonan churchyard. Another tragedy during the year was the death of John Quirk, 13, who was employed at Gawne's corn mill. While cleaning the mill near the wheel he was caught in it and suffered bruising in a frightful manner. He was conveyed to the hospital in Douglas but died the day after.

The spiritual needs of the villagers are well catered for with

The scene of the Laxey Fair held on the field at the bottom of the glen

the Wesleyan Chapel in Glen Road, rebuilt four years ago, and the Primitive Methodist Chapel down by the harbour. Both have thriving Sunday Schools. And now the Anglicans have their own church in the village following the completion of Christ Church, more popularly known as The Miners' Church. It has been built with the support of the mining company and stands on the elevated ground which forms the garden of the Mine Captain's house. The building is in Early English style, the open benches, pulpit, reading desk, rafters and all the woodwork stained a dark oak colour. While the miners are generally regarded as fine, upstanding men, sermons continually warn of the evil of drunkenness which leads to disgraceful scenes, especially when the miners receive their monthly pay packets. Services were formerly held in the licensed Glen School below the church. The indefatigable schoolmaster works well with the children who gain good examination results. It is hoped that a woman assistant will be appointed shortly to teach the females and prepare them for taking up employment in service.

The major annual event in the village is The Fair held on the field at the bottom of the glen. It is a great social event when the natives are joined by visitors from as far away as Douglas. The price of cattle is the main concern of the farmers while their wives deal in dairy products, poultry and eggs. There is also a good trade in toffee, gingerbread and jough, the latter causing many a sore head before the day is out! For the rest of the year there is much village life with an abundance of Societies and meetings to attend. What, with the busy mining activity and the New Road bringing many visitors to view the Wheel, Laxey is now well and truly on the map!

OUR JUST DUES

Students of the Manx political scene have found the events of the past twelve months absolutely fascinating. It will be remembered that the political restlessness began when the British Government took it upon itself to revise our Manx Custom Duties without even bothering to ask the House of Keys and the Manx people about it first. The raising of our duties on spirits and tobacco to those of the United Kingdom undoubtedly sounded the death knell to the smuggling trade that a century ago and less dominated Manx life. However the manner in which this was done, the arrogance shown, affronted nationalist sentiment to an unparalleled degree. Furthermore, the point blank refusal of the English to discuss the question of the Surplus Revenue offended everyone whatever their political persuasion. A petition containing over 7,000 signatures was ample indication of the anger felt.

For too many years the money raised from the Isle of Man has not been completely spent. But the surplus instead of being used here to improve harbours, maintain roads and so on, has vanished to the bottomless pit of the British Treasury. The recent uproar, especially the alleged comments from officials of the British Government, that financial control could hardly be given to a self-elected body of men, has undoubtedly fuelled the ambition of our Reforming Party. This group, it will be recalled, have agitated for the last quarter of a century for the abolition of the undemocratic Keys that represents, they say, only a small group of landed families who manipulate the affairs of the Island in their own interests. It will be interesting to see for how long the present system can survive.

Castle Rushen and Harbour by G Pickering, 1832

Peel Bay and Town, published by T. Carran, c.1850

Laxey Village and Bay by J. Burkill, published by J. Mylrea, Douglas, 1857

Ramsey Town and Harbour by J. Burkill, published by J. Mylrea, Douglas, 1857

TOWN COMMISSIONERS AT LAST!

After many years of protracted negotiations and haggling, Tynwald finally consented to the passing of the Douglas Town Act (1860) earlier this year. Leading residents of Douglas have been moved to make various approaches to Tynwald to invest them with the responsibility of controlling the affairs of the town which continues to grow, six hundred houses having been added during the past ten years while the population has grown to over 12,000. Tynwald's main concern has been, through its Highway Committee, the development of roads throughout the Island which has resulted in the four towns becoming the main centres of trade and communications – Douglas in particular. Apart from performing parochial labour on the highways the townspeople have also had to maintain the paving of their streets and contribute to the Highway Fund. Since 1777 the High Bailiff of each town has assumed the role of the Captain of the Town with responsibility for good maintenance and cleanliness of the streets though he has had little resources to do this. Such important matters were highlighted during the cholera outbreaks of 1832–33 followed by the smallpox epidemic of 1837. But things have moved slowly with the Governor, his council and the 24 self-elected Keys, mainly the country gentry, being accused of not representing the people and being irresponsible.

It is interesting to recall that at the Tynwald Court in February, 1846, High Bailiff John Kelly of Castletown presented a petition from the inhabitants of the town 'Praying the Court to have the streets kept in repair at the expense of the Highway Fund.' The people of Castletown complained of the hardships of having to repair at their own expense the streets which were being cut up by carts drawing seaweed, stones, lime etc. going to the farms in the country. Tynwald's response was that any assistance to Castletown should also apply to the other towns and Mr. Kelly was invited to prepare a bill for future consideration. There was a constant stream of letters appearing in the press such as that of a Douglas resident: 'Many of our drains and sewers are in a sadly neglected state and some of our streets require the use of a scavenger, because there are middins, ashpits and other nuisances exposed to view.'

The Towns Bill, applicable to all four towns on a voluntary basis, was published in 1847 but was subject to constant delays with much time spent arguing over town boundaries. There was, however, a committee appointed to provide Douglas with an efficient fire engine which is stationed by the Court House. That was in 1849 and the following year saw the establishment of a Hospital adjoining the Dispensary which had been moved from Strand Street to Fort Street. The ladies of the town, through sales of work, raised the money to purchase the large building and maintain the Hospital of 27 beds. Miss Nellie Brennan, it will be remembered, was its first matron though ill-health forced her to relinquish her position shortly afterwards.

Tired of waiting, there were many meetings called in Douglas and one held in Wellington Hall in 1851 called upon the Legislature with the following appeal: '...that in sewering, paving, lighting and cleansing, this town is far behind. That the burthen of these improvements ought to be equitably apportioned upon the whole town, which can only be accomplished by an Act of Tynwald giving powers to the ratepayers of Douglas to assess themselves and to elect from among themselves their own commissioners to have control of their money. That a portion of the funds now raised out of the town for the Highways to be appropriated to the uses of the town.' The Towns Bill became an Act of Tynwald in 1848 but it was not promulgated until 1852. It was immediately rejected by the tenants and proprietors of Douglas as being of little benefit to them and falling far short of their wishes.

Governor Hope attempted to resolve the issue with new Bills but they were rejected at a meeting held in St. George's Hall in April, 1858. However, at this meeting a committee put forward recommendations which were fully supported by all present. These were that the High Bailiff should not be one of the commissioners; the maximum rate should be one shilling in the pound; bye-laws to regulate hackney cars and carriages, bye-laws for porters and bathing should be introduced; provision to purchase for the purpose of widening and improving the streets; the Highroad labour charge to be replaced by a sum of money in respect of each dwelling to be paid by the commissioners to the Highway Committee; powers to alter the town boundaries subject to Tynwald approval; that the Act be compulsory for the town of Douglas. The above points became the foundation of the Douglas Town Bill but the Highway labour still proved a major stumbling block, country members claiming that roads were of benefit to townspeople as much as those living in the country districts and therefore should pay the same. But the view prevailed that some relief should be made to the future ratepayers and a sum of three shillings per dwelling (equivalent to $1\frac{1}{2}$ days labour) should be paid. The way was clear for the approval of the Douglas Town Act which was promulgated at a special Tynwald Court held at St. John's on 1st May.

For the town elections held in July of this year there were 30 nominations for the nine commissioners; 398 voters recorded their votes at the Court House. The Douglas Town Commissioners held their first meeting a week later with Mr Samuel Harris, advocate, who topped the pole being elected Chairman. He agreed that the Old Seneschal's Office, his property, be rented as the Commissioners' Office. Mr. John Mylrea, a bookseller and printer who is also a commissioner was appointed Secretary and Mr. George William Dumbell was appointed Treasurer. It was also agreed that a Clerk/Collector be appointed at a salary of £100 per annum less the salary of an office boy. Deputations were appointed to wait on the Douglas Water and Gas Companies concerning their supplies. Six scavengers have been engaged to clean up the town which has been divided into four wards – Ballaquayle, Finch Hill, Old Town and Hills – with two commissioners responsible for each. Thus, by the end of the year, the Commissioners have shown considerable zeal in setting about the many problems regarding paving, cleansing, lighting, and underground sewers, the latter being the most pressing and certain to be the most costly. Meanwhile the Commissioners have presented the Hon. Charles Hope with an address on his departure and a public meeting has adopted an address to the incoming Governor – Francis Pigott – who is due to arrive in February next year.

Mr Samuel Harris, advocate, first Chairman of Douglas Town Commissioners.

THE ARRIVAL OF GOVERNOR PIGOTT

Great rejoicings took place at Douglas, Isle of Man, on Thursday week, consequent upon the arrival of His Excellency Francis Pigott, the newly-appointed Lieutenant Governor of the Island, to take up his permanent residence at Villa Marina, near Douglas. 'It was,' says the Manx Sun, from which we extract a few particulars of the new Governor's reception, 'both a holiday for all classes and a triumphal entry for His Excellency such as has not been accorded to any previous Governor within the memory of the oldest Manxman.' A little before three o'clock a signal gun from Douglas Head conveyed the welcome intelligence that the packet containing Lieutenant Governor Pigott was in sight, and, shortly after, repeated salutes from the packet and shore announced her nearer approach. Exactly at three o'clock the "*Tynwald*", under the command of Captain M'Queen, gaily decorated with flags, steamed gallantly up the harbour, and was moored opposite the Steam-Packet Office. His Worship the High Bailiff, Major Pollock, Mr. Burham, Mr. Harris, Mr. Gell, and other gentlemen, then went on board to greet the Lieutenant Governor, who shortly after made his appearance on deck and was loudly cheered.

His Excellency landed accompanied by Mrs. Pigott, escorted by His Worship the High Bailiff; the two Misses Pigott escorted by Lieutenant Lindsey and S. Harris Esq.; together with Captain Pigott, and his two brothers. The Artillery Corps presented arms, and His Excellency entered the carriage provided for him amid the cheers of the assembled thousands, the band playing 'God Save the Queen.' A procession was then formed and proceeded along the North Quay, up Bank Hill, along Athol Street, up

The Villa Marina, belonging to Mr Samuel Harris, has been leased by Lieut. Governor Francis Pigott for a term of years.

Prospect Hill, along Finch Road, and Marina Road to Castle Mona. The whole route was thickly thronged with enthusiastic spectators, who loudly cheered His Excellency as he passed.

On the arrival of the procession at Castle Mona gates the societies formed in double line, and, allowing the carriage to pass up the centre, they entered the grounds of the castle, where His Excellency was received at the entrance to the hotel by a guard of honour of Volunteer Rifles. The mansion of Villa Marina, situated a short distance from Douglas, has been leased by Lieutenant Governor Pigott for a term of years. (*From the Illustrated London News 23.2.61*)

THE LIEUTENANT GOVERNORS AND THEIR HOUSES

Since the death of the fourth Duke of Atholl, in 1830, the Island has been governed by a Lieutenant Governor as the sole representative of the British Government. During the last years of the fourth Duke this post was ably filled by Colonel Cornelius Smelt who died at Castle Rushen in 1832. His many admirers saw fit to erect a memorial, in the form of a Doric column, in the Market Place, Castletown. Colonel Smelt had steadfastly refused to move from the Derby House accommodation within the Castle walls in order that extensions to the cramped Court House could be carried out. Colonel Smelt was succeeded by another military gentleman – Colonel John Ready. Such were the encroachments on Derby House as the Court House was being enlarged, Colonel Ready was obliged to leave the Castle, the British Government making it clear that, in future, he and his successors would be responsible for finding their own accommodation with an allowance to assist them. At this time Lorne House, which had long been in the possession of the Taubman family of Bowling Green House, Castletown, was vacant and Colonel Ready took a lease on the house which lasted until his departure from the Island in 1845.

The new Lieutenant Governor in 1845 was The Hon. Charles Hope who took up residence at Lorne House which was now referred to as Government House. It was unfortunate that he was blamed for the fiasco concerning the Royal Visit of 1847 when Queen Victoria and the Royal Consort coasted down the east coast of the Island on their return from Scotland. It will, of course, be remembered that the Prince came ashore at Ramsey and the proud townsfolk have since built the 'Albert Tower' on the top of the wooded height from which the Prince viewed the town and the north of the Island. Governor Hope will be remembered as an energetic and liberal administrator who brought considerable benefits to the Island during this difficult time of stringent control by the British Government. Governor Hope left in 1860 and the lease on Lorne House was terminated by the owner who wished to occupy it himself. It was proposed that a new residence be built, as Government House, at an estimated cost of £7,000. The proposal was promptly rejected by the British Treasury who placed the onus on the Manx Government, although it was prepared to continue the old allowance of £150 a year to the Lieutenant Governor who would be responsible for making his own arrangements.

In February, 1861, Francis Pigott, M.P. for Reading, arrived in Douglas as the new Governor amid great rejoicings among the townsfolk. He stayed at the Castle Mona pending a decision concerning his permanent residence. Only ten days after his arrival he reported that he had heard of nothing suitable in Castletown, either a house or prospective site. He therefore accepted the offer of Villa Marina mansion, the home of Mr. Samuel Harris, at an annual rental of £200.

Mr. Harris received much praise from the recently elected Town Commissioners of whom he is Chairman. This could well lead to Douglas being declared the Island's new capital despite the strong protests and resentment of Castletown.

Under Governor Pigott's instructions the gradual removal of various Government Departments and several Law Courts began to take place with Douglas being generally accepted, because of its size and central position. However, the process was interrupted with the sudden end of Governor Pigott's promising administration as a result of his death from cancer at his Hampshire home in January, 1863. During his two years as Governor, a harbour improvement scheme was initiated and land at the Strang purchased for a lunatic asylum. As the appointment of a new Governor was awaited Mark Quayle Esq., Clerk of the Rolls, became Deputy Governor and promptly ordered the return of the Law Courts back to Castletown where he lived!

The news that Henry Brougham Loch Esq. had been appointed as Lieutenant Governor was greeted with general approbation. He had achieved much distinction in India and the Far East where he had been involved in the signing of Treaties with both China and Japan.

In February Henry Loch accompanied by his wife arrived unexpectedly on board the "*Tynwald*" at Douglas. He was the guest of Deemster Drinkwater at Kirby where he received a deputation from the Douglas Town Commissioners pressing their case to make their town the centre of Government. He said he would give their request his most serious attention; this was followed by an announcement that the new Governor had decided to take up residence at Bemahague, a handsome seat just two miles from the outskirts of Douglas and in the parish of Onchan. The estate has been the property of the Heywood family since the end of last century.

When Governor Loch returned in April his reception in Douglas was overwhelming but he was in no hurry to commit himself regarding the claims of Castletown and Douglas. Diplomatically he is calling meetings of Tynwald in both places, besides the open-air meetings at St. John's. Meetings of Tynwald in Douglas are being conducted in the Court House in Athol Street, formerly the Oddfellows' Hall which was built in 1840–41 and latterly used as a theatre. It therefore seems likely that before long Douglas will be declared the Island's modern capital. Meanwhile Governor Loch is concerning himself with much more serious matters. He is working tirelessly to advance the interests of the Island and has undertaken prolonged negotiations with the British Government to secure control of the Island's finances which he regards as a prerequisite for future developments. It is also known that His Excellency considers the reform of the House of Keys as equally important and it is anticipated that important constitutional matters will be laid before Tynwald before very long.

Lorne House, Castletown

Bemahague House, Onchan

HERE IS THE NEWS: 1866
HOUSE OF KEYS TO BE REFORMED

After four centuries of self-election and autocratic rule the House of Keys is to become a democratically elected body next year. The decision has been made following a series of meetings between the Keys and the Governor, Mr. Henry Loch, who has played a significant part in bringing about what constitutional reformers are hailing as the end of medieval control of the Island's affairs, and the start of a new and enlightened era of Manx history. We have this report:

'The situation really began to develop last year when the Governor had discussions with the British Treasury on giving the Island more control over its finances, and its surplus revenue in particular. This was followed by long discussions with the Keys and the outcome, announced today, is that the House will become elective early next year. In return Tynwald will have control of Manx revenues, subject to "veto" by the Governor and the Treasury. It is also agreed that the Island should pay £10,000 a year to the British Government for defence and other external matters. The present House will be dissolved on March 16th next year, just 12 months from now. This will enable free elections to take place the following month. Great credit is being given to the Governor for his "able" and "far-sighted" part in the development, which the Keys have resisted for many years. But many observers date the real start of events leading to the change to two years ago. This was when Mr. James Brown, editor and owner of the Isle of Man Times, commented in severe terms on the undemocratic nature of the Keys and was called before the Bar of the House where he was deemed guilty of contempt and a breach of privilege. When he refused to purge his contempt by way of apology the Keys committed him to Castle Rushen for six months. This caused an uproar throughout Britain and the illegality of the Keys action was exposed in the Queen's Bench Division which ordered Mr. Brown's release and awarded him £518 **damages and costs for wrongful imprisonment. The constitutional position of the Keys was undermined, and has remained so since then. For next year's election there will be ten electoral districts with Douglas returning three members, Peel, Ramsey and Castletown one each; and Glenfaba, Michael, Ayre, Garff, Middle and Rushen three each. Candidates will have to be owners of real estate worth at least £100 and personal property worth a similar sum. Voters will have to be males of full age owning real estate to the value of not less than £8 or tenants not paying less than £12 a year rent.'**

SUMMER VISITORS ON THE INCREASE

The number of summer visitors coming to the Island continues to increase. There are now 50 to 60 thousand a year coming to Manx shores, twice as many as 20 years ago. They arrive mainly on the Steam Packet Company service from Liverpool to Douglas – and they are not deterred by difficult landing conditions. At low tide in Douglas they have to be ferried to the shore by small boats because of the lack of harbour works. Businessmen in the Island are now calling for the building of a pier upon which passengers can be discharged at all states of the tide.

WOODEN BREAKWATER DESTROYED

Meanwhile the destruction of the half-built new Douglas harbour break-water by storms last year has been blamed on economies imposed by the British Government. The original plan of Admiralty engineer Mr. James Walker was for a sturdy stone structure. But this was abandoned in favour of a creosoted wooden framework built on a foundation of rubble and known as Abernethy's Birdcage after its designer, and it could not withstand the winter gales. Five hundred feet of the new breakwater extending from Douglas Head battery were destroyed and there is now no sign of work restarting. Engineers say only a complex of solid stone blocks will provide a proper breakwater for Douglas.

WORK STARTS ON SEWERAGE SYSTEM

Work has started on the construction of a mains sewerage system for Douglas and it should be completed in two years time. This is one of the measures being taken to try and prevent a repeat of the serious epidemics of typhoid fever and smallpox in the Island over the last two years, which have been responsible for a death rate of over 20 per cent. The Town Commissioners of Douglas, where 30,000 of the Island's population of more than 50,000 people now live, have been granted full powers to control sanitary conditions in houses. To facilitate control all houses in the town will be numbered from next year.

LUNATIC ASYLUM COMPLETED

The Island's first specially built lunatic asylum near Strang village, just outside Douglas, has admitted its first inmates. It is intended to house 110 altogether. Work on the building, plans for which were first drawn up two years ago, is continuing rapidly and completion is expected in 1868. The cost, £21,781, is being shared between the Manx authorities and the British Government. The offer of this arrangement was originally made by Britain nearly 15 years ago and £1,500 was raised by public subscription in the Island. But there was a major setback when this money was lost in the collapse of Holmes Bank in Douglas in 1853. From 1849 to 1864 the lunatics were housed alongside the debtors and criminals in the Island's prison at Castle Rushen and since being moved out have been accommodated at Oatlands awaiting completion of the new asylum.

THE FIRST ELECTIONS

This year, 1867, has seen the most exciting spring in the Isle of Man for many, many years. The first few days of April produced the greatest furore imaginable for, at last, here in the Island we have an elected House of Keys! True, this happy state of affairs has come about much later than in the rest of what may be termed as the civilised world, but it is perhaps even the more welcome for that.

There have been demands for this reform since before the outset of the nineteenth century. There have been petitions organised, public meetings arranged, sermons preached, leader columns in our newspapers written. There have been accusations and counter-accusations but until last year all came to naught. Then, it will be remembered, notice was properly taken of the suggestions made over a decade ago by officials of the British Treasury when discussing control of the Manx Revenue. It was hinted that such control might more easily be vested in an elected House of Keys. The surprise really was that last year there were no meetings, no petitions, no vitriolic pamphlets. But by then we had a comparatively new Governor – Henry Brougham Loch – whose perception and wisdom resolved with speed and efficiency this apparently knotty problem. He re-opened negotiations with the Treasury proposing that financial concessions should be granted on the condition that the Keys became an elected body. The Treasury agreed. The matter was laid before the Manx Legislature at the beginning of March and by the end of the same month Tynwald had agreed. To describe the initial response of the populace as euphoric would be an understatement. There was universal and unanimous delight. But it was short-lived and the unanimity soon vanished and the abuse returned.

The battle was fought on the field of the details of the Reform Bill, and the Reformers believe they lost. To be a member of the House of Keys one has to be a male, over 21, a property owner to the value of £100 or have an annual income of £100. To vote one has to be a male, over 21, own property of £8 or pay rent of £12 per annum or over. It was said, "*This Bill is at best a narrow piece of class legislation providing the vote for a posse of grub worms and leaving a far more intelligent class of the community disenfranchised.*" Furthermore, as the Island is divided into electoral districts, the four towns and six sheadings, the townsfolk claim thay are being ignored. The North are objecting that they are outnumbered 15-9 by the South and Ramsey feels insulted by her one member status. The path of Reform never runs smoothly!

Once the Act had been promulgated in late December last year political activity began to increase. Candidates announced themselves and numerous committees were formed to advance a multitude of causes. In towns and villages those new phenomena, political meetings, were held and as they were new their management had to be learnt. Indeed, there are several reports of such meetings breaking up in disorder as everyone there insisted on speaking and often at once! At others, chairmen refused to put resolutions, with which they disagreed, before the meetings which naturally ended in uproar. In Douglas the entry of Richard Sherwood, solicitor, as a fourth candidate added spice to the

At the election for three members to represent Douglas, Mr. Sherwood received 317 votes. Mr. Moore polled 471; Mr. Dumbell 464 and Major Goldie-Taubman, 457; so that these three were duly elected. They returned thanks on the hustings where also Mr. Sherwood acknowledged his defeat, amidst a great deal of uproar, and the proceedings of the day were closed by escorting the newly-elected members home in their carriages drawn by men instead of horses, with a line of cars and omnibuses conveying their committee men and other friends. A barrel of ale was tapped to flow gratitude in the middle of the market place; but we do not hear of any riot or fight inspired by the heady liquor. Mr Marshal Wane favoured us with some illustrations of the hustings outside the Court House in Athol Street, one of which has been engraved and is shown above. (The Illustrated London News)

candidatures of Mr. Dumbell of Belmont, Major J. S. Goldie-Taubman of the Nunnery and Mr. W. F. Moore of Cronkbourne. By the end of March the political temperature was high and the Manx in general had had an exciting couple of months.

In five consituencies, Castletown, Peel, Ramsey, Ayre and Michael there were no contests. In the remaining five the actual hustings produced no clear result by show of hands and so polls were demanded. In Douglas, as bank clerks from Dumbell's Bank had been appointed as poll agents, it was claimed that this influenced many votes with business interests. The odd barrel of beer available at the polling stations did not pass without pointed comments either!

There seems little doubt that popular election has been adopted all over the Island with great enthusiasm even though the restricted franchise has resulted in the return of 15 members who at one time or another have been in the old House. The First Election has been a great event. It will occupy a rightfully important place in Manx history. And although radical departures from previous policies seem unlikely at present there can be little doubt, that now the first step has been taken, succeeding generations of Manxmen will go further. Will Universal Male Suffrage be seen? Will the Secret Ballot be introduced? Will the boundaries of the constituencies be redrawn? Most controversial of all, will women ever be given the vote?

SOME PROMINENT MANX POLITICAL FAMILIES

With the first elections for the House of Keys over and the Members, new and old, safely settled into their task of guiding the Island's destiny for a certain term of five years, it would appear to be a good time to review the fortunes of some of those involved.

EDWARD MOORE GAWNE (b.1802)

Edward Moore Gawne was Speaker of the old House having held that position since 1854. He had been selected as a member under the old system in 1829 and for some years prior to becoming Speaker himself had acted as Deputy Speaker to his uncle, John Moore of 'The Hills' near Douglas. Mr. Gawne was one of the three members of the old House who voted against the change to popular elections and because of his opposition to the new system would not offer himself for election. On the dissolution of the non-elected House, Her Majesty offered Mr. Gawne a knighthood in consideration of his distinguished service, but this he refused. His colleagues of the old House, however, presented him with the antique Speaker's Chair belonging to the House.

Mr. Gawne is well known for his work to improve the state of agriculture in the Island and was elected the first President of the Agricultural Society when it was reconstituted in 1841. He now has more time to devote to his family home and lands at Kentraugh, Rushen, although he was born at Mount Gawne, being the son of Edward Gawne and Catherine Moore of Pulrose. Through his grandmother Jane Gawne, alias Taubman, of Ballagawne, he is related to the Taubman family who have an unequalled record of service in the Keys. In 1835 Mr. Gawne married Miss Emily Maria Murray, the daughter of Colonel Richard Murray and Catherine Bacon, and they lived at Ardairey, Arbory, until the death of Mr. Gawne Snr. two years later. Mrs. Gawne was born at 'Hills House', Douglas, but before her marriage she lived at Mount Murray, her father being the son of Lord Henry Murray, and the grandson of the third Duke of Atholl, the last Lord of Man before Revestment.

JOHN SENHOUSE GOLDIE-TAUBMAN (b.1838)

Mr. Goldie-Taubman was selected as a member of the non-elected House of Keys in 1859 and having offered himself as a candidate for Douglas in the recent election was duly elected. The new House chose him to serve as Speaker and a wise choice it is proving to be. If Mr. Goldie-Taubman continues as he has started it would be fair to say he is likely to be awarded honours similar to his predecessor.

The Nunnery, home of the Goldie-Taubmans. The obelisk situated in the grounds commemorates General Thomas Leigh Goldie who was killed in action in 1854 during the Crimean War.

It is a remarkable fact that Mr. Goldie-Taubman's father, grandfather and great-grandfather all served as Speakers of the House of Keys. His father was John Taubman Goldie-Taubman of the Nunnery and his mother Ellen, daughter of Humphrey Senhouse of Netherhall, Cumberland. Mr. Goldie-Taubman, the new Speaker, was educated at Eton and travelled widely before returning to live in his family home at the Nunnery. In the grounds of the Nunnery is an obelisk commemorating Mr. Goldie-Taubman's uncle, General Thomas Leigh Goldie, who died of wounds received at the Battle of Inkermann in 1854 during the Crimea War. Beside the obelisk is a Russian gun captured at Sebastopol where Colonel Goldie lies buried.

Rumour has it that the Speaker's step-brother, Mr. George Goldie, has recently eloped to London with a Miss Elliott who was formerly employed at the Nunnery in the post of governess. Mr. Goldie had joined the Royal Engineers – all his forebears had been in the Brigade of Guards, indeed his father had been a Lieutenant Colonel in the Scots Guards – but some two years after being commissioned he inherited some monies and left the Army in somewhat mysterious circumstances. Apparently he went to Egypt where for three years he lived in the desert. He only returned to the Island when an Arab girl with whom he had formed an attachment died of consumption.

WILLIAM CALLISTER (b.1808)

Mr. Callister was nominated on a number of occasions for the House of Keys prior to accepting in 1847. For over ten years before this he had been campaigning vigorously for reform of the Keys and, indeed, was leader of the reform movement in the north of the Island. He seems to have decided that he could bring about reforms more readily from the inside rather than battering the walls of power from the outside. He soon became a most influential member, notable for his force of character and unusual power of oratory.

In 1853, with Mr. George W. Dumbell, he interviewed the Treasury regarding customs duties and obtained great advantage for the Island. Both members were presented with silver plates by their colleagues in the Keys to mark their success. In more recent years he went to London with regard to the Port Erin breakwater and also about the Common Lands issues. Having at last seen some of his ideas on reforms come about, Mr. Callister offered himself as a candidate for the Sheading of Ayre and was subsequently accepted at the hustings without the need of a poll. Some of his friends wished to see him elected Speaker but Mr. Callister declined,

Edward Moore Gawne, of Kentraugh, Speaker of the House of Keys from 1854 to 1866, and John Senhouse Goldie-Taubman of the Nunnery, the new Speaker of the House of Keys.

William Callister, M.H.K., of Thornhill, near Ramsey, and William Fine Moore, M.H.K., of Cronkbourne, near Douglas.

lending his support and influence in favour of Mr. Goldie-Taubman who now holds the office to good effect.

Mr. Callister was educated off the Island (at the Liverpool Institute and at Daresbrough, Cheshire) and then joined his father in the family business of timber merchants. It will be remembered that he is one of the founder directors of The Isle of Man Banking Company Limited. He had issued copper tokens for one halfpenny for use on the Island and dated 1831. When the need for them had passed they were redeemed by the issuer at no loss to the users.

Mr. Callister resides at Thornhill, just outside Ramsey, which he built just over twenty years ago. His daughter, Isabella, is married to Edward Curphey Farrant who is another Member of the House of Keys for Ayre. Another daughter is married to John Thomas Clucas, Secretary to Governor Loch and Clerk to the Council. Since the Isle of Man Customs Act was passed Mr. Clucas has become Treasurer of the Isle of Man.

WILLIAM FINE MOORE (b. 1814)

Mr. Moore was a member of the old House since 1857 in which year he was also appointed a magistrate. From the beginning he supported the few members pressing for the reform of the Keys. He was a member of the Board of Harbour Commissioners and served on many Tynwald Court Committees. His support for reforms as well as his undoubted ability saw him returned at the head of the poll as a member for Douglas in the recent elections.

Mr. Moore lives at Cronkbourne, near Douglas, where he was born the youngest of five surviving brothers, children of James Moore and Elizabeth Jeale. Mr. James Moore had erected the sailcloth factory alongside the River Glass near Cronkbourne and Mr. William Fine Moore joined his father in the business when he was only 14. Mr. Moore senior died in 1846 since when Mr. William Moore has run the business. He is also much involved in The Isle of Man Banking Company Limited and in The Isle of Man Steam Packet Company Limited and is a major shareholder in various mining companies.

It will be recalled that a few years back Mr. Moore's Company supplied the sails for the iron tank ship "*Ramsey*" built at Ramsey for the Petroleum Trading Company of Newcastle. Amongst other ships supplied with sails from this same factory are "*Euterpe*", also built at Ramsey, and the mammoth steam ship "*Great Britain*". Mr. James Moore built Cronkbourne House but his sons have added to it and also seen to the building of the village of Cronkbourne, together with its chapel, for their workers. As architect for many of their works they have used the services of their kinsman Mr. Ewan Christian who has designed a number of churches on the Island including the recently completed new church for Marown. Mr. William Moore was given Cronkbourne House by his eldest brother Archdeacon John Christian Moore who, of course, resides in the Andreas rectory and is not married. Archdeacon Moore has spent much of his own money on the Andreas parish church, school and glebe. He is the great grandson of Parson Edward Moore who, as Vicar General, was imprisoned in Castle Rushen with Bishop Wilson.

WILLIAM FARRANT (b.1826)
EDWARD CURPHEY FARRANT (b.1830)

William is the oldest and Edward the second son of William Farrant of Ballamoar, Jurby, and Susannah Eleanora Curphey of Ballakillinghan, Andreas. William was educated in Ramsey and Douglas before going to Magdalen College, Oxford. He then travelled widely including visiting the Crimea during the war with Russia. He returned to the Island in 1856 and was made Captain of the Parish of Jurby, a post his father had held. Two years later he was selected as a Member of the House of Keys and in 1860 was appointed along with Mr. William Callister to go to London to negotiate with the Commissioners of Woods and Forests.

Edward was educated at King William's College and selected as a Member of the House of Keys in 1852 to fill the vacancy caused by the death of his father. Mr. Farrant at that time was only 21 and is thought to be the youngest member ever to sit in the Keys. He was one of those who opposed reform of the old House and was one of the three who voted against the Reform Bill. However, he allowed himself to be nominated as a candidate for Ayre and was accepted at the hustings without the need of a poll.

Mr. William Farrant chose not to allow his name to go forward in opposition to his brother in Ayre Sheading so avoiding the necessity for a poll. It is thought probable that Mr. Farrant will return to the political field at the next election by allowing his name to go forward for a different constituency. He lives in the family house of Ballamoar which had been inherited through his grandmother Margaret Moore of Pulrose, she being the daughter of William Christian of Ballamoar, Receiver General of the Isle of Man.

Mr. Edward Farrant lives at Ballakillinghan which he inherited through his mother who was the last of the Curpheys of Ballakillinghan. Throughout the years, the Curphey family, or Curghey as it used to be known, has supplied many who have held important positions in church and state. Mr. Farrant is married to Isabella, second daughter of his fellow member for Ayre, Mr. William Callister.

William Farrant, M.H.K., of Ballamoar, Jurby, and Edward Curphey Farrant, M.H.K., of Ballakillinghan.

HERE IS THE NEWS: 1872
JOHN KEWISH HANGED AT CASTLE RUSHEN

At 8 o'clock this morning John Kewish was hanged in Castle Rushen for the murder of his father at their home in Glen Moar, Sulby, in March this year. Kewish, who was 40 years old, went to his death on a scaffold erected in the debtors' yard of the castle with no visible sign of emotion. Only senior officials and representatives of the Island's newspapers were present at his execution. We have this report

'August 1st, Castle Rushen. There has been much controversy in the Island over its first hanging for 40 years. Kewish was a man of low intelligence, there was a conflict of medical evidence in the case, and he had to be tried twice, the jury failing to agree at the first attempt. He was sentenced to hang at this second trial a month ago. Kewish and his parents lived in a remote cottage in Sulby Glen and doctors who examined the body said the fatal wounds had been caused by a pitchfork. But in the condemned cell Kewish made a full confession, saying that he had accidentally shot the old man with his gun as he removed it from its usual place on the beam. This was clearly in conflict with the evidence presented in court over the cause of death. A petition for a reprieve was raised in the Island and sent to the Home Secretary, but he refused to commute the death sentence. But this failed to allay the widespread feelings of disquiet.

This morning the officials were led by Castletown High Bailiff, Mr. J. M. Jeffcott, who had to witness the execution, and who had to be summonsed by the Coroner to attend. There was then difficulty finding a firm of joiners to make a new scaffold, the old one having fallen into disrepair. Neither was there anyone on the Island willing to carry out the death sentence and the famous executioner Calcraft had to be sent over from England. At seven this morning Kewish was awakened from an untroubled sleep and ate a hearty breakfast. When Calcraft entered the cell Kewish shook his hand then walked to the scaffold unaided where a white cap was placed over his head as he stood on the trapdoor. Calcraft then sprang the trapdoor and the body dropped eighteen inches. The reporters there said a terrible silence fell over all as the body swung at the end of the rope. The body was left there for thirty minutes before being placed in a black coffin and buried in the castle grounds.

The last Manx hangings were in 1832 when two Peel men were hanged for assaulting and robbing an advocate. In 1823 a man and woman were publicly executed at Castletown for poisoning the former's pregnant wife. The sentence on that occasion was carried out by Mr John Cowley, Crammag, by virtue of his office as Coroner of Ayre. These two, like Kewish, were from Sulby. These are the only executions since before 1800 thus making Kewish the fifth to be hanged this century. This morning's execution adds greatly to the view that such a punishment, especially for someone of poor intellect such as Kewish, should be abandoned. And there is a lingering resentment that the Home Secretary did not see fit to respond favourably to the appeals made, on behalf of the condemned man.

COMPULSORY EDUCATION FOR ALL

The introduction of compulsory state education into the Isle of Man is provided for in a new Act of Tynwald taking effect this year. It is modelled on the 1870 Public Education Act in England, but there are important differences. The Manx Act actually enforces attendance at school by law, which the English Act does not. It also makes religious instruction compulsory. There are 59 schools of various kinds, including parochial and private, in the Island and most of them are expected to come under the control of the new district school boards to be set up.

NEW PIER NAMED AFTER QUEEN VICTORIA

The new passenger landing pier in Douglas harbour, which was officially opened to traffic last month, is to be named Victoria Pier after Her Majesty the Queen. The Lieutenant Governor, Mr. Henry Loch, has declined the honour of having it named the Loch Landing Pier in his honour. Work on the £46,000 structure started in 1867. Last month's opening ceremony was celebrated with lavish hospitality and paying for this out of public funds has led to criticism. The Mona's Herald has described the big occasion as a 'well-organised fuddle'.

FURTHER INCREASE IN TRADE

Figures issued today show a continuing expansion in trade to and from the Isle of Man. Exports now cover livestock of all kinds along with food and also lead and zinc ore from the mines. Imports are mainly coal, salt, iron and tobacco and spirits. Trade has improved as a result of the Imperial Act of 1853 which allowed dutiable goods to be bonded in the Island and finally abolished the trader licensing system which had long been a hindrance to local businesses. The expansion has led to increasing numbers of joint stock companies being set up in the Island—and new legislation is being drafted to control their conduct.

FISHERMEN WIN CASE

Finally, the fishermen of Peel and Port St. Mary have been given assurances by Governor Loch that they will not have to pay harbour dues—as long as their home ports are not protected by breakwaters. This follows a mass protest at the Tynwald ceremony at St. John's last month by 400 fishermen. The demonstration was the result of an announcement that harbour dues were being introduced now that Tynwald had taken over responsibility for the Island's ports and harbours. The fishermen said as neither Peel nor Port St. Mary Harbours have any protection they did not feel they should be made to pay for using them.

EDUCATION FOR ALL

The Island has at last come to terms with the new demands of our age. In May of this year 1872 at St. Johns the Act establishing Compulsory Education for Manx boys and girls and accepting the principle of State support for the educational system was finally promulgated.

Many will hope that this Act will at last restore the Island to the pre-eminent place in educational provision that, according to some historians, it once enjoyed. As early as 1704 the Established Church, then the initiator and organiser of what we today would call all social provision, enforced compulsory attendance at its schools through the authority of its ecclesiastical courts. A little later every parish in the Island could boast of having its own parochial school. Some of these were excellent and the children who attended them, bare-footed or not, were well served by their teachers. Among agencies contributing to their improvement was the National Society which received schools into their union with itself on condition that the children were instructed in the principles of the Church of England, supervised by the parish incumbent, and that they attend the Established Church. There were other schools, however, maintained in buildings hardly worthy of the name where, for example, when it was time 'to get yer dinner', boys would sail boats in the pools of water on the floor of the schoolroom. There were also schoolmasters who, it was said, could just about distinguish "a round O from a crooked S and wield a strong stick."

Furthermore, each town during this period had a 'Free' School or an endowed Grammar School. Indeed, Peel for the past two centuries or so has boasted of both, of which perhaps the Clothworkers' School is the best known. More recently as the towns have expanded to accommodate the increased population smaller private schools have appeared in ever larger numbers on the Manx scene. Some years ago in the first half of this century a Report on the educational system here, produced by the Reverend Henry Moseley H.M.I., commented that there existed 'a state of things in some respects remarkable' in that the principle of State education appeared to have received legal recognition long before it was accepted elsewhere. That the situation as he saw it in the 1840s was less than satisfactory he attributed to 'some administrative neglect.' To be fair other reasons, such as poor teachers and poor teaching, directly produced by poor pay for teachers, were more responsible.

Since then our population has increased rapidly, new skills and techniques are ever more in demand and quite clearly a positive and thorough overhaul of our existing system has been needed to provide an adequate response to such demands. Fortunately, the Government possessed the perception to undertake such an overhaul. Indeed, as early as 1851 an attempt had been made to provide support to the existing parochial schools by establishing machinery for raising a parish rate. A recent estimate has shown that over 6,500 scholars, from under four years to over twelve, are receiving instruction in 59 parochial, grammar, 'dissenting' and 'village' schools in the seventeen parishes and four towns.

It will be recalled that some three years ago Lieutenant-Governor Loch announced to Tynwald his intention to review the educational system. This announcement immediately aroused considerable opposition from a variety of groups throughout the Island. Some argued vehemently that the notion of compulsion in education was quite unacceptable, or that it would force parents to take children from work and send them to school. The viewpoint of farmers was expressed by Mr Cadman of Howstrake, Onchan, and President of the Agricultural Society. He foresaw the calamitous results of children being taken from their labours in the fields. Others argued that if education were to be removed from the control of the Church and given to the State, the only consequence would be the production of generations of Godless sinners. Attempts were made to head off this particular criticism by making the Vicars and their Wardens ex-officio members of the School Commissioners and by making Religious Instruction compulsory. The immediate and irate result of this was a petition of several thousand signatures from the Noncomformists who objected to the extension of the authority of the Established Church! Indeed, those responsible for the initial construction of the Bill must have wondered what sort of hornets' nest they had managed to stir up.

However, all opposition notwithstanding those who advocated the support of the State for its educational system, for schools over which no church had final authority, persevered with their policies. And after three long years they were rewarded. On 2nd February, 1872, the House of Keys passed the Act establishing the principle of Compulsory Education here. For the first time the Manx State undertook directly to

GRENABY SCHOOL-HOUSE.

'Grenaby has a considerable population spread over Mount Barrule. There must be at least fifty families in the district, some of them as far as six miles from their parish church of Malew. They need more zeal than is usual amongst our peasantry to induce people to walk six miles over rugged, dirty roads to church on the day of rest.

'There is a good school at Grenaby, and a good master, who usually attends the parish church himself and brings a portion of his flock with him. But there are many who never go to church and would have no church instruction but for the visits of the worthy vicar to the sick and aged in their own homes.'

From 'Manxland: A Tale' by B. Stowell, 1863.

provide funds, some £2,300 per annum. There are to be 21 School Districts, with School Commissioners elected by ratepayers, charged with providing educational facilities in their areas. From the age of 7 up to 13 children will be compelled to attend school with fees varying from 2 to 5 pence a week, although the poor will be excused fees altogether.

That this is a major step in the creation of a modern community cannot be denied. Equally it must be said that bitter, bitter battles lie ahead. It can be expected that the supporters of the Church Schools, Established, Noncomformist and Roman Catholic alike, will maintain their fierce opposition to what is predicted will soon become known as 'Board' Schools. And the term Board School will undoubtedly be used as one of scorn and perhaps contempt. Indeed there have already been indications that personal, and it must be said, vulgar abuse might come to characterise the exchanges from both sides. Not that those in favour will be over-awed or less than equally hard-hitting. Already voices are being heard demanding that the lower age should be 5 years rather than 7 and that the principle of Free Education should be accepted and implemented without delay.

In view of the turmoil one cannot help thinking of the Manx boys and girls who are going to be subjected willy-nilly to these new and more rigorous scholastic regimes. What was it Shakespeare said? *"The whining schoolboy, with his satchel, and shining morning face, creeping like snail unwillingly to school."* There could well be a few unwilling snails to be found around the Island in future.

FIRST DOUGLAS BOARD SCHOOL COMMITTEES

At a meeting of Ratepayers at the Douglas Court House in July, 1872, a School Committee of nine persons was elected for three years, the Nonconformists, who are strong in the town, being well represented. They chose to meet in a room in St. James' Hall in Athol Street and a Clerk was appointed who also acted as enforcing officer. As the Committee had no money a bank loan was arranged in order to pay the Clerk his first salary of £70. To overcome this situation a rate of two pence in the pound was levied on all real estate. The Clerk is acting as Rate Collector as well, in return for which his annual salary has been increased to £85 though he has had to give security of £100 for the faithful execution of his new duties.

The first responsibility of the Committee was to find suitable accommodation for the 239 children of compulsory age who have been refused admission to the existing denominational or private schools. A long search resulted in a room being rented in Wellington Buildings, a lane which disappeared during the construction of Victoria Street. It can hardly be described as 'suitable' as it is situated in a coal yard in a room over an open shed in which guano manure is stored. For a closet the children have to make do with an open trough with a seat over it, two children being detailed to clean the closet each day. Called the Douglas Wellington Board School, the teaching staff consists of a Schoolmaster at a salary of £80 per annum, his wife as sewing mistress at £15 p.a., and two monitors teaching under probation at a shilling a week. Free breakfasts are being given as an inducement to attend school and numbers have risen to 120 though many of the children, unaccustomed to regimentation, are decidedly unruly. Strong opposition to this new Board School has been led by the new incumbent of St. Barnabas' Church, the Reverend W. J. Hobson, who has been supported by the *Manx Sun* in whose columns the most vicious and insulting attacks have been made on those who have been most active in providing the first school for the deprived children of the town. The recent re-election has seen an almost complete new Committee appointed, mainly composed of candidates who see little point in providing a school for such children. Ironically, it is one of the new members who, realising the true position, has displayed considerable courage in suggesting that the children deserve much better accommodation and has proposed that a new school with proper classroom facilities should be built. A suitable site might be the land known as the Fair field. The gentleman in question is Mr. William Isdale, the Postmaster of the Isle of Man. His humble origins have not helped him in his fight. His father, a shoemaker, died when William was only five leaving a widow and three small children almost destitute. They were found accommodation in the Widows' Home and the congregation of St. Barnabas provided the mother with a mangle to enable her to take in washing. The children attended St. Barnabas School free of charge.

Mr. Isdale is now being accused of turning on the very people who had helped him and the attacks on him appearing in the Manx Sun have grown more vicious with every issue and many think they have passed the bounds of libel. But Mr. Isdale is standing firm and is gaining the support of more and more townsfolk. He is also gaining support from the *Times* and *Mona's Herald* who see him as the champion of the School Board's cause. Perhaps Douglas will one day have a school worthy of the name and equipped so that its pupils can obtain an education as good as, if not better, than can be obtained in any other educational establishment. Should this be the case it will be to the credit of Mr. Isdale, the almost lone protagonist acting on behalf of the poorer children of the town.

DEATH OF HEAD CONSTABLE GOLDIE

The Island's first Head Constable has died following a period of illness and after completing nearly ten years in charge of the Isle of Man Police Force. He was appointed to this position in September 1863 after the Head Constable elect failed to have his appointment ratified. He had been observed driving his pony and trap down Prospect Hill at a furious pace and was promptly booked by a Douglas 'Bobby' for Drunken Driving. Governor Loch then approached Captain George Patrick Goldie to accept the appointment as Head Constable with responsibility for combining the police forces of the towns and districts into one body. Captain Goldie, a member of the well-known family, lived at Ballagarey, Marown and was a Member of the House of Keys from 1853 to 1862. He was also Captain of the Parish of Marown. Following his appointment Captain Goldie was accused of being 'favoured' and unsuitable for the job. However, he worked tirelessly for the benefit of his men and moulded the Island's police into a more efficient and effective force despite limited resources.

The first Constables were appointed nearly a century ago, in 1777, following the time when civil duties were removed from the soldiers. The High Bailiffs of the four towns, Castletown, Douglas, Ramsey and Peel, were required to appoint and control Constables, under a Chief Constable, for each district. The men were paid a pittance, little more than that of a labourer, and were forced to carry on other work, such as tailoring or shoemaking, to support their families. Whilst on duty, extra pence were earned by carrying out errands for business people. As the present century progressed, and crime, drunkenness and disorderliness increased, especially in Douglas, there were many calls for improved protection for the public. Many of the Constables were old men and were something of a laughing stock for locals and our summer visitors. There were various attempts to form a 'private' police force for mutual protection, such a case being that of the Douglas Police Committee of which High Bailiff Quirk and Sir William Hillary were leading members. Such attempts came to nought as the wages offered (ten shillings a week) failed to attract the right calibre of men. In 1833, a small rise in pay, to £40 for Chief Constables and £30 per annum for Constables, was awarded. At that time there were eight Constables in Douglas and three or four in the other towns each with a Chief Constable. The small Court House built as part of the Red Pier was replaced in 1856 by the purchase of the Oddfellows Hall in Athol Street, built in 1840, which was extensively altered to create a new Court House and Police Station with a lock-up.

The Constables' duties were many and varied ranging from enforcing law and order, reporting bad sanitation, raising the alarm by a rattle where a fire was discovered, to meeting arrivals of the Steam Packet ships. The latter was carried on outside normal duty hours and extra money could be earned from the Packet Company. Intoxicating liquor was cheap and disorderly conduct in Douglas among the seamen was frequent. The number of visitors, well over 100,000 a year, also brought problems. Letters in the newspapers reflected the growing concern about the inadequacy of the Constables and the urgent need for improvements. Reports received from the High Bailiffs were one of the first matters attended to by Governor Loch. Approaches to the Secretary of State in London received favourable support and the Governor was able to instigate the first measures of reform. A Head Constable for the whole Island was appointed and Constables' pay was raised to £32. 10 shillings per annum.

In 1861 the Island population was 52,252 of which 12,381 lived in the confines of Douglas with its ten miles of streets and lanes. Captain Goldie strove to increase the police force and to attract more suitable and better paid men. For Douglas, with its attendant problems, he recommended that there should be one Inspector, as Chief Constable for the town, two Sergeants and 24 Constables. Ramsey is a flourishing town with a population of 2,839, though it is rarely visted by strangers. There is extensive shipbuilding going on with some hundreds of the lower orders residing there. The recommendation was that there should be one Sergeant as Chief Constable and five Constables. Peel, with 2,818 people, is reported as a quiet town except during the fishing season when it is crowded with Manx, English, Scottish and Irish. One Sergeant as Chief Constable and three Constables were regarded as sufficient. Castletown, it was reported, had an efficient Force of one Sergeant as Chief Constable and four Constables.

As regards the Rural Constables, Captain Goldie recommended that these be increased from 12 to 17, one for each parish being 'badly needed.' Supervision of these men, on £10 per annum, is difficult with the distances being so great. Captain Goldie wished to see a mounted officer, with the rank of Sergeant, appointed to help in this supervision. He should be provided with a horse and extra salary to feed and stable the animal. Captain Goldie was to see his recommendations implemented but there were other matters in which he was not so successful. There was no money forthcoming for improved salaries despite many Memorials signed by the men themselves. There is no provision for times of sickness or injury and the men still have to meet their medical bills. Then there is the question of lock-ups in the country districts. As yet the Constables are expected to confine offenders against the laws in their own houses. Captain Goldie drew up many schemes including plans for purchasing existing dwelling-houses to which could be added lock-ups, but nothing has happened. Even the generous grant of the Great Laxey Mining Company to help provide a lock-up in the district has not been accepted. There is much work for the new Head Constable to do when he takes up his appointment in March 1874. He has been named as Captain David Munro, a retired officer of the Madras Regiment, Indian Army.

Men of the Ramsey Division in 1865 wearing their uniforms of neat belted frock coats with gilt buttons which had been introduced in 1863. Since this photograph was taken Chief Constable William Kermode (left) has been appointed Gaoler (in 1871) of Castle Rushen. Next to him is William Boyde who took over as Chief Constable of Ramsey with the rank of Sergeant, with Constables John Kneen, Leece Clucas, Henry Radcliffe, Thomas Martin and Henry Killey. In 1874 William Boyde was offered, and accepted, the post of Chief Constable of Douglas with the rank of Inspector.

HERE IS THE NEWS: 1878
PENAL SERVITUDE FOR BANK CASHIER

A sentence of ten years penal servitude was passed at the Court of General Gaol Delivery in Castle Rushen last night on Andrew William Gray, the man who carried out the sensational robbery at the Bank of Mona in Douglas in April this year. The jury brought in a verdict of guilty at 11.00 p.m. after a retirement at the end of a trial that lasted nine days. We have this report:

'The dramatic story goes back to Sunday April 21st when the theft of nearly £9,000 in gold from the bank's strongroom was discovered. Gray, who was the bank cashier, had told the police and bank officials that it must have happened the previous night. He had been walking home along the Peel Road, on the outskirts of the town at about midnight when two or three masked men sprang out on him near the bottom of Lazy Hill. They shot at him with pistols, but missed, and then knocked him to the ground and chloroformed him. He said they left him lying unconscious in the road after taking the bank keys off his person and when he came to at four o'clock in the morning the robbery must by then have taken place. But the story aroused instant suspicion and within hours of his telling it, Gray was put under arrest and brought before High Bailiff Samuel Harris on that Sunday afternoon. During the trial at General Gaol the Attorney General said the story had been a complete fabrication designed to cover misappropriation of funds from the bank by Gray himself and his falsification of books of account. This had happened after the manager, Mr. John Greig, had told him he must either leave the bank or withdraw from certain business undertakings he was involved in. In his summing-up Deemster Drinkwater said Gray's story had been undermined by a witness who had seen him walking in Peel Road long after midnight. This meant his assailants could not have got into the bank strongrooms before the manager had dropped the night bolt on it, at fourteen minutes past twelve. In giving their verdict the jury recommended mercy, pointing out that Gray had been exposed to great temptation because of lack of supervision by his superiors at the bank. In passing sentence Deemster Drinkwater said he agreed with this – but pointed out that Gray had refused to say where the stolen money was hidden. After being sentenced Gray made a dramatic outburst from the dock, saying he could have given information which would cast a different light on affairs. He then declared that before God and Man he was innocent. He was then taken to the cells, but it was midnight before the large crowd that attended the trial had dispersed after the excitement of the day.'

FUND FOR LOST FISHERMEN'S FAMILIES

A fund has been raised for the dependents of the twelve Isle of Man fishermen who were lost at sea off Ireland earlier this year. They left behind seven widows and a number of fatherless children. Eight of the men were lost in the '*Sonnet*', of Peel, and four in the '*May Lily*', of Port St. Mary, while they were with the Manx fishing fleet at Kinsale in March. They were caught in a gale off Carnsore Point. There were three survivors among the crew of the '*May Lily*' which was setting out from Kinsale to return home to the Isle of Man when the gale struck. But the entire crew of the '*Sonnet*' was lost.

COMPULSORY VACCINATION

The House of Keys has decided that vaccination should be made compulsory in the Island. This follows continuing outbreaks of smallpox, the latest occuring only last year. A spokesman for the House said this had been on such a large scale that it had been the critical factor in taking a decision on compulsory vaccination. There is also to be further legislation to prevent adulteration of food and drink, and to appoint public analysts. The spokesman for the House said these new public health measures combined with a vaccination programme should virtually eradicate smallpox in the Island.

CALL FOR POOR RATE

The increasing problems of caring for the poor in the main towns of the Isle of Man have been spotlighted by the committee of the House of Industry in Douglas. In a report they say they are not getting enough money in to carry out their work properly and that trying to run poor relief on a voluntary basis is not working. The report says the time is fast approaching when there will have to be a poor rate levied. It adds that the problem is largely in the towns. In the country the poor and needy are adequately cared for by the vicars and churchwardens in the parishes.

VOTES FOR WOMEN

Finally, the Isle of Man is likely to lead the democratic world by giving the vote to women. There is agitation in many quarters for an Act of Tynwald which will extend the franchise to spinsters and widows who are property owners. This will put them on the same footing as male property owners. The move comes only twelve years after the decision was taken that the House of Keys should become a democratically elected body. Electoral reform organisations in the Island said the latter was something which had been long overdue when it happened. But in giving the vote to women the Isle of Man would be striding ahead of Britain and the rest of the world.

GOVERNOR LOCH POINTS THE WAY

The news that His Excellency The Lieutenant Governor has resigned has been greeted with profound regret in all quarters of the Island. His firm and enlightened guidance during the past nineteen years has brought many benefits to us all. He has worked tirelessly to lead the Island into modern times and has dealt with the many problems arising from the attitude of the British Government which only he, with his great diplomatic skills, could have solved. As plans are being made for his farewell, and that of his good lady, it is fitting to look back on the many achievements of Governor Loch which have put the Island on the road to its undoubted future prosperity.

With steam-ships plying the Irish Sea in ever increasing numbers it was realised that our ports should be improved to welcome their passengers to our shores. Many plans have been submitted to construct breakwaters and improve harbour facilities but progress has been slow. In 1861 Tynwald finally gave approval for the construction of breakwaters at Douglas, Peel and Ramsey, all to the design of Mr. Abernethy. They were to consist of a rubble foundation with a superstructure of creosoted timbers giving a 'bird cage' effect. Work began in Douglas in 1862 with an approach road along the south side of the harbour to connect with the breakwater at the foot of Douglas Head. The work at Peel and Ramsey was similarly commenced with little delay, an enthusiastic Governor Loch laying the foundation stone of the Peel breakwater in June, 1863, soon after his arrival. It was made an occasion of great public rejoicing at the headquarters of the Manx fisheries. However it soon became apparent that Mr. Abernethy's plan for the Douglas breakwater was not equal to the force of the sea, especially when backed by inshore winds. Various attempts to strenghten the structure were made, but in vain. Storms in May, 1864, washed parts of the rubble foundation away while several of the piles which supported the timber framework gave way. The following year the Island was hit by a ferocious storm which completely demolished the breakwater, scattering timbers along the coast. Governor Loch, undaunted by the disaster, and with little prospect of further funds from the British Government set about finding ways to replace the wrecked breakwater with a more substantial construction. He embarked upon arduous negotiations with the Home Department and the Treasury which, as we all know, were successfully concluded, resulting in the great constitutional reforms accepted by Tynwald in 1866. The matter of harbours was left until after the General Election of 1867 when Governor Loch was able to consider new plans, armed with between £20,000 and £25,000 available for harbour projects annually.

A Committee, including Governor Loch, began to consider various proposals for the development of modern harbour facilities at Douglas. After many meetings and consultations Tynwald finally agreed to expenditure which would first provide a substantial pier, to be known as the Battery Pier from the nearby cannon emplacement, on the site of the ill-fated Abernethy breakwater. This would be built of concrete blocks and thus provide the necessary protection, in most conditions, for the second development – that of a Low Water Landing Pier to project from the Pollock Rocks and parallel to the Red Pier. This New Pier would also be built of concrete blocks and would be connected with the Red Pier by a roadway. Work on the great harbour scheme, costing over £175,000, was completed in 1872 and Douglas could now boast a magnificent pier which would admit steamers at all states of the tide. It was formally opened on 1st July by Governor Loch and named the 'Victoria Pier.' A suggestion that it should be called the 'Loch Pier' was turned down by His Excellency. The number of summer visitors arriving was now approaching 100,000. Such numbers

Henry Brougham Loch, Lieutenant Governor, 1863 to 1882

brought into question the means of access from the new pier to the town. The only way to and from the new pier was through a succession of narrow streets in which it was impossible for two carriages to pass. These circumstances led to the revival of the old idea of reclaiming a part of the shore by a strongly-built sea wall. This had already been done by Mr. Samuel Harris, now the High Bailiff of Douglas. By public subscription he had levelled the shallow part of the shore in the centre of the bay and converted it into a promenade for the use of townsfolk and visitors. It became a favourite resort and Mr. Harris handed it over to the Town Commissioners in 1868.

In 1870, Mr. Ellison, an engineer from Liverpool, submitted a plan to connect the existing promenade with the Victoria Pier, with a road next to the sea to be called Loch Parade, after His Excellency. The Parade, 50 feet wide, would be connected by short streets with the main streets of the town. The following year a more revolutionary plan for gaining access to the town was presented by Mr. J. K. Greig, Manager of the Bank of Mona on Prospect Hill. His plan was to connect the Victoria Pier with a new street which would pass through the back streets behind the Quay, avoiding the Market Place, and thence across Duke Street and along King Street in a gentle curve to Prospect Hill, the entrance to the growing upper part of the town. The plans set the town alight with speculation, evoking much heated discussion which only delayed the Town Commissioners coming to any decision. They would need powers of compulsory purchase and claims for compensation would have to be met. It was then that Governor Loch, aware of the many difficulties, invited them to send a deputation to consult with him. He also called upon the services of Mr. Culshaw, an eminent surveyor in Liverpool. His report recommended proceeding with the New Street plan while condemning as 'almost impracticable' the idea of an embankment behind a sea wall on which a road would be built and building ground behind it. The arguments raged and Mr. Ellison was not without his supporters. In response to Mr. Culshaw's proposal he submitted a new plan by which both schemes were combined with the New Street now leading from the Parade, increased from 50 feet to 80 feet in width. He also calculated that the combined scheme would, in the end, cost no more than the New Street alone (estimated at £30,000), bearing in mind the high prices to be obtained when selling plots on the embankment together with sites on either side of the new street.

Mr. Ellison's plan slowly grew in favour and, after some five years of constant appraisal and considerable wrangling among the supporters of the two plans, the combined scheme was finally sanctioned by the Commissioners and the approval of Tynwald gained. The first block of the sea wall was laid on 24th June, 1874, and the last block on 21st October, 1875. The sea wall and embankment were constructed under the control of Mr. Powell, engineer to the Commissioners, while work on the New Street was the responsibility of the New Street Board made up of local businessmen. Work was completed by the end of 1877 and the new promenade was named 'Loch Parade', and the new street 'Victoria Street'. Such was the demand for building plots both in Victoria Street, mainly for shops, and along Loch Parade for hotels, that all plots available were sold by 1880.

Prior to these major developments, His Excellency was forthcoming with both advice and encouragement for the Town Commissioners as they grappled with the insanitary condition of the town, with sewage flowing in many places through the streets and polluting the shore. At Governor Loch's behest Mr. Stevenson, Borough Engineer of Halifax, was asked to plan for a complete drainage system for the town. This was in 1863 but it was not until 1866 that the Town Commissioners were in a position to commence work on the scheme. The first phase began opposite the Castle Mona from where a main intercepting sewer ran along the shore to Broadway, opposite the Iron Pier which had been recently built for the benefit of our visitors. At this point a second drain from Victoria Road and Derby Road was connected before the main drain continued along the Shore Road towards Castle Street where it received drains from Finch Road and the centre of the town. The drain then turned on to the shore along which it ran, receiving a further connection from Drumgold Street before crossing the sands to Pollock Pocks where it joined the main outlet, 42 inches in diameter. The south part of the town, between Drumgold Street and the harbour, had its own system of sewers which joined the main outlet of the Pollock Rocks. The outfall is carried along a natural slope through these rocks to below low water mark where it discharges the sewage into the sea. The Town Commissioners had gained further powers under the Town Amendment Act of 1864 despite strong opposition from certain country members of the Legislature who have persistently refused to relieve Douglas from the burdensome Highway Rate, which has slowed down completion of the new sewage system.

Imitating the example of Douglas, Ramsey, the 'capital' of the North and the most thriving and energetic town next to Douglas, began in 1864 to agitate for local self-government. Not without opponents, a Bill was passed in 1865 and in August the first election of Town Commissioner for Ramsey took place amidst great excitement. The Northern members of the Keys and Legislative Council have been remarkably uniform in their steady advocacy of Northern interests. It has followed that Ramsey has benefited from its share of the surplus revenue. However the town's development has been greatly impeded by its isolation from the rest of the Island. The collapse of the Ramsey Steamship Company in 1861 has not helped matters making the town more dependent on Douglas which can only be reached by way of difficult roads.

A view of Peel Harbour beyond which can be seen the Abernethy breakwater built of wood upon a rubble foundation. A similar 'bird cage' breakwater has been built on the north side of the entrance to Ramsey harbour.

Governor Loch has needed all his administrative skills to translate the acceptance, in principle, of Douglas as the Island's capital into a reality. The removal of the Legislature and its attendant Courts from Castletown has been subject to many delaying tactics, especially from the Southern members. These have mainly concerned the financing and design of new Legislative Buildings for which various architects have submitted their ideas. Members each had their own ideas and no two seem to agree with each other, resulting in much undignified haggling. The Southern members showed little interest while those of the west and north would have much preferred to see the £14,000, secured by Governor Loch, to be spent on harbour improvements at Peel and Ramsey. Biding his time, the Governor successfully played one faction off against the other. In a detailed statement concerning the Island's revenue he set forth a plan which would cover the construction of Legislative Buildings (£14,000); for harbour works at Ramsey (£28,000) and Castletown (£6,000). This received Tynwald's approval. Peel was considered at a later date and was granted £4,500 to effect repairs to the quays. The Governor flatly refused to consider a petition from the Peel fishermen to construct outer harbour works which were estimated to cost £25,000. This was progress but the general acceptance of a design for the Legislative Buildings was still no nearer, despite the Governor holding land in Bucks Road for some years. Years passed

Work on constructing the ill-fated Port Erin breakwater began in 1864 and brought the first steam locomotive to the Island, it being employed to move the concrete blocks and filling-in materials. The breakwater took twelve years to complete but a fearful westerly gale in 1881 caused severe damage which led eventually to its complete destruction.

and then, in November, 1879, the Bank of Mona on Prospect Hill was purchased for 'Government purposes.' The Bank of Mona was the local branch of the Bank of Glasgow which had failed. Thus was solved a problem that had confronted Governor Loch for many years.

It was also left to Governor Loch to implement the agreements of 1860 and 1864 between the British Crown (Woods and Forests) and Tynwald regarding the common lands on the higher hill slopes of the Island which, for centuries, have provided free grazing for animals, turf cutting and ling collecting for fuel and the right to quarry stone and slate. Since becoming Crown property following the purchase of the Duke of Atholl's manorial rights in 1826, the rights of access to these common lands has been divided between landowners and the Crown, with much of the areas now enclosed. This means that the humble crofter is now deprived of the amenities and many fear it will hasten the end of the crofting way of life which has persisted for centuries. It required Governor Loch, accompanied by the garrison soldiers and a number of police, to visit the mountain areas and quell the opposition of those objecting to the loss of what they regarded as their traditional rights. One newspaper records that, when visiting the south of the Island to confront the irate crofters, Governor Loch shared his lunch with those present after the position had been explained.

Returning to harbour works, Governor Loch inherited the scheme, funded by the Board of Trade, to provide a sheltered port at Port Erin. This was in response to repeated requests from fishermen from the south of the Island who were joined by their colleagues from Ireland and also from hundreds of merchants operating in the Irish Sea. They pointed out that the west coast of the Isle of Man afforded no shelter in stormy conditions when all shipping had to make for Port St. Mary. Work commenced in 1864 with Governor Loch suggesting that the breakwater, projecting from the south side of the near land-locked bay, should be increased from 600 feet to 800 feet. He envisaged steam-ships using the new port and work commenced amid great popular rejoicing. Governor Loch took part in the proceedings and hundreds of fishermen were present, afterwards partaking of a dinner provided by Mr. Milner (locksmith and safe maker) of Liverpool and Port Erin, through whose exertions the long-continued agitation for this work had mainly been brought to a successful conclusion. Two hundred workmen were employed in quarrying stone to form the rubble foundation, building the limited staging and forming the concrete blocks which would complete the breakwater. Huge quantities of gunpowder were required to blast the stone from the nearby cliffs. Such work had never been seen on the Island before and great crowds attended to watch the progress of the breakwater.

Work at Port Erin was nearing completion when, in 1868, the structure mostly lying in deep water, was struck by a series of storms which washed away a considerable part of the timber piles and staging, and did great damage to the rubble foundation. Governor Loch and Legislative members inspected the damage and received reports from the Harbour Commissioners. Expense had so far amounted to nearly £50,000, paid by the Imperial Government, but now a further £13,000 was required to repair the damage and extend the breakwater to 900 feet at the request of the fishermen. This was agreed by Tynwald. The fishermen had asked for an extension to 1,200 feet, costing a further £15,000 but this was turned down though Governor Loch agreed to an enquiry at which the fishermen said the further extension would shelter between 600 and 1,000 vessels. At this point the Peel fishermen made strong protests as they could see their ambitions for Peel being passed over. Instead, Tynwald sanctioned the building of a low water landing pier. It was now 1874 and, wearily, the work on the breakwater was eventually completed in 1876 to the agreed length which did little to satisfy anyone, least of all the fishermen. Matters were exacerbated by the British Government decreeing that the Insular Legislature should collect harbour dues from all vessels using Manx ports but those using Port Erin should be free of dues at all other Manx ports. This led to the men of Peel and Port St. Mary marching in protest at the Tynwald Meeting at St. John's signifying they would pay no dues until proper provision had been made in their home ports. Disappointed by the paucity of revenue from Port Erin, the Treasury, which had advanced a total of £58,200, made it known it was to be regarded as a loan. This caused the utmost alarm within the Manx Legislature and Governor Loch was confronted with a most serious situation. The matter was to drag on with the annual charge on the Port Erin Loan amounting to £2,600 annually. The Loan Commissioners also threatened to withhold any support for any further harbour developments.

In May, 1879, a deputation, including His Excellency the Governor, travelled to London and met with the Financial Secretary of the Treasury and the First Commissioner of Customs. In July Governor Loch was able to present the result of their deliberations to Tynwald as follows: 1. The Postmaster had been authorised to accept an offer from the Isle of Man Steam Packet Company to carry out a mail service between Liverpool and Douglas six days a week throughout the year. 2. The Board of Customs to calculate and remit duty on imported goods to the Island. 3. The

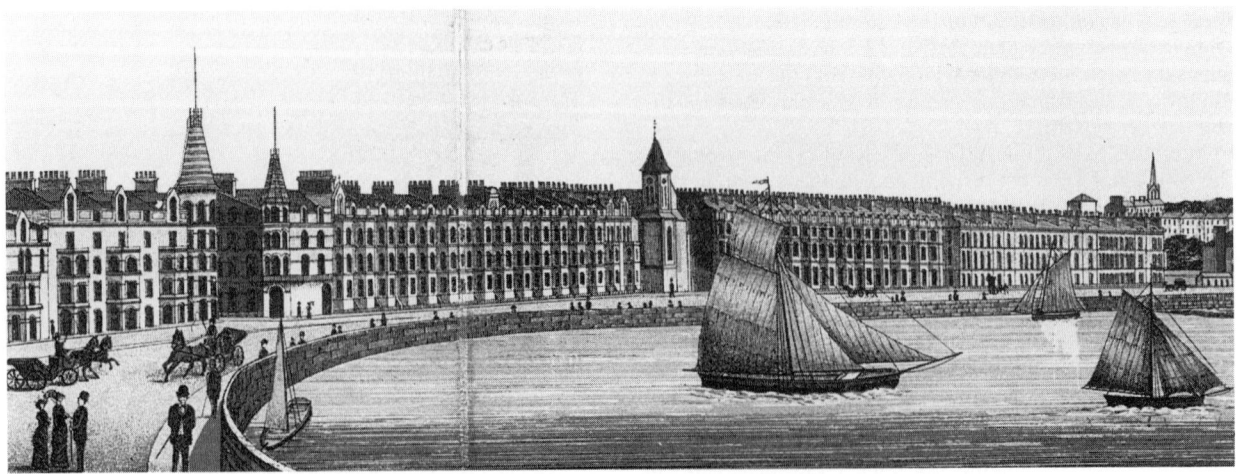

The magnificent panorama of the Promenade, named after Governor Loch, complete with the imposing rows of new hotels.

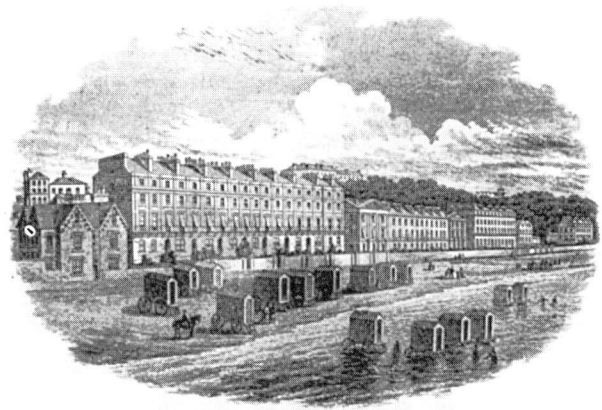

First boarding houses to appear on Douglas sea front were those of Clarence Terrace and The Esplanade built in the 1840s.

Another amenity for our visitors is the Iron Pier built in 1869. Whilst providing an invigorating walk it is also used as a convenient way of separating male and female swimmers.

Commissioners of Woods to give the same credit on rates in respect of Crown property on the Island. 4. The granting of power to the Insular Government to borrow on debentures. 5. Regarding the Port Erin Loan of £58,200 the Treasury is prepared to accept a sum of £20,000 in full discharge of all liabilities and that dues received at Port Erin should be set free and become part of Insular revenues. These measures were cordially accepted by Tynwald with much congratulation and thus was the threatened serious conflict between the two parties averted and a spirit of mutual compromise achieved which augurs well for the future. Our ports can now look forward to the long-awaited harbour improvements and there is even talk of extending the Queen Victoria Pier.

The process of Manx Law has been modernised and the Criminal Code revised under the guidance of His Excellency. Many ancient practices have been abolished and legal procedures brought into line with that of the United Kingdom through a series of measures such as the Limited Liability Act, the Real Property Act, the Wills Act and the Register of Deeds Act. His Excellency has been keen to extend the franchise and abolish the property qualification for aspiring Members of the House of Keys. The plight of the poor has been looked into and though a Poor Rate has not been as yet accepted, measures to improve the administration of existing funds have been introduced. He created the Industrial School for orphan children which continues to do its good work at Strathallan, Onchan. His Excellency has also appointed a Public Analyst and is pressing the Town Commissioners to close all wells still being used within the town. He would like to see the provision of housing for those still living in cramped and insanitary conditions. He has also suggested a new central hospital in Douglas and the establishment of dispensaries throughout the Island. He was quick to introduce compulsory vaccination following the outbreak of smallpox in 1877. As regards the Castles he is anxious to preserve their fabric and at Peel he has had the walls repaired and the Cathedral area cleared. Nor must it be forgotten that Governor Loch was instrumental in appointing an Archeological Commission and in 1879 the Isle of Man Natural History and Antiquarian Society was founded. This has awakened public interest in preserving the Island's heritage and it is hoped that one day it will lead to the establishment of a Manx National Museum.

Governor Loch was the first to take measures to provide elementary education for all and, despite many prejudices and a lack of enthusiasm in some quarters, this is likely to lead to one of the greatest social improvements of all. He has encouraged agriculture and great progress has been made under the stimulating influence of the Isle of Man Agricultural Society and the Isle of Man Farmers Club. New methods of cropping and the introduction of new machinery together with the improvement in livestock are paying dividends and satisfying the needs of the visiting trade. And the Island now has a network of railways and the coach services, which often suffered from a lack of passengers, have been replaced by well-filled trains. The busy scenes at Douglas Railway Station are in wonderful contrast to the starting of 'the coach' from the Market Place in the old days.

As, regrettably, the time approaches for the departure of His Excellency and Lady Loch, there have been many addresses praising Governor Loch for his many great services to the Island. We have taken a giant step forward and are indebted to him for laying the foundations for our future prosperity. He has given us a sense of independence so we can go forward, united, and face the future with confidence. His memorial is all around us in his many good works, not least in the impressive buildings now appearing in Victoria Street and the fine hotels under rapid construction along the Loch Parade. Farewell, Sir Henry Brougham Loch; we earnestly hope that your new Crown appointment with the Commissioners of Woods and Forests, with whom you have worked for the Island's benefit, will be a means of continuing your connection with a grateful Isle of Man.

THE FISHING INDUSTRY

Over the last decade or so one of the most important changes on the Manx scene has been the harbour improvements carried out in the ports around the Island. The important political and financial reforms inaugurated by Governor Loch in the 1860s provided for the first time funds for harbour works to be undertaken. Undoubtedly the most dramatic impact has been made by the Pier at Douglas with its immediate advantages for our ever increasing numbers of visitors. But what is equally important for the balance of our economy as a whole is the tremendous benefit the piers and breakwaters have been to that most traditional of our occupations, Fishing.

For centuries Manxmen and boys have gone to the Fishing and its importance in the life of the nation is revealed in the oath sworn by our Deemsters as they undertake to dispense justice as impartially 'as the herring backbone doth lie in the midst of the fish.' Manxmen have served in the Royal Navy with great distinction and throughout have shown a stalwart independence. In 1872 some 400 turned up at Tynwald to protest about the possibility of harbour dues while in 1880 a thousand went along. Indeed on that occasion the Governor had to protest that such a large group was intimidatory! For some years now Fishing has made a major contribution to our economy. Indeed it has been calculated as recently as 1883 that those directly concerned in the industry with those immediately dependent on it amount to a little short of a quarter of the population of 53,000 or so.

Our harbours at Peel, Port St. Mary and elsewhere are full of Manx, Scottish and Irish boats. The kippering houses work at full blast, their smoke stinging our eyes; the quaysides are crowded with the fisher girls gutting and salting the herring. Nets are draped over walls and hillsides to dry while the flash of needles can be seen everywhere as holes and tears are mended. Even the stones are worn down by fishermen sharpening their knives as they dig out the flesh from flitters and buckies as bait for their long lines.

Keen observers of the scene will have noted that of late years the old Manx fishing lugger with its six or seven man crew has largely been replaced by the 'Nickies.' These were originally boats from Cornwall that the Manxmen realised had more speed and weatherly ability with their different rig. They were first noticed at the Irish mackerel fishing. It is said the first such boat brought here was called 'Nicholas' and from this the others built locally were named. However some are talking of newer rigs, especially one from Scotland on boats that they call 'Nobbies.' It will be interesting to see if they challenge the Nicky for popularity.

The Manx boatyards, too, have profited from the general prosperity created over the last few years. There is no doubt that the reputation for speed and safety established by the Manx-built schooners many, many years ago has been well maintained as the skills have been handed down in many cases from father to son. All our ports have their yards, some a considerable distance from the sea. Boats are dragged down streets, man-handled over the brooghs, pulled over the shores, all to reach the tide. The net lofts and sail rooms of our small ports, with their dark corners and the pungent smell of Stockholm tar, are objects of curiosity and interest to our visitors. Our frantic, bustling and colourful harbours and quays must provide fascinating sights, sounds and smells for people from the cotton mills and coal mines of England's industrial North. Indeed, the two major contributors to our Island's wealth seem to move hand in hand.

All in all, there is a feeling of success and stability in the air. The value of the produce from the sea in 1883 was over £140,000; the value of boats and nets almost £250,000. In Peel alone in that year there were 240 herring boats, with undoubtedly well over another 100 in the other Manx ports, especially Port St. Mary. The fishing grounds range from those off Southern Ireland, with boats based at Kinsale, to those of the Shetlands.

Yet for all this air of permanence there remains the undoubted fact that throughout our history, fishing as a staple of the Manx economy has been hazardous in the extreme. Our records are full of accounts of its failure. Bishop Wilson in the last century prayed that 'the blessings of the sea' be restored to the people while in 1827 there was the first of what will surely be a series of investigations into the difficulties faced by the fishermen in finding the fish. Various reasons have been and will continue to be put forward. Shooting the nets before sunset has been suggested as a cause for the absence of the herring. Trawling over the banks is another; nets with too small a mesh yet another. Protection of the spawning beds has also been proposed while the seagulls are already protected as an indicator of the shoals.

Given these circumstances and the fact that the wanderings of the herring shoals remain something of a mystery, it would perhaps be prudent now to look to the day when the herring might be sadly reduced in number. In such a case the steps necessary to prevent over-fishing and to encourage the numbers to increase again should be devised now and be ready to be implemented without unnecessary delay. Fortunately no such possible fate seems to lie in wait for our other source of income, our visitors.

The Nickey XEMA, PL 37, leaving Peel for the night's fishing.

Some of the 240 Nickeys of Peel moored along the quayside. On the left is a trading smack used for exporting the herring from the curing yards.

Nickeys at rest in Port St. Mary Harbour. In the foreground is the Peel schooner KATE built in 1872, one of many used for the exporting of herring to ports of the Baltic Sea in the north and the Mediterranean Sea in the south. They return with timber and fruit.

OFF TO KINSALE FOR THE MACKEREL

Prior to 1864 there was no recognised fishing for mackerel in spring and early summer. But Robert Corrin, of Knockaloe Beg, formed a theory that the mackerel shoals, which appeared regularly at Peel grounds in July and August, came in from the Atlantic by the south-west of Ireland and up the Irish Sea. To prove his point he equipped one or two of his own boats with his own new make of mackerel nets and sent them south. This pioneering venture was immediately successful and within a few years some 800 vessels from the Isle of Man, Cornwall, Scotland, France and Ireland were involved. Robert Corrin was, indeed, a very astute man and is known to have made a small fortune by being far-seeing enough to buy up cotton just before the outbreak of the American Civil War.

And so, with the coming of the Nickies and their splendid sea-keeping ability, it is now possible for our fishermen to venture south to Kinsale to take part in the mackerel fishing which starts early in March. Boats are made ready with the boy, a lad of 13 or 14, cleaning out the cabin which is pretty dirty after the boat has been laid up on the beach during the winter. The galley funnel has to be swept, lockers washed out and the floor well scrubbed, as all meals are eaten off the floor, no table being provided. Then the men turn up and scrape the spars, set up the rigging and raise the foremast. The bulwarks are painted and the outside tarred. Then the sails go on board and the nets collected from the warehouses. Fifty nets or more make up a mackerel train with the heavy springback coiled down below deck. Water and provisions are then loaded: two sacks of potatoes, two stone of barley, a box of raisins, three dozen boxes of condensed milk, two sacks of sea biscuits, a sack of bread, about twenty pounds of beef and half a pig, one pound of tobacco for each man, some tea and a few cabbages, two stone of rice and some butter and cheese. Given a good north-easterly the two hundred miles to the mackerel shoals can be covered in about 28 hours. Ports along the south coast of Ireland are used as bases and a return made to the Island in time for the herring fishing to start later in the season.

RAILWAY REVIEW

At Foxdale on 16th August 1886, Captain Kitto of the Isle of Man Mining Company at Foxdale hosted the celebrations for the inauguration of the new railway between St. John's and Foxdale. A special train brought shareholders and their families to the village and the Foxdale Brass Band led the procession to Captain Kitto's residence of 'Brookfield' where lunch was served on the lawn. Unfortunately, heavy showers dampened the proceedings and the toast list had to be completed indoors. One speaker said they hoped to proceed shortly with a southern connection with the Isle of Man Railway to Port Erin. He called for support from the whole Island to meet the estimated cost of £25,000. Captain Kitto, in congratulating the Foxdale Railway Company, hoped to see all the lines, now totalling 46 miles, operated by one company. At present the Isle of Man Railway operates the highly successful lines from Douglas to Peel, completed in 1873, and from Douglas to Port Erin completed the following year. The Manx Northern Railway opened their line from St. John's to Ramsey in 1879 but the number of passengers, both locals and summer visitors, has so far been disappointing.

The rich lead mines in the Foxdale area are the foremost of their kind in the British Isles, producing some 4,000 tons of ore a year. At one time the ore had to be horse-carted to Peel for exporting, the carts returning with coal to fire the steam pumps of the mines. Following the opening of the Peel line, the Isle of Man Railway undertook this transfer of materials between St Johns and Peel and at first appeared interested in the mining company's suggestion for a line up to Foxdale. However the railway company withdrew having decided the expense was unjustified. Nevertheless, the Foxdale Railway Company was formed in 1882 and, despite strong opposition from Isle of Man Railway about the layout at St. Johns, Tynwald gave approval to the proposed line. At this point Manx Northern, in some behind-the-scenes negotiations, managed to gain a 50 year lease to operate the line, guaranteeing to pay a 5% dividend to the Foxdale Railway shareholders. Work had not even started and it seemed a bold stratagem on the part of MNR, thinking it would make a fortune in transporting the ore on their line to Ramsey, with an extension to the quayside. Sacks of ore would be loaded on to wagons at Foxdale station and transferred to ships at Ramsey, returning to Foxdale with Cumberland coal to supply the mines. Agreement reached, MNR ordered a fourth engine, this being 'Caledonia', the most powerful engine on the Island. No expense has been spared on the construction of the railway which links with MNR's terminus at St. Johns.

When the Isle of Man Railway Company declared it had

Map showing the 46 miles of Manx railways as operated by the Isle of Man Railway, the Manx Northern Railway and the Foxdale Railway.

abandoned any idea of constructing a line northwards from St. Johns to Ramsey it caused considerable bitterness in the northern town. Sponsors came forward to rectify matters and capital was forthcoming for the Manx Northern Railway. A Tynwald Committee looking into the matter agreed that Ramsey, now the second largest town, should have a railway being the market town for the northern agricultural district and now equipped with improved harbour facilities. Tynwald gave an undertaking to pay a minimum dividend of 4% for the first 25 years on half the Preference Share capital. With Mr. John Thomas Clucas, as Chairman of the new company, approval was given to proceed with the construction of the line along the agreed route. The most difficult part of the line was that along the uneven coast as far as Kirk Michael which required a series of cuttings, embankments and bridges. The embankment at *Gob-y-Deigan* (Devil's

A view of Port Erin Station with engine 'Mona' and train ready for the return to Douglas.

The memorable scene at Douglas Railway Station on 1st July 1873 as the first train to Peel prepares to depart. The engine 'Sutherland' is suitably bedecked and bears the message 'Douglas and Peel United'.

Elbow) is 70 feet high and the line climbs to 200 feet above sea level. The bridge at Glen Mooar is 75 feet above the river and the viaduct at Glen Wyllin is 55 feet high. Two Sharpe Stewart engines named '*Ramsey*' and '*Northern*' were purchased and later joined by a Beyer Peacock engine which has been named '*Thornhill*' after the residence of the Chairman. Mr. Clucas is also a director of Isle of Man Railway and no doubt has helped to create a spirit of mutual co-operation between the two railways. This year, 1886, has seen the two stations at St. Johns connected so now passengers can travel in MNR carriages between Douglas and Ramsey. This now means it will also be possible to travel from Ramsey to Port Erin and back in one day.

The call for railways goes back to 1860 in order to provide a cheap form of travel for visitors and allow other parts of the Island to join in the growing tourist industry. Many of the roads of the Island were still in a primitive state. Various attempts were made to form a company but lack of local finance saw them come to nought. In 1870 another attempt was made and this resulted in the Isle of Man Railway Company being registered; the capital was to be £200,000. Only £30,000 of this was raised and Governor Loch used his influence to interest other parties outside the Island. Various railway enthusiasts responded including Liverpool M.P. Mr. (now Sir) John Pender and the Duke of Sutherland. The latter agreed to accept the position of Chairman of the new company and things began to move rapidly.

Work began on the Peel line in June 1872 and, as many will remember, the Island was taken by storm as the contractors moved in machinery, transport and hundreds of navvies. Many local men left their crofts to earn money never before dreamt of. Normal life just about collapsed and those with carts and horses were hired much to the neglect of the farms. The marshy ground known as The Lake at the top of Douglas harbour was filled in and the rivers diverted to provide a spacious station and sidings. Work on laying the lines to Peel went on apace and work was completed a year later. Three engines, suitably named '*Sutherland*', '*Derby*' and '*Pender*' had already arrived. Thursday, 1st July, 1873 was granted as a holiday to many and they came from far and wide to join in the great national occasion of the opening of the railway. The Duke of Sutherland took his seat in the Directors' Saloon with the engine named after him hauling the train of twelve crowded carriages on the first journey to Peel. On the way they stopped at all the stations until Peel was reached where huge crowds joined in the celebrations. On the return journey an average speed 25 miles per hour was achieved in a demonstration of speed and safety never seen on the Island before.

The longer and more difficult line to Port Erin was completed by August 1874 and two more engines, '*Loch*' and '*Mona*' were obtained. A combination of prudent management (under founder Manager and Director Mr. G.H. Wood) and increased traffic has seen the railway go from strength to strength. The annual number of passengers has already passed the half million mark and is well on the way to a million. To locals it has been a boon enabling them to make journeys hitherto barely possible. Women carrying their baskets of produce to Douglas Market are now rarely seen. Farmers have also benefited by being able to move livestock to marts and in obtaining lime for the land. Two more engines, '*Peveril*' and '*Tynwald*' are now in service to cope with the increasing traffic. All the engines are of the Beyer Peacock type which have proved eminently suitable for the gradients of the 3' 0" gauge railway.

Whether the Foxdale line will see the end of railway developments is uncertain. A branch line for the MNR from Ballaugh northwards to Andreas through Jurby was turned down by Tynwald. The line extending from Foxdale to Castletown will largely depend on the success or otherwise of the Manx Northern. Nearer Douglas a company has been formed calling itself the Douglas, Laxey and Ramsey Railway Company with plans to branch a line from the I.O.M.R. Peel line from the Quarterbridge area northwards through the difficult and hilly terrain of Onchan and then to Laxey. This would certainly be a boost to Laxey now somewhat isolated and with those wishing to visit the Great Wheel still having mostly to make the journey on foot. There is also talk of a steam railway being constructed to the summit of Snaefell. So it could be that the railway mania that has swept across Britain has at last reached the Isle of Man!

Manx Northern Railway's powerful engine 'Caledonia' which is now busy at work hauling the lead ore from Foxdale to the quayside at Ramsey.

NEW HOSPITAL TO BE BUILT

The foundation stone of a new hospital in Douglas was laid by Mrs Rebecca Noble on July 26th, 1886, and it is expected to be completed in two years time. It is to be known as Noble's Isle of Man Hospital and Dispensary in recognition of the munificence of Mr. Henry Bloom Noble who has endowed the hospital to the extent of £20,000 to build and equip what will be one of the finest hospitals anywhere. The Douglas Hospital Committee has for some time been looking for a site within easy reach of the poorer part of the town but could not agree either on its position or the amount of money to be spent. The old hospital in Fort Street since 1850, with its 14 beds, has proved woefully inadequate, especially in times when smallpox is prevalent. Their search was ended when Mr. Noble's wife, Rebecca, inherited the estate of her father, Mr. Samuel Thomson, a retired Sea Captain, who lived in Clifton House, No.14 Mona Terrace. It is the plot of ground above Clifton House and adjoining the top of Crellin's Hill that Mrs. Noble donated for the purpose of building the hospital. It is to have two main wards of 18 beds, one for men and one for women. There will be consulting rooms, an operating theatre, kitchen, stores and accommodation for doctors and nurses.

Mr. Noble is now one of the wealthiest of our local businessmen and has come far since arriving from Whitehaven in 1835 as a young man of 19. His father had been a Customs Officer in the port and following his death young Henry and his mother, Mary, came to settle in Douglas. He is reported as saying he arrived with 'the single pair of breeches and the patches' but was determined to make his way in life and support his mother. She is the only child of Daniel James Bloom, a carpet weaver of London, and only recently has Henry added Bloom to his name following his success as a financial and property speculator.

On arriving in Douglas Mr. Noble was fortunate to be taken on by the highly respected firm of Alexander Spittall of Douglas and Whitehaven. From undertaking a variety of humble jobs in the wine trade he rose to being in charge of the firm by the time he was 24. This was at the behest of the young widowed Mrs. Jane Spittall and her children. Much to the chagrin of the Spittalls, Henry Noble left the following year and applied his experience to setting up his own enterprises, dealing in timber and wine and spirits. No doubt he foresaw the potential of Douglas as a holiday resort.

As a wine and spirits merchant Mr. Noble had offices at Fleetwood Corner, midway up the North Quay. In 1852 he purchased land from Mr. Samuel Harris in Upper Church Street and built new premises which have recently been leased to Messrs Bucknall. His timber and slate business was started in Georges Street but the timber yard is now in Hill Street where he had room for expansion. Very soon he owned a fleet of schooners which trade with English and Continental ports. They are also used to carry away the ore from the Great Laxey Mine in which he has a large holding. The ships return from North Wales loaded with slate for the building industry. He also lends money and is noted for his stringent conditions; failure to pay means a visit from the Coroner. It has been said Henry Bloom Noble is not the most popular of men, no doubt because of the envy aroused in his business rivals. He is now a major shareholder in the Douglas Gas Light Company and was a director of the Isle of Man Steam Packet Company until he parted company with his fellow directors upon their refusal to adopt his scheme for introducing the new propeller-driven steamers in place of the paddle boats.

Perhaps his greatest business acumen has been shown in gaining a controlling interest in the Douglas Water Works Company which owns the reservoirs at Burnt Mill Hill and the pipe system upon which the town depends for its water supply. The Town Commissioners will one day have to gain possession of the system and already Mr. Noble is asking £146,000, insisting on cash. This has met with furious indignation by the Commissioners and the whole Island. But Mr. Noble is unmoved and is content to bide his time. It is said he has little confidence in the Commissioners' bankers, the Dumbell's Banking Company managed by Mr. Alexander Bruce, who is also the Town's Treasurer. Mr. Noble's Waterworks Company is with the Isle of Man Banking Company Limited which was formed in 1865 and of which he is a founder director. Feelings at the moment are running high but it is predicted that Mr. Noble will get his price in the way he has demanded.

When Villa Marina, the property of Mr. Samuel Harris, came on the market following the untimely death of Governor Pigott at the end of 1862, Mr. Noble purchased this prestigious residence where he, his wife and elderly mother continue to live. The house and its spacious grounds were bought for £7,000 which some said was foolishly high. Today it is worth at least ten times as much! The land to the south west of Villa Marina was later purchased for £5,400 by Mr. Noble. He has since disposed of the land, making £10,000 on the sale of the plots on which it is planned to build a theatre and a grand hotel overlooking Harris Promenade.

Mr. Noble also owns the estates of Brundell and Ballalheanagh in Lonan, the latter being his favourite as a summer house from which he drives daily to Douglas in his carriage. His mining interests have resulted in charitable help for the miners and he is always ready to help those who are prepared to help themselves. It is in this spirit that he has helped the Douglas Hospital Committee and, it is said, he is happy to repay the town of his adoption for his good fortune.

HERE IS THE NEWS: 1887 ANOTHER RECORD FOR VISITORS

A huge increase in the Isle of Man's visiting industry is revealed with publication of the number of people who arrived during this summer. It was just under 348,000 which is the highest on record and double the total recorded last year. With increasing numbers of people in Britain now being given paid holidays from work it is expected that this comparatively new Manx industry will bring about a new era of great prosperity in the Island. We have this report:

'The growth in visitor numbers has been remarkable over the last ten years. In 1877 there were fewer than 90,000 people recorded and before that the yearly average was about 60,000. One of the reasons for the success is recognised to be the rapid development of the facilities that Douglas can now offer visitors. Two major steps forward were the completion of the Victoria Pier in 1872 to enable people to land from the steamers at any state of the tide, and the building of the Loch Promenade where new hotels and boarding houses have been springing up since the sea wall was completed twelve years ago. One of the most imposing of the new hotels is the 140-bedroom Villiers put up by English builder Mr Charles Udall, who won a substantial bet by getting it completed in time for Whitsun 1879. Next year Mr Udall plans to further develop the Villiers by building what he is to call the Octagonal Saloon at the front of the premises. The increasing number of visitors has also contributed to the growing success of the horse-car service which now runs the length of Douglas seafront from Summer Hill to the Peveril Hotel. There is a fleet of more than 20 cars in use, compared with only three when the service started eleven years ago, in 1876.

A great deal of credit for the development of all this prosperity is given to Governor Loch, who caused considerable dismay when he resigned his Isle of Man post in 1882 after 19 years. He is now Lord Loch and is Governor of Victoria in Australia. But his example in initiating new projects is being continued. It has just been announced that the Victoria Pier is to be extended over the next five years to improve steamer landing facilities even more.

It is forecast that the number of summer visitors is likely to go over the 400,000 mark by the turn of the century.'

REDUCTION IN CRIME FIGURES

A reduction in the Island's crime rate is revealed in a recent report. It says that since criminal statistics were first kept nearly twenty years ago serious crime had been found to be rare. And in the last two years the overall number of indictable and summary offences has shown a steady reduction. This is attributed to the increase in the size and efficiency of the Manx police force which now numbers nearly 50 constables. But offences of drunkenness remain high. There were 855 dealt with by the courts last year which was well above the national average for Great Britain.

NEW PRISON TO BE BUILT

Meanwhile, Tynwald has decided to buy the two-acre site at Victoria Road and Tod's Lane in Douglas in order to build a new prison there. This follows last year's report by the Official Inspector of Prisons, Sir Edward du Cane, who condemned the use of Castle Rushen for detaining prisoners. He said its medieval conditions made it unsuitable from the point of view of both humanity and prison discipline. The architect for the new prison will be Mr James Cowle, who was responsible for the conversion of the old Bank of Mona buiding at the top of Prospect Hill into the new offices of the Manx Government. The prison is to be ready for occupation by March, 1891.

POOR RELIEF RATE

Action has been taken by Governor Walpole for the establishment of a community system of poor relief. This follows what he describes as the failure of the system of relying on voluntary subscriptions, which had resulted in spending the lowest possible sums consistent with decency. In a Bill which will become law next year Tynwald will have power to enforce the provision of poor relief by way of rating. It also provides for setting up a poor asylum near Ballamona Hospital and the establishment of bodies to be known as Boards of Guardians of the Poor.

PORT ERIN BREAKWATER ABANDONED

After years of conflict between the Manx and British Governments efforts to build a breakwater to protect the bay and harbour at Port Erin are to be abandoned. This follows the serious storm damage done to the breakwater works three years ago, which were the worst since building operations started in 1864. There was also storm damage in 1868 and 1881 which resulted in disputes with Britain over who should meet the cost of repair. This has now cost the Manx Exchequer more than £45,000 and it has been decided that no further effort should be made to build a breakwater for Port Erin.

THE JUBILEE CLOCK

Finally, work has just been completed on the handsome tower clock at the end of Victoria Street, Douglas, which has been erected to mark the Queen's Golden Jubilee this year. It will be known as the Jubilee Clock and it is the gift of Mr George W. Dumbell, the well-known Douglas merchant and banker. There are drinking fountains at the base of the column for people, horses and dogs, and the faces of the clock are illuminated by gas. The water and gas companies are providing their services free of charge. The clock has been built by the Glasgow firm of W. McFarlane and Company and there is only one other like it – at the resort town of Hastings in Sussex.

LOOKING AFTER OUR VISITORS

We have seen an advance copy of yet another in the long line of guide books intended to assist visitors to our shores. This one is in the series of Shilling Guides issued by Ward, Lock and Bowden, Ltd. of London, New York and Melbourne. The series runs to 39 guide books to various regions of England, 14 of Scotland, 11 of Ireland and 4 on the Continent, in addition to that of the Isle of Man seen by us. Not only is it part of a large series but the publishers claim that they will keep their guide books revised in coming years.

There is general information about the Isle of Man and its history together with detailed descriptions of various areas and outings. Another section tells how to get to the Island, yet another where to stay and there is a large and scholarly appendix entitled 'The Natural History of the Isle of Man'.

Prospective visitors are advised of the various ports from which they may embark on steamers for the Island – Liverpool, Fleetwood, Barrow, Holyhead, Whitehaven, Silloth, Glasgow, Greenock, Dublin and Belfast. It advises that the charges to Douglas from London are: First Class 68/3; Second Class 51/6 and Third Class 34/6. Holders of third class tickets who wish to use the saloons of the steamers may purchase special supplementary tickets at a cost of 2/6 single and 5/- return. Crossing times are also given with the shortest being two hours and a half from Whitehaven to Ramsey, and the longest being ten hours from Glasgow to Douglas.

The Isle of Man is stated to be *par excellence* the land of boarding houses... 'They are of all sorts and conditions – all of them the best of their class; and their terms are so arranged that they will suit the requirements and the pocket of the thousands of visitors who resort thither in the summer – except those whose purses are quite empty.'

'Hotels – many of a very high order, and all of them good; they multiply year by year as the requirements of 'our visiting friends' (as the toast at every banquet runs) need them. Their charges are not unreasonable...'

(Abbreviations: R bedroom, b breakfast, l luncheon, d dinner, a attendance, t afternoon tea, fr from)

CASTLE MONA, Douglas. R for 3/-, b, l or t fr 2/6, d fr 5/-, a 1/6 Pension 73/6 per week.

ATHOL, Loch Promenade. R and a 4/-, b or t 2/6, l 2/-, d 3/-Pension 8/6 per day or 60/- per week.

ADELPHI, Church Street. R and a 3/-, b, l or t 2/-, d 2/6 Pension 7/6 per day.

GRAND, Victoria Street. R 3/-, b or t 2/6, l 2/-, d 3/6, a 1/-Pension 9/- per day.

SALISBURY, Victoria Street. R 2/-, b or t 2/6, l 2/-, d 3/-, a 1/-Pension 9/- per day.

TALBOT, Athol Street. R 2/-, b or t 1/9, l 2/-, d 2/6, a 1/-Pension 6/6 per day.

WATERFALL, Glen Maye. R and a 2/-, b l or t 1/6, d fr 2/- Pension 5/6 per day or 35/- per week.

COMMERCIAL, Laxey. R 2/6, b or l 2/-, d 2/6 to 3/6, t 1/- Pension 6/6 per day or 42/- per week.

MANX ARMS, Onchan. R 2/-, b or t 1/6, l 2/-, d 2/6 Pension 6/6 or 40/- per week.

CREG MALIN, Peel. R 2/6, b 2/6, l or t 2/-, d 3/6, a 1/- Pension 8/6 per day.

GEORGE, Castletown. R 2/- to 5/-, b l or t fr 2/-, d 2/6, a 1/6 Pension 7/6 per day or 50/- per week.

BELLE VUE, Port Erin. R and a 2/6, b, l or t 2/-, d 2/6 Pension 6/6 per day. Weekend 15/6.

PROMENADE, Port Erin. R and a 2/-, b or l 1/6, d 2/-, t 1/- (Boarding House) Pension 6/- per day.

ALBERT, Port St. Mary. R and a 2/-, b, l or t 1/6, d 2/- Pension 6/- per day or 42/- per week.

MITRE, Ramsey. R 2/- to 2/6, b or l 2/- to 2/6, d 3/- to 4/6, t 1/- to 2/6, a 1/- Pension 8/6 to 10/- per day or 60/- per week.

CAINE'S, Ramsey. R and a 1/6, b or l 1/3 to 1/6, t 1/- (temperance) Pension 5/- per day or 30/- per week.

In the description of the town of Douglas the Guide book explains that as new arrivals come off the steamers – 'Large hotels face them; houses, where good apartments may be secured, stretch along the Promenade; cars and wagonettes are waiting at the end of the pier, with drivers asking the visitors to employ them; and porters, who apparently live for no other object, leap on board and express their readiness to carry their luggage. Active lodging-house keepers, male and female, press through the crowd insinuating their cards into the hands of the wearied arrivals; and it will be hard indeed if in a very short time all these tired tourists are not comfortably housed, refreshed inwardly and outwardly, and discussing how they may best enjoy the beauties and wonders of this picturesque Island.'

Before leaving Douglas and turning to the more picturque parts of the Island our Guide book says – 'of course, the usual seaside entertainments are to be found on the Promenade – instrumental bands, solo vocalists, the blackened artistes who (though in a different sense from that in which Hood used the words) 'rattle their bones over the stones', very juvenile female violinists, and singers of comic ditties. As there is plenty of room in the roadway for these various artistes, the promenades are not incommoded, and can, if they prefer to do so, enjoy the ever changing beauties of the sea or criticise the costumes of the visitors, as their fancy may incline.'

PEVERIL HOTEL,

DOUGLAS, ISLE OF MAN.

(*Victoria Pier and adjoining the Loch Promenade.*)

A FIRST-CLASS HOTEL for families and Tourists. Replete with every modern convenience. Spacious Coffee Rooms, Smoking Room, Billiard Room, Ladies' Drawing Room, Reading Room, and Library.

ALL LOOKING ON TO THE SEA.

Miss MASON, Manageress.

STRATHALLAN PARK.

THE RESTAURANT, SULBY GLEN.

Places of entertainment described include: 'The PAVILION originally, known as the Marina Palace, erected in 1892 in eleven weeks and devoted to dancing and concerts, sacred concerts and so forth. The CENTRAL HOTEL, one of the many large 'houses of entertainment' in Douglas. OLYMPIA, a recent addition to the pleasure and recreational grounds of the town...it is chiefly devoted to athletic sports. The PALACE and OPERA HOUSE, the former, the largest building in Douglas, devoted entirely to amusement in which concerts are held every Sunday during the season. It cost nearly £100,000. The Opera House was opened in 1893. The DERBY CASTLE owned by the Derby Castle Hotel and Pleasure Grounds Company. The VICTORIA TOWER (Strathallan) which contains a camera obscura and galvanic machines, and other attractions. From the summit of the Tower, it goes without saying, a glorious prospect can be obtained. The BELLE VUE PLEASURE GROUND, on the Peel Road, is one of the most recent additions of the town. Erected in 1892 for the Exhibition they held, it has been acquired by a company and is now a very popular place of recreation. It has a good racing track, available for athletes and cyclists.'

Of that supposed health-giving pastime beloved by visitors – bathing – our Guide has this to say: 'One of the Bathing Places of the neighbourhood is the beach opposite the Castle Mona Hotel. Here are drawn up, in rows at a respectful distance apart, bathing machines for ladies and gentlemen. It is rather amusing to see them called 'male and female vans', but that is only a matter of detail. They are well constructed and comfortably fitted up; and their tariff – sixpence for one bather, ninepence for two – is reasonable.' But in Victoria Street 'are some Baths, alike unexceptional in their construction and management; they include two large swimming baths, as well as others of the usual description. However, at PORT SKILLION is the (free) popular bathing resort for gentlemen. A little creek flows into the sea, and some small caves are utilised as dressing rooms; and there are concrete piers from which a good header may be taken, and enclosed places where persons unable to swim may bathe in safety.'

Away from Douglas other places of resort and amusement are the MARINE DRIVE leading to PORT SODERICK, one of the most charming spots in the Island; and it contains an hotel and numerous refreshment rooms which 'do a roaring trade' on a hot summer's day. Its coast is very rocky, and on the south side of the bay are three caves, one known as the 'Smugglers' Cave'.

At DERBYHAVEN is found The Island Racecourse which instituted the 'Derby' now run annually at Epsom Downs, and constituting one of the chief attractions of the racing world. Latterly, the course has been laid out as a Golf Links under the eye of John Morris, of St. Andrew's. It is over three miles long and contains the statutory eighteen

PEEL, FROM THE PIER HEAD.

From a photograph] [by Keig, of Douglas.
PORT ERIN, FROM THE SOUTH CLIFF.

holes; it is well looked after, and it is usually in excellent condition. Tickets can be obtained from the Secretary, Malew Street, Castletown.'

Very near to the centre of the Island, at INJEBRECK, an excellent hotel which has been recently built and a pleasure-ground opened here. A short distance to the north but over the hills is THOLT-E-WILL and the Alt Waterfalls, and pleasure-grounds – one of the most popular resorts on the Island. They are situated at the foot of Snaefell, and contain within their own grounds of nearly 200 acres the most thickly wooded and picturesque portions of this far-famed glen. Visitors from Douglas will find the drive this way to Ramsey delightful. It utilises the mountain road – still called 'new' in comparison to the others – along the base of Snaefell and commands, at it nears the glen, the grandest mountain scenery to be seen anywhere in the Isle of Man.... Near the lower entrance gate...stands a large restaurant, with a dining room, in which an enticing bill of fare is provided during the season... Tennis, quoits, swings etc. combine to make a visit pleasant.'

Another similar place glowingly described is GLEN HELEN with the Rhenass Waterfall and boasting a Suspension Bridge, aviaries, a monkey house and seals basking in the river. At RAMSEY is the Park and Marine Lake with tennis, bowls and similar amusements, and on the lake 'is a fleet of substantial boats, any of which the visitor may hire for a small sum.'

The above are just a few of the many places now providing for the accommodation and amusement of our visitors which are described in this latest guide. The book is well illustrated but in this respect a word of warning is perhaps in order for whilst many of the engravings are prepared from photographs by Messrs Keig, Woodcock (Senior), Dean and Bradshaw it was noted that that on page 213 entitled 'Ramsey from the pier' was in reality of Port Erin. A similar warning about the descriptions and particularly the historical information must also be given and the above quotations from this most excellent publication are by your reviewer without thought or comment as to their specific accuracy. Indeed, the Editor of the Guide asks to be notified of any errors and any communications in this respect will be thankfully acknowledged, and the inaccuracies duly rectified.

RHENASS WATERFALL

From a photograph] THE PARK AND MARINE LAKE. [by Keig, Douglas.

MANX "RUMPY" CAT.

128

A view of the bustling Loch Promenade in the centre of which can be seen the splendid Loch Parade Primitive Methodist Chapel for use by locals and visitors alike.

It is usual to celebrate the centenary of any organisation with great acclaim and each decade leading up to it with lesser celebrations. In 1897 the Primitive Methodists celebrate 90 years since their persuasion was founded. They mark the beginnings of The Connection as the camp meeting, which was held on Sunday, May 31st, 1807, at Mow Cop in Cheshire, was attended by many thousands of people. For their part in this Mr Hugh Bourne and, later, Mr William Clowes were expelled from the Wesleyan Methodists and went on to organise their followers into what is now the Primitive Methodist Connection, often referred to as 'The Ranters'.

It will be recalled that John Wesley visited the Island twice, first in 1777 and then in 1781, and that as a result of this Wesleyan Methodism very early became an influential force in the Isle of Man. It was not until 1823 that the Primitives missioned the Island when the Bolton Circuit sent John Butcher on what was supposed to be a three month trial. It is said he arrived at Derbyhaven in a fishing boat and had encountered a storm during which he lost his hat. His response to this was perhaps typical in that he often said: 'The devil tried to wreck me and prevent me coming to the Isle of Man, but he only succeeded in getting my hat!' On arriving he held a service in a house at Derbyhaven – the first Primitive Methodist service held on the Island. Soon the word had spread to Castletown, Colby, the Howe and Ballasalla. Much of this work was carried out in the open air – reminding the older people of the early days of Wesleyanism, now long past – and the rest in hired rooms or the houses of converts and friends. Within two months this area became the Castletown Circuit with some 110 members.

The work spread through Foxdale and northwards with the first specially built chapel being at Clougher Farm, near Ballamodha. This chapel had a mud floor and a thatched roof. Another early building was Rhenshent (East Foxdale) where the land and stones had been given by the Mining Company, and a request for timber and slates was met with the promise that they would be forthcoming when a certain notorious poacher was converted! The conversion happened at a service led by Mr J. Graham who was now John Butcher's colleague. Mr Graham was heard to call out, as the poacher knelt at the penitants' rail, 'Praise the Lord! There's the timber and the slates for our new chapel!' The Cornish miners strengthened the Primitives at Foxdale, as did those from Cumberland at Laxey.

In March, 1823, Butcher was missioning in Douglas and preaching in the Market Place and on the foreshore. The following year the first of the town chapels, and still the largest, was built, the now Wellington Street Chapel. For twelve months in 1823/4 John Butcher was joined by Thomas Sharman who, during this brief period was said to have walked 2,200 miles and preached over 400 times. With such zeal success was inevitable. The years 1824–30 were troubled times in the Island with the Bishop attempting to enforce a tithe on potatoes and turnips, and the Duke of Atholl – then Governor–General – negotiating with the British Government for more money. By the time the Duke had sold out his last remaining rights and the troubles and riots subsided, membership of the Ranters had fallen from 640 to 300. Better times were to come, however, helped by a visit from Hugh Bourne himself in 1839. By 1842 membership had risen to 1,770 with over a hundred local preachers and six ministers. Today membership is nearer 1,150 with six ministers and some 110 local preachers. There are 32 chapels divided between the five circuits of Douglas, Ramsey, Castletown, Peel and Laxey. In comparison the Wesleyans have some 71 chapels served by 12 ministers and 170 local preachers.

With regard to the chapels Mr Samuel Harris, High Bailiff of Douglas and a staunch Anglican, was heard to say: 'When God builds a church, the devil builds a chapel!' Others in high office would disagree with him for Alderman Thomas Keig, now the first Mayor of Douglas, designed and supervised the building of the Loch Parade Chapel. This is a case where the past influences the present, for the scheme to build this chapel had run into difficulties and looked likely to fail when it was realised that this was the very part of Douglas foreshore used by John Butcher when first missioning Douglas all those years earlier. After that, the scheme went forward to success and now the splendid building serves not only the people of Douglas but also those of our visitors who are of the Primitive persuasion.

RAMSEY – 'QUEEN OF THE NORTH'

'Royal Ramsey' – 'Queen of the North' – these are just two of the flattering names being applied more and more to our major northern town. And indeed such flattery is well deserved. It has tremendous natural advantages. It has a salubrious climate, fine sea bathing, a magnificent bay with long shores of firm sands and all this with a marvellous background of mountain, glen and rolling Northern plain. The past two or three decades have seen these assets exploited with increasing skill and fervour. Indeed as recently as 1889 a famous Directory prophesied that the town would speedily become the finest resort not only here but in Great Britain as a whole!

Ramsey Town has always shone by the sea but the small cluster of fishermen's dwellings huddled precariously on what was really only a sandbank on the south side of the mouth of the Sulby River has most recently undergone the most astonishing development. Just as the rest of the Island blossomed under the impact of the 'Visitor' so has Ramsey. And just as elsewhere the improvements to the harbours and to transport, and communications in general, have been an essential factor in such development, so, too, in Ramsey.

The citizens of Ramsey had already made their statement of intent following the visit of the Prince Consort in 1847, and the completion of the Albert Tower in 1849, made that intent visible to all. The formation of the Ramsey Steam Packet Company with its famous 'Manx Fairy' in 1853, and the incorporation of the town in 1865 with its seven Commissioners confirmed their determination to take part in the general progress of the times. Yet the real stimulus remained the improvements in transport that quite simply made it both easy and cheap to get to the town.

The arrival of the Manx Northern Railway in 1879 at its newly built station near the stone bridge was a tremendous step forward while the line's extension down the south side of the harbour in 1882 not only increased the general sea traffic of the port but made it, remarkably enough, the outport for the lead mines of Foxdale The extension of the South Pier in 1876 was a further necessary improvement of the harbour but undoubtedly the most dramatic sign of progress was the construction of the Queen's Pier between 1882 and 1886. This magnificent iron pier, built to the design of Sir John Coode at a cost of some £70,000, now dominates the bay and provides a superb leisurely stroll straight out into the Irish Sea! More importantly, however, it gives a landing stage that is usable at all states of the tide, high or low.

These improvements enabled further dramatic changes in the landscape of the town to occur. In that decade of the 80's boarding houses and hotels such as the Queen's, seemed to

Land reclaimed in 1820 from the mud flats at the mouth of the Sulby River now forms the Market Square of Ramsey. It is overlooked by St. Paul's Church which was consecrated in 1822 by Bishop Murray to replace the little chapel at Ballure. In the centre of the Market Square public subscriptions provided a water fountain surmounted by a gas lamp to celebrate the incorporation of Ramsey as a town in 1865.

spring up like mushrooms. Near the old town, that was understandable; but 'north of the river bank' at first was not. From time immemorial that particular area had been little more than a tidal swamp, overgrown, and it must be admitted, more than a little smelly. In 1881, though, this vast stretch of waste land, some 200 acres in extent and known as the 'Mooragh', was bought for the town for £1,200. The highly ambitious scheme, or so it seemed at the time, was to turn the whole place into a pleasure ground that would be the envy of the Island. Boating lakes, gardens, tennis courts, refreshment rooms, children's playgrounds, all were part of this far-seeing and, some thought, impractical vision. Today there is no thought of impracticality. The groundwork has been done and no-one can be anything but impressed by its appearance now and by its unlimited potential for the future.

With the construction of the Mooragh Park went inevitably the building of what is already called the North Promenade. The sea wall and the Promenade made their appearance in the middle of the decade and were followed by the building of the substantial and indeed elegant hotels and boarding houses, which it is believed will rapidly extend along the whole of the sea front as at Douglas. For some time, it must be confessed, access to these new areas from the

A view from Queen's Pier showing much of the developments undertaken by the South Ramsey Building Estate of which Mr Frederick Saunderson was Engineer. On the right can be seen the South Pier and the Abernethy Breakwater between which the Sulby River is now channeled.

The entrance to the Iron Pier, now known as Queen's Pier, which stretches 722 yards into Ramsey Bay. It was opened on 22nd July, 1886 and welcomes passenger ships at the seaward end at all states of the tide.

old town centre posed a problem. To go by means of the stone bridge at the top of the harbour and then back along the north side was clearly something of a nuisance. A partial but, as it proved, inadequate solution had been found in the provision of a small ferry and wooden footbridge; a similar problem in Peel to reach the castle and breakwater has been solved by the same methods. But here in Ramsey the problem has been finally solved by the provision of another permanent bridge nearer the harbour mouth. Because of the shipping it had to be a swing bridge, as indeed it has been found necessary in Douglas. Many will recall that there has been considerable delay and dispute over the depth of the foundations that were necessary. However, at long last and to everyone's relief, the new bridge finally opened in 1892. In the years to come it will surely prove of great benefit to the town as further expansion North of the harbour inevitably goes on.

There is today, then, a confidence in the future in Ramsey that is most stimulating. It has always been well provided with schools, with churches and chapels. Its population increases steadily and the building of the fine new Town Hall in 1889 reflects this. The successful completion of the proposed extension of the Electric Railway from Laxey to Ramsey will complete the links that will, it is believed, enable the town to challenge Douglas as the premier resort of the Isle of Man.

Another symbol of Ramsey's determination to become a leading holiday resort is the 225 feet long swing bridge to link with the developments to the north of the river. Bedevilled by delays, it was not until June, 1892, that the contractors, Cleveland Bridge and Engineerimng Co., were able to open the bridge to traffic. It is hoped that the bridge will lead to the construction of further hotels on the Mooragh Promenade.

RELIEF FOR THE POOR

The recent declaration by His Excellency Lieutenant-Governor Walpole that the existing system of poor relief was totally ineffective, has come as welcome support, albeit very belated, to those who have long argued the same as they have witnessed abject poverty and distress in our towns. For many years now there has been ample evidence that widespread destitution, especially in the winter months, has existed on the Island. The rapid expansion of our main towns, especially Douglas, has created substantial areas of crowded and dilapidated dwellings, hopelessly insanitary, lived in by the unfortunates who seem for one reason or another unable to break out of their circumstances. In such conditions few can deny that the existing ways of helping the distressed poor are utterly inadequate and far too haphazard to cope with enormous problems that the rapid pace of modern development has created.

Traditionally the Church has always been responsible for the relief of the poor. The parishes looked after their own and in most cases did it well, until at least the general expansion in the eighteenth and nineteenth centuries. Then, it must be confessed, the wardens of the parish churches found that they were being forced to provide what can only be described as very meagre help as demand for help increased and their resources remained more or less the same. Begging, sheep stealing, petty thievery of one kind or another were rife as people responded to poverty and hopelessness in the only way they could find. It was only the widespread emigration in the early and middle years of this century that prevented such despair leading directly to even more serious outbreaks of disorders than those that occurred. As it became clear that the Church could no longer cope unaided, various voluntary efforts emerged to tackle the situation. The nineteenth century has become the age of Friendly Societies represented by such bodies as the Castletown Artificers and the Andreas Benevolent Society. Then there have been the Oddfellows whose original magnificent building in Athol Street marked their importance in Manx life. However, important though these groups were, they were supported by the more prudent of our citizens. They did not address the problem of the real poor; that became the pre-occupation of others.

As early as 1814 a small group of people had managed to establish premises in Sand (now Strand) Street where as many as 85 of the poor were fed daily. Still it was not until 1835 that a properly organised effort, stimulated by a grant of some £400 from the funds of St. Matthew's Church to purchase land, was able to go into operation. Many of today's Douglas citizens are familiar with the building known as the House of Industry which was opened in 1838 and built on the old 'Brick Field' in the newer part of the town. That this venture was a response to the upsetting and undesirable activities of the poor in the main streets of the town, a procession nick-named 'The Beggars' Parade,' is clear. Equally clear is the fact that within a few years it was housing some 80 inmates and indeed by mid-century was doing duty as a hospital as well, a necessary supplement, some argued, to that in Fort Street which was struggling manfully to cope with hopelessly inadequate accommodation and resources.

The House of Industry has continued to perform a most valuable function in relieving distress but for many years now it has relied heavily on voluntary subscriptions. And while the inmates may have enjoyed, for example, the roast beef and plum pudding sent by George Dumbell on the occasions of his daughters' weddings, that dependence has meant that its continued existence has always been in doubt. Yet it has already won a firm place in the hearts of the citizens of the town and although the new legislation ensures that the Government has taken over primary responsibility for the needy it is to be hoped that our House of Industry, with perhaps wider financial support, will continue to be a landmark for many years to come.

The new proposals to be implemented in the forthcoming Act are highly controversial in that one of them stipulates that Poor Relief is to be funded out of General Revenue. While this may not be as clear and specific as a Poor Rate, nevertheless those residents who felt that the Rate was objectionable are certain to find this method equally unpalatable. Some £12,000 is to be provided to build the House for the Poor and poor people from all over the Island will have the right of admittance. The only condition as far as can be discovered is that the district from which the poor come must bear the maintenance cost.

It is not suggested that this new system will solve all problems. Indeed, the rapid pace of development at present enjoyed by the Island continually produces new ones. However, a start has been made in establishing some form of structure that will ensure that the poor in our community will not in future be left to suffer, and perhaps die, in abject poverty and misery.

House of Industry, Douglas. 1838

THE HOUSE OF INDUSTRY 1838

The cholera epidemic of 1832, more than anything, brought to everyone's notice the plight of the poor and there were those who advocated that steps should be taken to alleviate the dreadful conditions that prevailed. In 1833 a Douglas Town meeting was called by the High Bailiff and a committee was set up to raise money to build a House of Industry. Its purpose was to serve as a poor house, medical dispensary, orphanage, lunatic asylum, a place for out-of-door relief and a mortuary. It was something of a pioneer project but has proved to be a constant source of succour for the poor and destitute. To help off-set the cost of their keep, and the salaries of the superintendent, matron and doctor, able-bodied males undertake tasks such as gardening and rearing pigs while females do mangling, sewing and teazing hair. Approaching its 50th Anniversary, the success of the House of Industry is a tribute to all who have supported this great charitable enterprise.

HERE IS THE NEWS: 1895
ISLAND HIT BY SNOW BLIZZARDS

The Isle of Man has been brought to a complete standstill by the worst blizzard in living memory. All roads are impassable, people are trapped in their homes, business life in the towns has been suspended and there are a number of reports of people freezing to death. There has also been at least one ship lost at sea. We have this report:

'The first week in February will go down in Manx history because of the blizzard which has raged for two days and two nights. It is estimated that at least two feet of snow has fallen and the fierce gales have left drifts up to 14 feet deep in country areas. All roads and railway lines are blocked and people who have managed to dig their way out of their homes have found commercial life virtually halted. In Douglas hardly any shops are open because of ten foot drifts – and gentlemen like Major Stephen and Major Spittall have been making their way about town in a carriage whose wheels have been replaced by steel runners. The worst disaster of the blizzard involved the sailing brig 'Nelson Rice' which was driven ashore on the rocks below Douglas Head. All her ship's company are feared drowned. A vessel also went aground in Ramsey Bay and when the lifeboat put to sea, her crew braving frozen spray and huge waves, they found two men alive after hanging in the rigging all night, sheltering in the belly of the topsail. They had icicles inches long on their faces. On land it is reported that Mr. George Thomas Morris, tenant of the Slieau Lewaigue Hotel, was frozen to death while on his way home and there are reports of two shepherds dying with their flocks. Work on constructing the Snaefell Mountain Electric Railway has been halted and there have also been some narrow escapes for children. One had to be dug out of a drift at Rosemount in Douglas – after a hand was seen sticking out of the snow.

At Maughold School most of the children have been marooned since the start of the blizzard, but they are believed to be safe and well in the schoolhouse. Now that the snow has ceased a severe cold has set in and there has been 18 degrees of frost recorded. The River Dhoo has been frozen over for half a mile out to Braddan with ice five inches thick. Where the river flows through his estate at Kirby, Deemster Drinkwater has invited ladies and gentlemen to be his guests at skating parties. But for the moment there is no sign of a thaw and it is forecast that the snow will still be lying in the Island well into March. Only then will it be possible to assess the trail of damage that has been caused, and the loss of life.'

THE MUNICIPAL BOROUGH OF DOUGLAS

Douglas is to be incorporated as a municipal borough from next year. The Town Commissioners are to be replaced by a Town Council consisting of 18 councillors, six aldermen, and a Mayor. The move reflects the growth of Douglas in the last few years and the need for a local authority of greater power. The town's population has risen to more than 20,000 people and the rateable value of property has gone up in the last seven years from £85,000 to £123,000. The incorporation of the new Borough of Douglas is to take effect from January 7th 1896.

FRANCHISE TO BE EXTENDED

Voting in the next House of Keys General Election will not be confined to property owners in the Island. Under a new Act of Tynwald any man of full age will be entitled to vote, whether he owns property or not. The Act also extends the women's franchise originally granted in the Island in 1881. In future it will include spinsters and widows who are the occupiers of real estate. Before this only those who were the actual owners of real estate could vote.

FISHING TO BE CONTROLLED

A Committee of Tynwald is to be set up to make bye-laws for the control of sea fishing round Manx coasts. It is proposed that they should include a prohibition on trawlers operating within three miles of shore. This is because of the damage done to fish stocks by the trawling method. The Committee will also be asked to consider the establishment of a hatchery for flat fish and lobsters at Port Erin. Conservation of fishing grounds is being proposed to try and prevent the major catch failures that have hit the Manx fishing industry in the past. The size of the fleet may be reducing but it still consists of about 350 vessels and it still provides employment for 2000 men and boys.

GOVERNOR'S SHORT STAY

Finally, after what is the shortest term of office on record for a Lieutenant-Governor, the Right Honourable Sir Joseph West Ridgeway is leaving the Island to become the Governor of Ceylon. His move comes after less than two years in the Isle of Man. His genial disposition and his conciliatory attitudes have already endeared himself to the Manx people and his statesman-like qualities have brought about many improvements. He will be particularly remembered for introducing the highly controversial Boarding House Act which allows lodging houses in the Island which take in visitors to serve them with intoxicating liquor. Governor Ridgeway's successor is to be Lord Henniker.

TRAMWAYS FOR ALL

The residents of Upper Douglas have at last got what they have long been demanding – public transport, in the form of a cable tramway. For many years they have felt their boarding houses and businesses have been neglected while resources have been concentrated on the promenades where the new hotels and boarding houses are well served by the Bay Tramway, now owned by Mr. Bruce's Isle of Man Tramways and Electric Power Company. While the older and higher parts of the town languished, property values fell and annual rents reduced from £40 to £25. Even then there have been court cases for non-payment. Horse buses have failed as many refused to see the horses struggle up Prospect Hill. Public meetings and petitions from ratepayers pressed the Town Commissioners for alternative transport. Many schemes were put forward involving some form of mechanical power with the cost of a cable tramway, similar to the successful one in San Francisco, put at £25,000. The matter was 'pigeon-holed' for a while until the ambitious Mr. Bruce put forward his ideas. His Dumbell's Banking Company has been behind the construction of the Douglas and Laxey Tramway, completed in 1894 during which year the Douglas Bay Tramway was taken over and the Isle of Man Tramways and Electric Power Company was formed. With the lease of the Bay Tramway from the Town Commissioners due to be renewed in 1897, Mr. Bruce and his associates offered to construct a tramway to Upper Douglas and to supply electricity free for lighting the promenades and Victoria Street, in return for a 21 year lease. The Commissioners were slow to respond but a determined Mr. Bruce made fresh approaches which secured him the lease in return for 15% of receipts from the Bay Tramway and agreeing to construct the Upper Douglas cable tramway. It was also agreed the tramway company would provide an interim bus service and move the horse tram sheds at the foot of Burnt Mill Hill to new buildings at the entrance to Derby Castle. Tynwald moved with alacrity to give its consent to the Upper Douglas Tramway Act finalised in January 1896.

Work on the 1½ mile tramway began immediately with a twin track of 3 feet gauge, each track incorporating a conduit for the underground cable. The lines run from the Peveril Hotel, past the Jubilee Clock thence up Victoria Street and Prospect Hill to Bucks Road and Woodbourne Road, past the top of Murray's Road to Avondale Corner, from where a

Prospect Hill in May, 1896, with tracklaying in progress for the cable tramway connecting Victoria Street with upper Douglas.

single track turns down to Ballaquayle Road finishing at the bottom of Broadway. At the same time it has been necessary to widen Prospect Hill to accommodate the tracks.

One of the finest red brick buildings in Douglas is the new tramway depot built in Laureston Avenue where the two existing houses have been purchased and rented to tramway staff. The building is of two parts with the upper one housing the trams and the lower one containing the boilers and engines to power the tramway. It is from here that the 20 ton cable starts its 3 mile underground journey guided by intricate sets of pulleys. The trams are equipped with grippers which the drivers have to control skilfully in conjunction with the wheel brakes ensuring that the cable is pulling and never the car.

On Saturday 15th August 1896, the first three cars began the service providing a ten minute frequency. Five more cars are expected shortly and they are to be numbered from 71 leaving 1 to 70 for the horse trams. The cable trams are remarkably smooth and quiet requiring frequent ringing of the warning bell. Bystanders can hear eerie sounds from the underground cable passing over the pulleys while children have found a new game in dropping pieces of paper and string down the conduit to see them whisked away.

The year has seen much to celebrate. The new Corporation

In August, 1896, the first cable cars came into operation, one being shown here in Woodbourne Road before the line turns right to the depot in Laureston Avenue.

of Douglas has taken over from the Town Commissioners with the well-known photographer Alderman Thomas Keig J.P., F.R.P.S. becoming the first Mayor of Douglas. At first it was thought the honour would go to Mr. Samuel Harris who has been in the forefront of town developments since becoming the first Chairman of Douglas Town Commissioners in 1860, and later High Bailiff. However, he has declined the offer. The year has also seen the completion of the promenade scheme which now stretches continuously from Victoria Pier to Strathallan. But the greatest cause for celebration has been the completion of the cable tramway. For this bands from the Palace, Derby Castle and Foxdale led a procession around the cable tramway route and then from Broadway to the Derby Castle end of the new Queen's Promenade. The procession then gathered outside the Palace grounds for the speeches headed by Lieutenant-Governor Henniker. Pains firework displays from the Derby Castle pier and the Tower of Refuge ended the day. The following evening the Tramway Company and the tramway contractors, Dick, Kerr and Co. hosted a sumptuous dinner at the new Douglas Bay Hotel which proudly boasts of being the first to be illuminated by electricity.

Mr. Alexander Bruce of the Dumbell Banking Company is very much the hero of the times. Mr Bruce arrived on the Island to work in the Bank of Mona, a subsidiary of the Bank of Glasgow. When the Scottish bank failed in 1878 Mr. Bruce moved to the Dumbell's Banking Company and became its became its general manager. The prestigious premises of the Bank of Mona built in 1855 on Prospect Hill was subsequently purchased by Tynwald and in 1880 was converted into Government Offices and a Council Chamber for the House of Keys. This sufficed until the new and adjoining Legislative Building was opened in 1894. Mr. Bruce's forceful and captivating personality has seen the Dumbell's Bank grow in stature. He is also the Treasurer of the town, a Justice of the Peace and vice-chairman of the Board of Advertising responsible for publicising the Isle of Man as a resort. He is also something of a tramway visionary and he has been the driving force behind the creation of the electric tramway which reached Laxey in 1894 and then the Snaefell Mountain Railway completed last year. These mean that any plans for steam railways in this area have now been abandoned. It is believed that the Isle of Man Tramways and Electric Power Company, of which Mr. Bruce is Chairman, plans to extend the Laxey line to the northern 'capital' of Ramsey before the end of the century.

In 1896 the Douglas Bay Horse Tramway was extended to its new terminus at Derby Castle where an ornate shelter brings passengers close to the electric railway station.

Mr. Bruce is held in the highest regard in political and financial circles. It was he who saw the possibilities of applying the new invention of electric motive power and he sought the best advice from Drs. Edward and John Hopkinson of the Salford firm of Mather and Platt who have supplied the generating plant and who are in the forefront of this new form of traction. Much of the equipment is experimental and the building of a railway of such proportions is causing considerable interest in many parts of the world.

At the same time, Mr. Frederick Saunderson, civil engineer, is deserving of much credit. He had gained experience in Ireland on railway construction and in 1865 came to the Isle of Man and became involved in real estate promotion, especially in the South Ramsey development now completed. He then turned his attention to the Howstrake Estate, Onchan and joined with Mr. Bruce in purchasing part of the estate. Ostensibly it was for housing on a grand scale. Tynwald approval was sought, and given, one of the conditions being that a road should be built from Derby Castle Gate to Onchan Harbour. It was after this that the idea of building an electric railway as far as Groudle was conceived while, Mr. Broadbent of the Groudle Estate was proceeding with building a hotel and converting the Glen into a visitor attraction. To construct the road it was first necessary to fill in Port-e-Vada creek between Derby Castle and Port Jack and it is on the reclaimed land that the electricity generating plant has been built, along with a depot for the trams. Electricity is also now being supplied to private

The electric railway of Isle of Man Tramways and Electric Power Co reached Laxey in 1894 since when the Rencell Road cutting has been bridged to give easier access to the terminus of the Snaefell Mountain Railway opened in 1895.

residences in the area and Onchan village is proud to be first with electric street lighting. Mr. Bruce has also offered to illuminate the promenades in return for the concession of supplying the town with electricity. The Corporation has still to decide between gas and electricity for its street lighting.

To the south of Douglas there have also been developments with the creation of the Marine Drive which invites visitors to take the air along this magnificent stretch of coastline. An imposing entrance was built in 1891 with accommodation for the gate keeper who takes tolls from vehicles and pedestrians. To attract more people there was a proposal to build a suspension bridge across the harbour to the top of Douglas Head. This came to nought and lack of finance slowed the completion of the Marine Drive, though some fine rustic bridges were built across the deep clefts in the cliff face allowing Keristal to be reached. Then came the formation of the Douglas Southern Electric Tramway with the Electric and General Construction Company of London providing most of the finance. In places the cliff face has had to be blasted to provide a ledge for the tramway while lattice-girder bridges take the track of single standard gauge across Pigeon Stream (where the power station is situated), and over the viaducts at Wallberry and Horse Leap. The tramway now reaches Keristal and it is planned to complete the tramway to the clifftops 180 feet above Port Soderick in time for next season. A promenade at Port Soderick is also to be built and a cliff lift to connect with the railway. A similar lift on Douglas Head would greatly ease the climb to the railway terminus although Sir John Goldie-Taubman of the Nunnery, who owns all this stretch of coast, has permitted the construction of a road through his land from North Quay up to Douglas Head. Sir John is now Chairman of the Douglas Southern Tramway Company which has bought out the interests of the Construction Company.

Meanwhile, along the sea front, the Bay Tramway continues to flourish with passenger figures fast approaching $1\frac{1}{2}$ million a year. It is now 20 years since the first horse trams ran from Burnt Mill Hill to the Iron Pier (demolished in 1894) at the bottom of Broadway. The tramway was the idea of the late Mr. Thomas Lightfoot. He was a 'retired' engineer from Sheffield who took up residence in Athol House beyond Castle Mona. His ideas were quick to gain Tynwald approval and the single line with loops was soon extended to Victoria Pier for the benefit of passenger arrivals. It is also proving a great boon to people from the Onchan district who can now reach their places of work in the town considerably quicker

The imposing entrance and toll gate of the Marine Drive which was opened for pedestrians and vehicles in 1891. The Marine Drive has since been taken over by the Douglas Southern Electric Tramway Co who have completed their single 4' $8\frac{1}{2}$" track as far as Keristal with plans to continue to Port Soderick in 1897.

and without having to brave the winter elements. The line has now been doubled in most parts and extended to Derby Castle, the terminus of the electric tramway. Mr Bruce's plan to electrify the Bay Tramway has met with strong opposition from the horse-bus operators but future developments will, no doubt, depend on the success of the Cable Tramway of Upper Douglas.

While the emphasis has been on electrical traction power in recent developments, a novel steam railway is now operating in Groudle Glen which has been developed into a major tourist attraction by the enterprising Mr. Broadbent. The railway – advertised as 'The Smallest Railway in the World' – runs for three quarters of a mile along the upper side of the Glen as far as the zoo where sea lions are accommodated in a rocky inlet in the cliffs which has been dammed and closed off with iron bars. A single engine (appropriately named 'Sea Lion') and three passenger coaches began plying the two foot gauge line at the beginning of the 1896 season. With the electric railway bringing up to 100,000 visitors a year to the Glen, the success of the little railway seems assured.

The construction of the Douglas Southern Tramway imposed many engineering problems not only in cutting into the cliff face but also having to cross three deep gullies. The largest of these, shown above, is at Wallberry where two lattice girder bridges span the 256 feet gully over 250 feet above the shore line.

HERE IS THE NEWS: 1897
DISASTER AT SNAEFELL MINE

Poisonous carbon monoxide fumes have now been identified as the cause of the deaths of 20 men in the Snaefell mine disaster. The source of the deadly gas which filled the mineshaft is not yet known, but it is believed to have been old timbers which had become ignited and started smouldering. We have this report:

'Monday, 10th May. One of the worst disasters in Manx history happened this morning after 34 men had reported for work at the mine at six o'clock in the morning. Sixty fathoms down the shaft they encountered poisonous fumes and immediately began struggling back to the surface. But only 10 of the miners escaped to safety. The mine manager, Captain Kewley, immediately led a rescue party down the shaft and began helping men out to safety. A series of further rescue forays were made below ground in spite of the air continuing to be foul. It was at the 60 fathom level that the first bodies were found. In the afternoon Her Majesty's Assistant Inspector of Mines, Mr. Williams, who was on a visit to the Island, arrived to take charge and he and Captain Kewley continued rescue efforts at the risk of their own lives. Five men were rescued alive but unfortunately one of them has since died. Bodies were sent back to the surface by way of the kibble which is normally used for transporting the ore, timber and other materials. Death appeared to have been instantaneous and peaceful, with the men's eyes closed as in sleep. Efforts to retrieve the bodies of the remaining nineteen men continued over the next two days, with Mr. Williams collapsing twice from the effects of the fumes, so that he has emerged as one of the heroes of the disaster. Eventually all the bodies were brought up save for one which was at too hazardous a depth. Of the dead men eight were married with 26 children between them. The oldest was 57 year old John Oliver of Agneash, whose 22 year old son died with him. The dead also included two sets of brothers, William and Walter Christian of Abbeylands, and William and Robert Kewin of Baldhoon.'

There is to be a full inquiry into the disaster which is the worst of any kind known in the Isle of Man since 1852 when 29 men were killed in an explosion as they tried to salvage the cargo of the wrecked Liverpool brig 'Lily' on Kitterland.

KEYS DIVIDED ON LIQUOR ISSUE

A new House of Keys is now in office following the General Election, and it faces a bitter controversy over the so-called Permit Bill by which boarding houses are allowed to serve intoxicating liquor to their guests. The House is divided on the issue with 12 successful candidates declared for the Bill and 12 against. Opposition is led by temperance organisations, but the permit system is being upheld strongly by the Douglas licensing bench. At the same time the Manx Licensed Victuallers Association is campaigning for the Sunday opening of public houses, which has been illegal since 1857. A petition has been raised in the Island by the LVA.

ELECTRICITY FOR STREET LIGHTING?

The new Douglas Town Council set up by the incorporation of the Borough last year, is facing the major decision of whether to use gas or electricity for street lighting in the future. The Douglas Gaslight Company has been providing the lighting for more than half a century but there are growing demands to adopt the more modern medium of electricity. The Council is to seek expert advice on the matter, but a Corporation spokesman said it could be well into the 20th century before the matter is finally resolved. Meanwhile following the untimely death of the first Mayor of Douglas, Alderman Thomas Keig, his successor has been named as Major Robert Stephen MHK, son of the late Deemster Stephen.

BRITISH ARMY UNIT LEAVES

The British Army has finally withdrawn from the Isle of Man after a standing presence dating back to the Napoleonic Wars. The military establishment was reduced after 1815 to a half-company of infantry from a Regiment of the Line, quartered in the barracks at Castletown. But this has been withdrawn by the War Office – now that the threat of foreign invasion no longer exists. Still maintained in the Island is the detachment of the Royal Naval Reserve stationed at Peel, whilst the new Drill Hall and Headquarters of the Isle of Man Rifle Volunteers was opened in Peel Road, Douglas, during June last year.

MR. CAINE'S LATEST NOVEL

The famous Manx novelist, Mr. Hall Caine, has just published his latest work, called the 'The Christian', and its contents are arousing criticism and controversy. Mr. Caine's writing is noted for its frankness – which is believed to be one of the reasons for his success. His last book, 'The Manxman' achieved great acclaim on both sides of the Atlantic three years ago with 40,000 copies sold. Mr. Caine, who is 44, was born in Douglas and went to London to work as a journalist 16 years ago. His first novel, 'The Shadow of a Crime' published in 1885, launched him on his career. He returned to the Isle of Man to live four years ago.

T. E. BROWN MOURNED

Finally, that other great Manx literary figure, the Reverend T. E. Brown, known as the Isle of Man's national poet, has died. A widower, he leaves two sons and three daughters.

Recently he wrote: 'Old Manx is dying, dying in the tholtans'. He was, of course, mourning the passing of a way of life which has belonged to the Island for centuries, and in which Manx Gaelic was universally spoken. No doubt he would have been pleased to learn that Mr William Radcliffe, Master of Andreas School, has seen fit to introduce Manx lessons to his pupils so that our native language will survive at least in one part of the Island.

Laxey Village and Glen

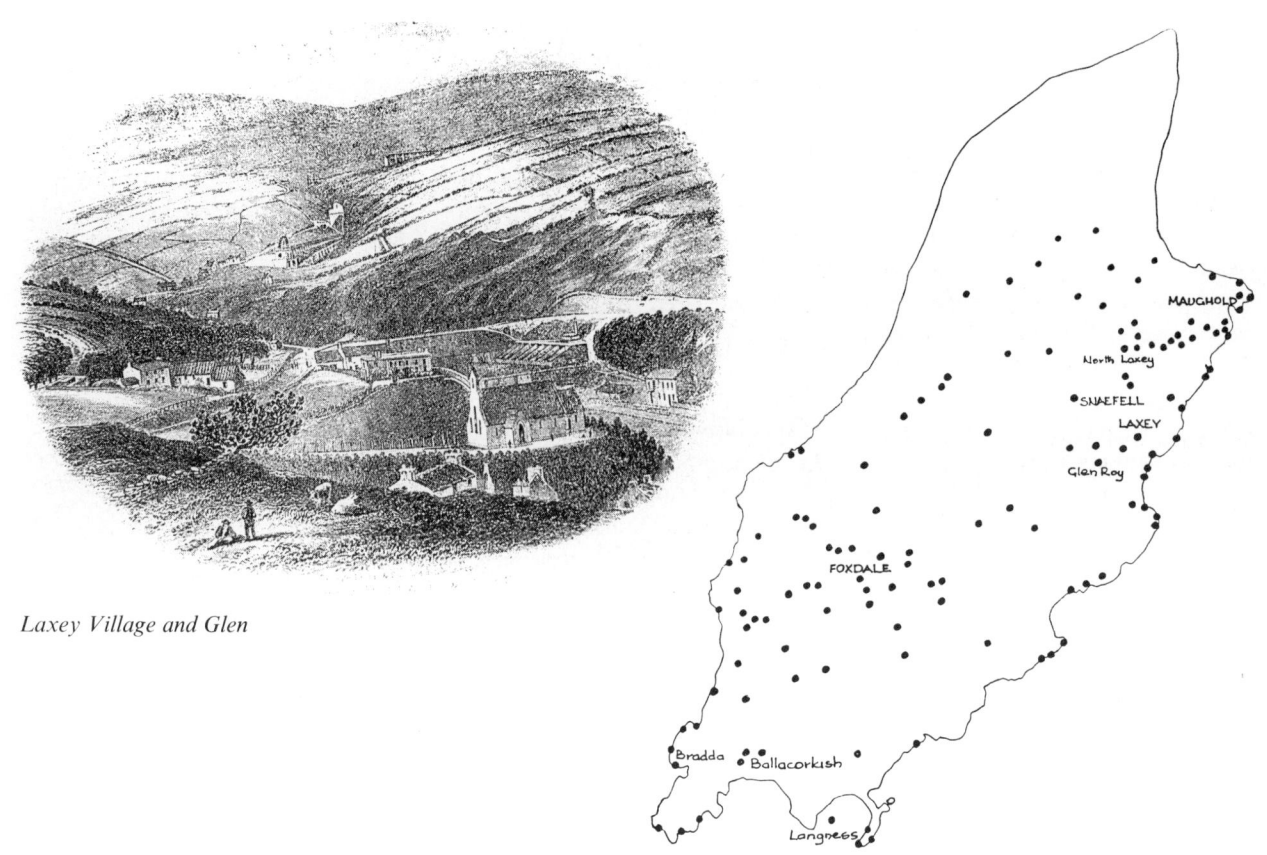

MAP SHOWING ALL THE KNOWN MINES AND MINE TRIALS IN THE ISLE OF MAN

Miners pose for the camera at Foxdale

Seated centre is Captain Kewley of the Great Snaefell Mine with the rescue team which was assembled from many parts of the Island to assist in retrieving the bodies of miners lost in the disaster.

THE MANX MINING INDUSTRY

It now seems certain that the report on the Snaefell mine disaster will show that the 20 men who died did so as the result of carbon monoxide poisoning. The gas was produced by an underground fire over the week-end break and, with the restricted flow of air available, the fire produced the deadly poisonous carbon monoxide rather than the more normal and less deadly carbon dioxide. The body of Robert Kelly which could not be reached for some time after the disaster has been recovered and lovingly buried, and every effort is being made to bring the mine back to full production.

Mining started at Snaefell about 1856 on ore exposed by the river. This work was carried forward by The Great Laxey Mining Company Ltd. who developed the mine and then issued shares making it a separate Company in 1871. The early work was not very profitable but more recently a large ore body has been discovered which, barring accidents, should keep the mine in production for some years to come.

Laxey, the parent mine, not only of Snaefell but also of Glen Roy, North Laxey and many smaller mines, is one of the 'Big Two' mines not only in the Isle of Man but in the British Isles as a whole. Today Laxey soldiers on despite the depressed state of mining generally in the British Isles. New mines in far distant countries with huge ore bodies mean large quantities of low priced ore are available to the smelting houses in spite of the increased costs of transport. These new mines, whilst on the one hand causing great difficulties for the long established home companies, do, however, have the advantage of needing skilled men. As a consequence, as activity at Laxey and all similar centres has reduced, there has been a movement of miners emigrating to work in the new mines.

Whilst some of these men have left vowing never to return, others have gone with the intention only of earning good money and then coming back to the land of their birth. This last group and their colleagues, who have been sending money home to their relatives here on the Island, are responsible for the rash of exotic names now being applied to new buildings in Laxey and the other mining areas of our Island.

Laxey is much visited by visitors to our shores who pay good money to climb the steps to the top of Lady Isabella (the Laxey Wheel) or who stand and stare at the activity on the Washing Floors or the Mine's Yard. A whole series of fun fair stalls, photographers booths and cafes line the route from the electric trams up to the Great Wheel to beguile those visitors and to persuade them to part with yet more of their money. These visitors, however, see nothing of the underground workings where the real miners spend their working day deep below the ground in the dark and damp complex of narrow tunnels. These tunnels stretch from the village of Laxey to well beyond the hamlet of Agneash and take the miners down to a depth almost equal to the height of Snaefell. Whilst the number of men employed (once over 600) has had to be reduced, Laxey continues to prosper albeit with a reduced yield. It is very noticeable, however, that the quantity (and value) of the zinc ore produced at Laxey now far outstrips that of lead.

The Island's other great mining complex – that of Foxdale – is still a major producer of lead with an annual production of 4,000 tons whereas Laxey is now producing nearer a tenth of this. These three mines (Snaefell, Laxey and Foxdale), together with some sporadic working at the Maughold iron mines, are all that remains of the giant Manx mining industry which, at its peak only some 20 years ago, was producing half of the mineral ore mined in the British Isles. This year has seen the cessation of work at North Laxey and within the last couple of years Ballacorkish and Langness have both closed. Bradda closed some 14 or 15 years ago and was perhaps the earliest identifiable mining site. It is mentioned in records as far back as 1656 and even then had old workings.

It is thought that some of the mines still have ore bodies in place that could be exploited in the future should the price of ore rise to its former levels. However, many mines by then could be so damaged as to make it impracticable to reopen them, and this would apply with more rigour to Bradda than to most. Bradda had engine houses clutching the front of the vast cliffs for support and to which access was only possible via tortuous and steep pathways. Furthermore, many of the working levels extended under the sea with the additional problems and risks that this involves.

So one of our oldest industries, which has in the last hundred years soared to prodigious production and profits, has now sunk back to a steady if restricted output but seems likely to be able to hold its own against the new competition, at least in the foreseeable future.

A view of Foxdale Mines as they were some 40 years ago.

The Washing Floors of the Great Laxey Mine as seen from the New Road passing through the village.

The Great Snaefell Mine showing, on the right, the shaft down which the miners perished in the recent disaster.

Perched on the cliff can be seen the office of the Bradda Mine. The mine has now closed after over two centuries of activity in the area.

OBITUARY: REV. T. E. BROWN, M.A., SCHOLAR AND POET

The Reverend Thomas Brown was born on 5th May, 1830 in New Bond Street, Douglas, and was the fifth of ten children born to the Reverend Robert Brown and his truly heroic wife, Dorothy Thompson Brown. Both parents were Manx born and when Thomas Edward was born, his father was the minister of St. Matthew's Church and master of Douglas Grammar School. In 1832 the Browns moved to Braddan where, after being curate, the Reverend Robert Brown became Vicar, a post he held until his death in 1846. Thomas had attended the local parish school but in the year of his father's death he entered King William's College as a day boy, travelling on foot each day. From here he entered Christ Church College, Oxford, in 1849. This was made possible by a 'Servitor' Scholarship – a kind of 'poor relation' educational concession which Brown endured until graduating with Double First Honours in Classics and Modern History. In 1854 he was elected a Fellow of Oriel College, Oxford, and the following year was ordained by Bishop Wilberforce of Oxford and appointed Vice-Principal of King William's College.

In 1857 T. E. Brown married his charming but very shy cousin Amelia Stowell in Kirk Maughold. He continued as Vice-Principal until 1861 when he secured the appointment of Headmaster of the Crypt School in Gloucester. He was neither happy nor successful there and in 1863 he was appointed Head of the Modern Side at Clifton College, a post he held as Vice-Principal for almost 30 years.

Although he had shown an inclination towards poetry in early life, it was not until 1861 that he wrote some lyrical poetry and it was 1872 when 'Betsy Lee,' the first of his 'FO'C'S'LE YARNS' was published – over 8 years after he arrived at Clifton. The narrator of most of his 'FO'C'S'LE YARNS' is Tom Baynes – a 'persona' invented by Brown, whom, when challenged, described as:

> *Old salt, old rip, old friend;*
> *Keltic, that is it. The Kelt emerging if you will,*
> *but the Kelt a good deal hardened and corrupted by the Saxon. That is Tom Baynes. That is myself in fact. I never stopped for a moment to think what Tom Baynes should be like; he simply is I, just such a crabbed text blurred with scholia 'in the margent.'*

Thus the Yarns were told by Tom Baynes – a person in authority – to the assembled crew in their quarters of a deep-sea sailing vessel. They were told in a type of Manx dialect which is not difficult for the listener or to be understood by a cosmopolitan audience such as one would expect to find in a ship's company. Thus, they have a world-wide appeal and

Rev. T.E. Brown, M.A.

are full of pure sweet Manx drama and seem to radiate Brown's love of God, of the Isle of Man, of the countryside and of his countrymen, old and young.

Between 1872 and 1892, twelve of these narrative poems, some quite long, were published by the Manx press and by MacMillan the publishers who were zealous, perhaps a little over-zealous, in ensuring that the tone of the Yarns was entirely suitable for the sensibilities of the reading public. However, the published editions are enjoying universal popularity and have placed Brown in a high place in the literary world. From 1892 until his recent death in 1897, the Reverend T. E. Brown lived quietly in Ramsey.

FROM CLIFTON

It was quite understandable that the sense of bereavement was most intense here at Clifton where T. E. Brown taught as Housemaster and Vice-Principal for nearly 30 years. As a most popular and respected Head of the Modern Side, he retired only five years ago, after a severe illness and although he took up residence in Ramsey, he maintained contact with many of his erstwhile colleagues and friends at the public school upon the life of which he had had such an influence almost since its opening in 1860, and upon its growth and development into what has become one of the great schools in England.

Only a fortnight ago he was on a return visit to Clifton to see the boys and to talk to them on 'The Ideal Clifton' – a subject very close to his heart. During his talk, however, he suffered a collapse and shortly afterwards died. This tragedy, on Sunday, 29th October, came as a very severe shock to Headmaster, teachers, pupils and parents alike, but many here felt a certain sweetness in their sorrow because in Redland Churchyard, where he was interred only a few days ago, lay waiting for him his devoted and beloved wife Amelia and Braddan, his adored son whom he lost at the early age of seven years.

Old Kirk Braddan, where Robert Brown was Vicar from 1836 to 1846.

His huge contribution to public school education in general, and to Clifton in particular, will surely never be forgotten. After almost six years of Vice-Principalship at King William's College and his time at Clifton, T. E. Brown gave almost 40 years of devoted service to the education and character building of hundreds of boys. A life-long friend wrote of him, 'It is impossible to convey to those who did not know him what his effect was on the school. His form appreciated his splendid teaching and his eye for genius of all kinds. His House was passionately loyal. The school overflowed with delight in his Sunday evening addresses. The writer of this note has heard the most brilliant lecturers from Faraday downwards but he could put none in the same rank with Brown.'

Thus, as a teacher he was a resounding success although, naturally, he resented the restrictions that the teacher's life made upon his poetic nature. As a minister of religion he was splendid and in great demand and his devotion to God, although sometimes considered by contemporary evangelicals to be a little unorthodox, was deep, intense and humbly filial. He advised one young man, '*Pray not as a midget; not as a perishing unit of poor, passing humanity, but as God's own child. Forget His omnipotence, we cannot understand it. Pray to Him as a loving Father.*' That was only a few months ago.

Here, back in the Isle of Man, we, his fellow countrymen, mourn his loss, not solely because of his life of literary excellence had a status unparalleled this century and possibly any other; not only because of the huge contribution which he made to the literature of the British Isles meriting the award of the highest honours for which he, in his touching modesty, never asked; and not only because he brought home to the Manx people the half-forgotten fact that we have a proud heritage to protect and respect, and when we can, enhance.

Probably the most poignant facet of our grief is that the Isle of Man has lost one who certainly could not have loved the Island more. This love was clearly expressed in his poems and letters but nowhere more graphically than in his 'F'O'C'S'LE YARNS.' By far the vast majority of his poems were written at Clifton but little was ever produced concerning his life at the College.

As has been said, not unnaturally and, indeed, like many other schoolmasters, he dismissed the monotony of the college routine as 'Grinding at the mill,' but he thanked God that his heart was ever in his beloved homeland, his Mannin Veg Villish Veen. This love never waned and indeed in his Poem of Dedication, written only ten years ago, he re-stated the Aims he expressed in 1881.

Dear Countrymen, whate'er is left to us of ancient heritage, Of manners, speech, of humours, polity, the limited horizon of our stage-Old love, hope, fear; all this I fain would fix upon the page, That so the coming age, lost in the empire's mass, yet haply longing for their fathers, here may see as in a glass, what they held dear. May say, 'Twas thus and thus they lived,' and as the time-flood onward rolls, secure an anchor for their Keltic souls.

*'To sing a song shall please my countrymen;
To unlock the treasures of the Island heart;
With loving feet to trace each hill and glen,
And find the ore that is not for the mart
Of commerce; this is all I ask.'*

That, indeed, was all he asked or wished. He never sought any public acclaim or fame, as well he might have done, but was content after retirement from Clifton to settle to a curate's life in Ramsey and to serve churches all over the Island, but particularly in the north, in charity and Christian humility. He steadfastly refused all advancement in rank within the church and said he sought no preferment anywhere and that literature was his calling; and that he wanted to remain free to the end without the responsibilities of high office. Nevertheless, in retirement, he still made himself available to all sections of local society and to help literary colleagues and friends such as Hall Caine, the well known scholar and author, with their researches.

Of the Isle of Man, very recently, he wrote, '*Be assured that you live in a happy Island. Don't do anything that will injure the character; sustain it in its purity, in its simplicity. Be proud of your Island. Be Manx. Be thoroughly Manx.*' And again, '*I want to make you love the past, especially you young people. It is to the young I look, convinced that I am, that when the old world vanishes, they will be smitten with regret and cast back longing lingering looks and wonder why their parents dropped the treasure they possessed and allowed it to be swallowed up in the whirl of change and so-called progress.*'

This places a trust upon us all, which in the years to come we should be careful not to refuse.

The poet on a recent visit to King William's College.

BLACK SATURDAY

Saturday, 3rd February, 1900, is already being dubbed 'Black Saturday' – one of the blackest days in the Island's history, the memory of which will live on for many years to come. The day the Dumbell Banking Company collapsed brought ruin to all parts of the Island. Families have been left without means, money frozen in accounts, marts and auctions have ceased, tradesmen and farmers bankrupted and clergy reduced to poverty. No fragment of Manx life has escaped the calamitous consequences of the crash of Dumbell's Bank. The charges of fraud brought against five of the bank officials are due to be heard shortly in the Court of General Gaol. But the man held to be mainly responsible, Alexander Bruce, will not be among them. He took to his bed in March and the High Bailiff withdrew the warrant on the grounds that his arrest would prove fatal. In fact, the man, once the hero of the Island's commercial life, died on 14th July in his 57th year. His death has produced almost every human emotion in most Manxmen and women – from grief to delight, bitterness to sorrow and satisfaction to sadness.

How did it happen? Dumbell's Bank has been a feature of Manx commercial life for almost half a century, apparently as solid and enduring as the Tower of Refuge. George William Dumbell himself was a businessman, lawyer and politician of towering stature, combining, or so it always seemed, financial commonsense with an imaginative appreciation of the opportunities to be seized on our Island. All the great Manx business ventures enjoyed the benefit of his expertise. In the 'fifties and 'sixties the Laxey Mining Company (later to become the Great Laxey Mining Company) became, under his Chairmanship and, needless to say, with his Bank holding the account, one of the most profitable mining enterprises in the British Isles. He was active, too, in the Isle of Man Steam Packet Company and an enthusiastic, if at times irascible, member of the House of Keys. On top of this he was undoubtedly the leader of the Island's social life. Indeed, the weddings of his daughters in the mid 'sixties were glamorous occasions, the like of which the Island had not seen before. The building of his new banking premises at the bottom of Prospect Hill was a recognition of the status he and his enterprises enjoyed even if a visiting English architect described it as the ugliest building he had ever seen!

Not that he always had his own way. In the highly

The late Alexander Bruce who was General Manager of the Dumbell Banking Co. Ltd since 1878. He died in July of this year, aged 56, so he will not have to face charges of fraud at the next sitting of the Court of General Gaol.

competitive world of banking, he found himself confronted with weighty rivals, of whom the Isle of Man Banking Company Limited, founded in 1865, has proved the most serious. In business, too, he was sometimes confronted by the other giant of the Manx commercial scene, Henry Bloom Noble – a gentleman of different personality but with no less expertise and determination.

In 1878 George Dumbell made an appointment to his Bank that was to have exceptional consequences. The appointment was that of Alexander Bruce. He was born in Banff, Scotland, in 1843 and had served his apprenticeship with the Bank of Glasgow being then transferred to the Island to become manager of the Ramsey branch of the Bank of Mona, a subsidiary of the Bank of Glasgow. Bruce was a man of powerful character and charisma and when the Glasgow bank collapsed in 1878 he was given his chance by Mr Dumbell who appointed him General Manager of his bank. Mr Dumbell was growing older and less concerned with the detailed running of the Bank. He died on December 13th, 1887. Alexander Bruce undoubtedly saw the almost unlimited potential of the visiting industry and was deter-

Mr Thomas Keig's photograph of the scene outside the Douglas branch of Dumbell's Bank on the morning of Saturday, 3rd February. The crowd of 500, full of anguish and bewilderment, could do little more than inspect the closure notice on the solidly locked door. Over 8,000 individuals and businesses now face ruin.

mined to profit from it. The Isle of Man was on the crest of a wave following the 1870s which saw the opening of the Victoria Pier and the first steam railways. It seemed speculators couldn't lose. The Bank made loans for all sorts of ventures. Businessmen were granted almost unlimited credit; hotel owners provided with funds secured against earnings to be made, it was hoped, later. A Chemical Company at Peel was allowed to run up an overdraft of some £8,000 at the Bank only to collapse later and be valued at about £500. In retrospect, the Bank was rapidly becoming unsound. And there were warnings. As early as 1890 the Douglas Water Company, then being bought by the Douglas Town Commissioners, refused to accept a cheque drawn on Dumbell's Bank and demanded, and got, cash instead. As Mr H. B. Noble was a principal of the Water Company this was taken as yet another 'locking of horns' between these two eminent men, rather than as a shrewd demonstration of business acumen by Mr Noble.

But if Bruce was alive to the dangers, he ignored them and in 1893 embarked on one of the most dramatic of his enterprises, the Douglas and Laxey Tramway Company, later to become the Isle of Man Tramways and Electric Power Company. The construction of the electric tram line along the spectacular scenery between Douglas and Laxey was an outstanding undertaking. The addition of the Snaefell line in 1896, built as a private undertaking led by Mr Bruce and then sold to the Tramways and Electric Power Company at a profit of some £4,000, has proved a tremendous tourist attraction. Finally the completion of the line as far as Ramsey in 1898 at a remarkable speed, with several hundred men working flat out, provided the east coast with one of the most scenic railways in the world. It was built as a result of heavy borrowings amounting to £150,000 arranged by Mr Bruce and underwritten by Parr's Bank. Unfortunately the line did not make money – in fact, it lost money at an alarming rate. Yet, even so, in 1899 many claim Bruce continued his speculative activities by backing what has become known as The Brewery Syndicate – a grandiose scheme to erect a structure combining breweries, hotels and other elements of the visiting industry which might well have dominated that aspect of the Island's economy.

When Alexander Bruce himself saw that the Bank was so far over-stretched as to be in imminent danger of collapse is uncertain. His illness towards the end of last year may have been the intense worry that the situation must, in all conscience, have been causing him. Certainly, in November the Chief Cashier resigned and acquainted the Chairman with his assessment of the dangerous situation in which the Bank found itself. At some point Bruce realised that the only solution lay in selling the Bank as quickly as possible. Two of the Directors, Messrs Nelson and Mylrea, went post haste to London to discuss the situation with Parr's Bank, and, Parr's, with certain conditions, agreed to buy.

Relief then was at hand, but it came too late. On that fateful Saturday morning, Dumbell's Bank in its fine building at the foot of Prospect Hill stood with its stout wooden door firmly closed. Notices on the door and side windows gave sparse information. Inside, Parr's employees began to sort out the mess. Outside, there was bewilderment and confusion, at first shown only by a few. But as news spread and rumour grew, so did the crowd of customers, who were worried, frightened and increasingly angry. Gradually it was realised with horror that the 8,000 depositors, including Douglas Corporation and several departments of the Manx Government, were in danger of losing their money and savings, if not all, then savagely reduced. Businesses large and small were ruined, farmers made destitute. Shareholders lost their investment and the commercial and business life of the Island stopped in its tracks.

Today, several months later, the effects of the disaster are still to be seen with businesses still closed and people broke. It is going to be a lean Christmas in many a household. Yet the world continues to go round and other ventures have already begun, and while undoubtedly things will never be the same again, while the free-wheeling daring that characterised the last decade has gone, we hope, for ever, surely prosperity will once more return to this Island. Alexander Bruce is dead; let his death mark the beginning of that new prosperity. And let those who are found guilty pay for the extraordinary ineptitude of their actions and for the ruin they have brought upon many a Manx family.

Mr Bruce was Chairman of the Isle of Man Electric Power and Tramways Company which, like the bank, has now collapsed. It was this company which constructed the Douglas Cable Tramway and one of its cars is seen here passing the Dumbell's banking office at the foot of Prospect Hill. It is said the cable cars are losing between £1,500 and £2,000 a year.

HERE IS THE NEWS: 1900
PRISON SENTENCES FOR DUMBELL OFFENDERS

Sentences of imprisonment have been passed after a fifteen day trial at General Gaol on the five defendants who faced fraud charges following the sensational collapse of Dumbell's Bank in Douglas in February. But the man held to be mainly responsible for the crash, Alexander Bruce, general manager of Dumbell's for 22 years, was not among them – he died five months ago. We have this report:

'19th November, 1900. Ramsey advocate Charles Nelson, 58 year old member of the bank's board of directors, was today given five years penal servitude. Assistant Manager John Shimmon, who is 55, was given a similar sentence. The bank secretary, 24 year old Joseph Drake Rogers was given 18 months hard labour. Accountants William Aldred, aged 77, and his son Harold, 33, were also given 18 months hard labour. The sentences obviously gave great satisfaction to the huge crowds gathered inside and outside the court. But during the trial it was made clear that Alexander Bruce, a Scot who became one of the Island's most prominent and respected men in public life, was the person most responsible for the bank's collapse. Fraud charges were brought against him but were dropped when he fell ill and it became clear that he had not much longer to live. The trial was told that the bank had nearly a quarter of a million pounds in dubious overdrafts and there were huge borrowings by Charles Nelson. It's all happened as the development of Douglas is going ahead rapidly and great fortunes are being made. But in the case of the men behind Dumbell's they were too reckless in their financial dealings. Since the collapse there have been many substantial bankruptcies, people have lost their life savings, and nearly every family in the Island is affected in some way. At the same time the national credit of the Isle of Man itself has been thrown into doubt. It now seems clear that there would have been no collapse if the founder of the bank, the late George William Dumbell, was still in charge. He was one of the Island's most successful entrepreneurs and he left a huge business empire when he died in 1887. His eldest son was Sir Alured Dumbell, who rose to the highest possible Manx office as Clerk of the Rolls and Deputy Governor. It will be recalled that he died suddenly a month after Black Saturday, another victim of the tragedy. Now the bank itself is in liquidation with hundreds of people hoping to save something of their money. But it is estimated that the bank's affairs could take 40 years to clear up.'

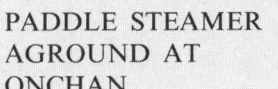

PADDLE STEAMER AGROUND AT ONCHAN

Nearly 700 passengers escaped to safety when the paddle steamer "*Lily*" went aground on rocks near Onchan Harbour in dense fog. With visibility reduced to ten yards the "*Lily*", owned by the Liverpool and Douglas Steamer Company, was well off her course for Douglas harbour. Passengers were taken off in boats. Others went down ropes lowered over the side and some were taken off by breeches buoy by the Coastguards. Eventually everyone was rescued without loss or injury. The vessel was refloated on the high tide the next day and berthed at Victoria Pier. Her master, Captain McShea, said the incident might have been avoided if there had been a fog signalling station on Douglas Head.

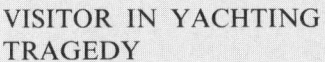

VISITOR IN YACHTING TRAGEDY

Meanwhile a local boatman and a visitor have died in a yachting accident in Port St. Mary Bay. They were 25 year old John Corlett and 23 year old George Stanley Roberts, of Egremont in Cheshire. They were on a pleasure trip when a south-easterly gale blew up. Their vessel, the "*Olga*", capsized 200 yards from the Alfred Pier as they were making for shore. Mr. Roberts had been staying with his father at the Cliff Hotel in Port St. Mary. The gale almost proved fatal for another sailing boat with a man and three members of his family on board. But they ran for the shelter of the Sound and were able to get ashore on the Calf.

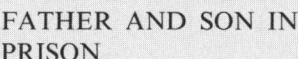

FATHER AND SON IN PRISON

Two Douglas butchers, father and son, have been sent to prison on manslaughter charges. The court heard that the charges had been reduced from murder. In May this year Robert Cowell died after a street fight outside the butcher's shop in Bucks Road run by Thomas Corlett and his son William following a personal argument. Thomas Corlett held Cowell while his son punched him, causing him to fall and strike his head on the kerb. He died in hospital shortly afterwards. Corlett senior was sentenced to three months hard labour and his son to six months.

RETURN OF WAR HERO

The Isle of Man has just had a visit from its hero of the war in South Africa, 15 year old Bugler John Francis Dunn, of the Royal Dublin Fusiliers. He was given a huge welcome by crowds at the Victoria Pier in Douglas and also at his birth place, Port St. Mary, after arriving by train. At the Battle of Colenso on December 15th last year his regiment attacked Boer positions. Bugler Dunn was sounding the charge and continued to do so after being wounded by shrapnel in the arm. Later he was received by the Queen who presented him with a medal – and a new bugle, his original having been lost in that battle. During his visit to the Island he was entertained to tea by the Lieutenant Governor, Lord Henniker.

HALL CAINE TO ENTER POLITICS

Keen students of the Manx political scene have been viewing with interest the strong possibility of the colourful and dynamic Hall Caine standing for the House of Keys at the next opportunity. Few would dispute that this gentleman is the most famous Manxman of our day. He was born with no silver spoon in his mouth and even his bitterest enemies must confess that what he has achieved, he has done on his own and with his inborn talents. Born in Cheshire in 1853, the son of a Manx blacksmith, he started to train as an architect, turned to journalism, and even had a short spell as a school teacher in Maughold. However, it was as a writer that he found the fame and, indeed, the fortune that he sought. Yet the fame brought with it a hostility from many of his fellow countrymen that must have wounded him very deeply indeed. In 1887 Hall Caine's first Manx novel, 'The Deemster' was published. It immediately established him as one of the foremost literary figures of our time and since that first novel he has become one of the most widely read of writers. His works have been translated into more than sixteen languages, including even Russian and Japanese. Some argue that he has been fortunate in that the recent educational advances in the United Kingdom and the Island have created a vast, new and comparatively untapped readership for the type of fiction that he produces. That may be so, but the runaway success of his novels demonstrates beyond doubt that these new readers enjoy what he writes. More serious, perhaps, are the allegations that he has betrayed his Manx heritage, that he has exploited the simplicity, even the ingenuousness of his fellow countrymen for his own personal profit and that he turned the Manx into figures of fun. 'Blasphemous' and 'seditious' are adjectives not often applied to popular novels; they are to those of Hall Caine.

However, it is Hall Caine's political views that today concern us most. Following the collapse of Dumbell's Bank it was argued by some that the existing system of government was unsatisfactory. The lack of representation of the hundreds of businessmen upon whom the Island's economy depends and what is seen as an uninformed executive guarantees that it is incapable of dealing with the problems, and indeed opportunities, of a new century. It is into this rather fraught political situation that Hall Caine has stepped with his vision of the future. His views are arousing considerable enthusiasm and many consider that he is just the type of man we need in the Keys. This is despite the fact that he has made it perfectly clear that his part in the Island's future is somewhat problematical because of the 'pressure of commitments' and the fact that he has to be off the Island for long periods.

Still, not many would find fault with his basic analysis of the condition of the Island, that it will stand or fall on its development of the Holiday Industry. Yet the sweeping reforms that he advocates seem too sweeping, indeed too revolutionary, to stand any chance of implementation. That banking, the steamship services, the railways. the electricity undertakings are all utterly essential to our national survival is obvious; that the right way to proceed is to nationalise them is, to put it mildly, open to debate! His perception of the need to reform the Manx Constitution is again supported by most people but it must be remembered, too, that since the Keys became an elected body in 1866 there has been a steady, if unspectacular increase in the democratic character of our institutions. Unspectacular is probably too moderate a word as not only has the Island witnessed the introduction of the Secret Ballot but as early as 1881 women as property owners were given the vote and in 1892 the franchise was extended to include those women who rented property also. There are few, if any, places in the world where women enjoy this as of right.

Whether Hall Caine can persuade a sizeable body of opinion of the correctness of his views is still doubtful. We shall have to wait and see, and while it may appeal to some to have an international figure in the House of Keys there are many others who, apart from their resentment over the portrayal of the Manx in his novels, believe that the business of Government is too serious to be left to someone who cannot guarantee his presence on the Island. Nevertheless, it is to be hoped that he will be persuaded to devote his perceptive and imaginative mind to our affairs; nothing but benefit to the Island would result.

Greeba Castle where Mr Hall Caine (inset) took up residence with his wife in 1897.

WELCOME, TWENTIETH CENTURY!

Now that we have entered a new century, it is meet and right that we should look back and count the many blessings that have transformed our lives during the past hundred years. To go back to 1801 is almost going back into ancient history and the Atholl Lords of Man. Douglas was a mere fishing village clustered around the river mouth, while Castletown was the metropolis and seat of the Insular Government. At that time the Manx language was generally spoken by most of the Island population of between 30,000 and 33,000. The old people loved to gather round the *chiollagh* in the lurid light of the old rush dip where they recounted old legends and traditions of their past history, the young gladly listening. They were warm-hearted, superstitious and industrious; their way of life simple, almost primitive, and free from all artificialities which, in their latter days, have almost changed their manners and customs. There was no visiting industry then and the industries of the Island were farming and fishing. Smuggling, it must be said, was still actively carried on by the rougher portion of the community, and it was a very profitable occupation.

Agriculture was in a very backward state, farming being carried out in a very primitive fashion. Nothing was known about our present day improved machinery for ploughing, winnowing, drilling, threshing, etc. The yearly rent of land at that time ranged from 10 to 40 shillings an acre and the right of pasture on the commons belonged to the public. Farm houses, with rare exceptions, were much behind town dwellings. The cottages were often built of earth. The cattle were rarely kept clean and fattening stock did not thrive well. Female labour was extensively used in the fields and the women, using sickles, were expert reapers. Threshing by the *flaills* was also performed by them. Fencing was often poor too and animals were lanketted to prevent them straying. The herring industry was much more important than today with upwards of 5,000 men being thus employed. Just about every full grown man was involved and this fact should serve to emphasise the importance of the change which has come over things.

Peat was generally used for fuel and the steel, flint and tinder box in general use. Now the common match is universally used and this has meant that no longer is it necessary to fetch a live coal or burning turf from a neighbour when the fire has gone out during the night. The dip light has been replaced in many homes by the incandescent gas burner. Those without gas have paraffin to give them light and fuel for cooking. The working classes fare differently from the beginning of the century when potatoes and herring, barley bread and oatcake were the staple diet of most. There was plenty of oatmeal porridge daily and, on Sunday, a bowl of Manx broth.

As regards clothing there has been little change. They wore good woollen cloth in the old days and country folk wore clothes almost exclusively made from pure Manx wool. Flax was grown and prepared for use. Perhaps the greatest change has been in footwear with the disappearance of the *carranes* made of hide and, being without a heel, were difficult to wear and slippery in wet weather.

Now, a century later, we have the benefits of the glorious inventions which have raised the well-being of people here as well as throughout the civilised world. Take, for example, the application of the power of steam which enables us to move more swiftly over land and sea than ever before. And what about the marvel beginning with Franklin drawing with his kite the electric sparks from the heavens and ending with Marconi sending the electric sparks across the trackless space bearing, as his servant, man's message. Now the stirring events which transpire all over the world are flashed to the Island in an incredibly short space of time, a far cry from waiting for the packet ship from Whitehaven! We are also acquainted with the electric light and electric traction. Perhaps in the future all our towns and homes will be illuminated at the touch of a switch rather than just the few that now have this almost magical facility.

Emigration has in no country in Europe played, proportionately, a greater part than here among the Manx people. The United States, Canada, Australia, New Zealand and South Africa contain a vast amount of Manx who have proved industrious, law-abiding, prosperous and constitutional citizens; and everywhere retain the fondest affection for their cradle Island. The second half of the century has seen the ancient constitution of our Tynwald Court change from its oligarchical character and, in respect of the House of Keys, become a free Constitution. The Island, let us hope, will retain honourably the prestige of unbroken connections with its historic past.

Control of our revenues has seen great improvements in our harbours and roads. Schools throughout the Island now provide education for the young. The poor are better cared for and the needs of the sick attended to. The towns are being developed following the appointment of Commissioners representing the people; local affairs in parish and village districts are now in charge of those who have been given increasing powers. Industrially, the Island has become the health resort and holiday field of the great industrial counties of Lancashire and Yorkshire. The whole Island benefits while Douglas now has the status and constitution of a municipality.

Unhappily, the closing year of the century has been disastrous for the Island, a year of unparalleled misfortune. The effects of the Dumbell Bank Smash are ubiquitous. All have suffered some deprivation;

some have suffered ruin. Yet there has been shown a high degree of heroic steadiness and, at this point, we can leave the dark year of 1900 behind us and learn the lessons of those who desired to make it rich in as short a time as possible. We now enter 1901, a new year and a new century. It is time for taking heart, grace, setting our house in order and making the best of those things that remain.

The Manx character has heretofore been sound and honest. It is so still. A wave of speculation has inundated the developing community; that wave has broken. The value of property will recover daily. If experience ever taught and disciplined a community for its good, the experience of 1900 in the Isle of Man will also see its values recover, materially and morally. Another season will, ere long, arrive and many of the financial terrors will be obliterated. At the closing hour of the nineteenth century, to those who say, 'Watchman, what of the night?' the answer is 'Patience!' and again to the same question the answer is, 'We bid you be of hope! It is the dawn – of the New Year and the Twentieth Century!'

LATE NEWS: THE ISLAND IN MOURNING

Within a short time of His Excellency Lord Henniker receiving the telegram of Her Majesty's death on Tuesday evening, 22nd January, 1901, the measured tolling of the church bells rang the news into hundreds of homes that the Queen was dead. St George's bell was the first, followed by St. Thomas' and All Saints; and in a brief time all the bells of the town had taken up the sad toll. And so throughout the Island. The sad news was sent shivering over Braddan from the old bell which has rung the knell of many a King and Queen of the British Isles. These death measures were the first news in mansion and cottage of the beloved Queen's death in her 82nd year following an illness we have all followed so closely. For 63 years she has presided over the destiny of the British Empire of which we are proud members. Thus it came about that in the morning, the Manx, who have ever boasted themselves as the most loyal to the Queen and Throne, rose perhaps the saddest people in the whole empire the world around and of which, geographically, the Island is the centre.

Saturday next has been proclaimed a national day of mourning and memorial services are to be held in church and chapel throughout the Island. The official Memorial Service will be held at noon in St. George's Church and will be attended by His Excellency Lord Henniker, Lord Bishop Straton and leading dignitaries from the towns, villages and parishes. Shops, offices and hotels will be closed throughout the day.

THE MARVELS OF PHOTOGRAPHY

To add to the recording of the news we have been able to take advantage of the marvels of photography and the talents of the photographer. Already it has been said that a picture is worth a thousand words. Photography has made tremendous strides from the dim and shadowy *daguerroetype* of half a century ago to the photographs of today with the clean-cut and sharp outlines that not only preserve the features of our loved ones but can also set upon a plate the stars of heaven for convenience and proper study. So, too, can be revealed the hidden parts of the human frame, expose its disease to the eye of the physician and surgeon for better diagnosis and treatment.

For most, photography is a graphic means of recording the many and varied delights of our Island, and of preserving for posterity the many developments that have taken place in recent years. Earliest photographer of local scenes was James Burnham, Clerk to Tynwald from 1851. Then there was Marshall Wane who took photographs between 1865 and 1882. One of his exposures is reproduced here, depicting Henry Bloom Noble, the well known businessman and philanthropist, with a group of orphans he cares for. Mr Thomas Keig, first Mayor of Douglas, began his career as a photographer in 1862 and set up his business at Allen Bank in Circular Road. Already he has created a library of scenes from around the Island which are much in demand. The greatest of all Manx artists, John Millar Nicholson, in recent years has turned his attention to the art of photography in capturing the lively scenes around the harbour and in the streets of Douglas. There are many others who have similarly applied their skills to this new art form and recently the renowned photographer Frederick Frith has visited our shores. It is thanks to such gentlemen that we are able to conclude with a survey of many parts of the Island in graphic form.

J. M. Nicholson

The paddle-steamer 'Snaefell' berthed at the North Quay, Douglas

J. M. Nicholson
Fish Market, North Quay

J. M. Nicholson
Jubilee Clock, Loch Promenade

J. M. Nicholson
Well Road Hill

T. Keig
Douglas Harbour

T. Keig
Harris Promenade and
Iron Pier, removed 1892

T. Keig
Victoria Pier extension
completed 1892

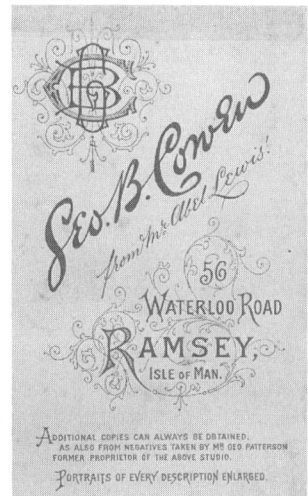

G. B. Cowen — *Bride Village*

G. B. Cowen — *Andreas Village*

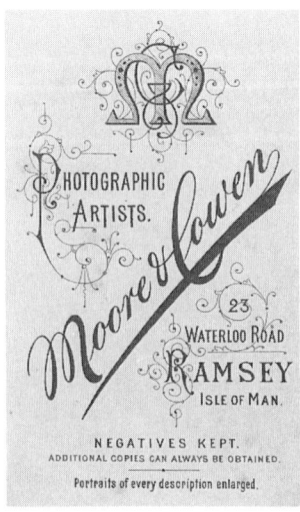

Sulby Village

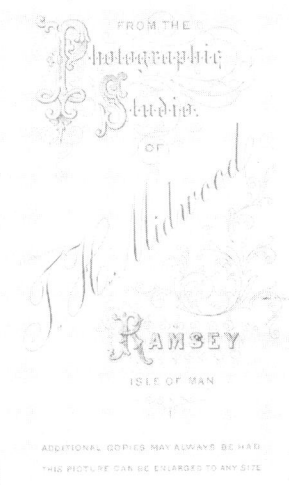

F. Frith Ramsey Harbour

F. Frith South Promenade, Ramsey

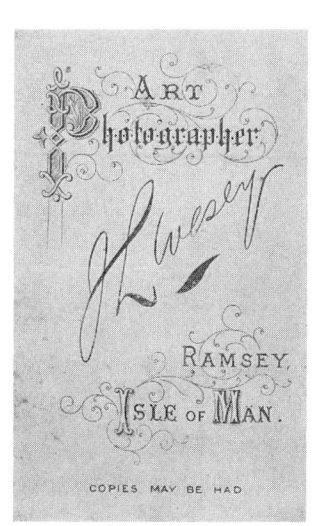

F. Frith South Beach, Ramsey

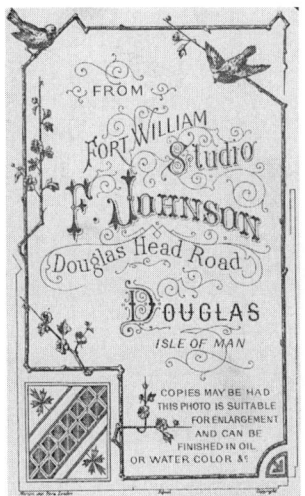

Union Mills

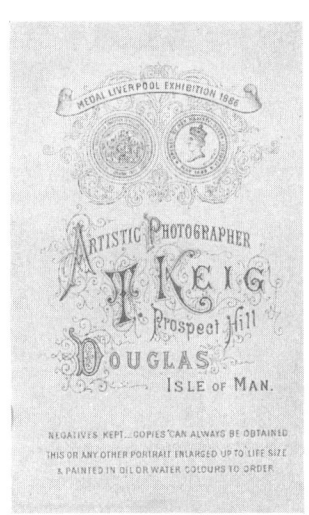

T. Keig   *On the road to Peel*

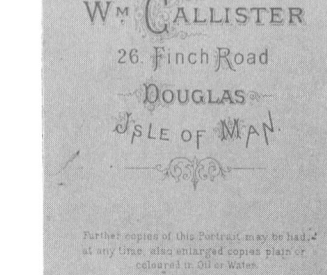

Kirk Michael

T. Keig   *Fenella Hotel and Beach, Peel*

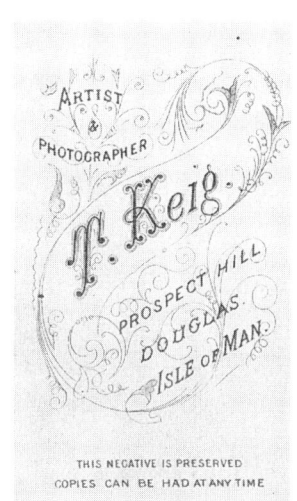

Peel Parade

Castle Rushen

F. Frith　　　　　　　　　　　　　　　　　　　　　　　　*Port Erin*

Port Erin Beach

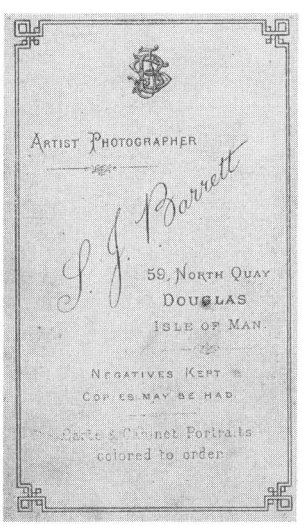

Market Place, Castletown

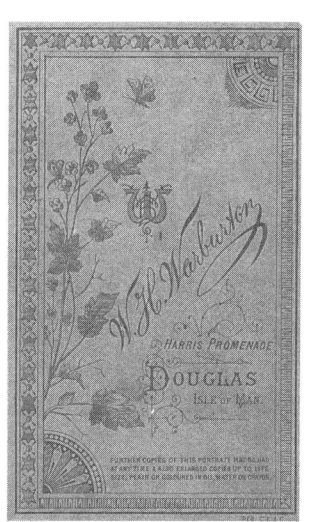

F. Frith   *Port St. Mary*

On the Underway, Port St. Mary

SHIPS OF THE ISLE OF MAN STEAM PACKET COMPANY CO. LTD.

The end of the century has seen the Isle of Man Steam Packet Company celebrate its seventieth anniversary triumphant in the knowledge that it has beaten off, or absorbed, its rivals in the lucrative passenger trade which, in turn, has made the Isle of Man a premier resort. There have been keenly fought races to establish the fastest crossings, and there have been punishing fare reductions. These the Company has survived and it is now in the position of being the leading passenger carrier in British waters. And so the Isle of Man Steam Packet Company, with a fleet of eleven ships including some of the finest in their class, sails into the new century ready for any eventuality. With annual traffic now over 400,000 it is confidently predicted that the million mark will be surpassed in the next few years. Here are details of the present fleet.

'Ellan Vannin' leaving the Red Pier. One of the most profitable ships of the Company was built in 1860 as the paddle steamer 'Mona's Isle' (11) but was converted into a twin-screw steamer in 1883 and renamed. She can carry 299 passengers.

King Orry
A handsome iron paddle-steamer built in Glasgow, 1871. Refitted and re-boilered in 1888 with tonnage increased to 1,104. Speed 17 knots and passengers 1104. Electric lighting installed in 1895.

Ben-my-Chree
Built in 1875 in Barrow-in-Furness. Reboilered in 1884, she was altered to carry four funnels in pairs fore and aft of the paddle boxes. Largest Company ship at time of building but speed is slow at 12 knots. Is shown here in Douglas berthed by the Imperial Buildings, Head Office of the Company.

Snaefell
Iron paddle-steamer built in Glasgow in 1876. One of the smaller ships of the fleet with tonnage of 849. Speed 15 knots. Now equipped with electric lighting.

Fenella
Built in Barrow-in-Furness, 1881, as iron twin-screw steamer. Of 564 tons, she was primarily built as a cargo ship but also does passenger runs as relief service in winter. Hard working ship seen on all routes including the Peel to Belfast run, though this is now no longer operated.

Mona's Isle
Steel paddle-steamer built at Greenock in 1882 with high pressure oscillating engines giving her a speed of 18 knots. Tonnage 1564 and, as with most of the fleet, was allowed to carry a similar number of passengers. The largest and most expensive Company ship at time of building, she was able to do the Liverpool crossing in under four hours.

Mona's Queen
Large steel paddle-steamer built in 1885 at Barrow-in-Furness. Tonnage 1559 and speed 19 knots. Can do the Fleetwood–Douglas run in under three hours. Used on the Liverpool route to compete with rival Isle of Man, Liverpool and Manchester Steamship Company.

Prince of Wales
With her sister ship 'Queen Victoria' was purchased from the Isle of Man, Liverpool and Manchester Steamship Company in 1888, having been built in Govan two years previously. These powerful and fast steel paddle-steamers are a great asset to the Steam Packet Company and can each carry over 1500 passengers.

Tynwald
Steel ship with twin screws built in Govan in 1887 to work the Douglas–Ardrossan run. Tonnage 937 and speed 18 knots. First of the fleet to use the latest in marine engineering – the triple-expansion engine. Her two boilers are each fired by eight furnaces. She is also the first to have full installation of electric lighting.

Empress Queen
Built in Govan in 1897 and named in honour of Queen Victoria's Diamond Jubilee. Likely to be the last paddle-steamer to be built by the Company, she is of over 2000 tons and powered by advanced engines giving her a speed of 21 knots. The pride of the fleet she is said to be the largest and fastest paddle cross-channel steamer to be built, and holds the record of 2 hours 57 minutes from the Mersey Light to Douglas Head. Capable of carrying 2000 passengers she has a crew of 95, 16 of whom are firemen working the 32 furnaces.

ACKNOWLEDGEMENTS FOR ILLUSTRATIONS

Front and back cover: From a lithograph by J. Needham based on the work of J. Burkill entitled 'CASTLETOWN'. Published by J. Mylrea of Douglas, 1857 (Rodney Quayle Collection)
Frontispiece: Ornamental title-piece of Peter Fannin's map of the Isle of Man, 1789, by kind permission of Manx National Heritage (M.N.H.)

Pages:
 2: Enchantment of the Triskele of Manannan, by Eric Austwick
 4: Celtic homestead – artwork by Susan Jones; Celtic Round House – M.N.H.
 6: Celtic keeill – artwork by Susan Jones
 7: Manx Cross designs by Maureen Costain–Richards
 8: Norse homestead – artwork by Susan Jones
10: Bishop Symon – Susan Jones; Rushen Abbey – Leeds University Archaeological Studies Centre
11: Viking King – artwork by Susan Jones
15: William de Montecute – Frank Cowin Library (F.C.L.); St.German's Cathedral – artwork by Susan Jones
18: Lord Thomas Stanley, First Lord of Derby – F.C.L.
20: Daniel King Drawings reproduced by kind permission of Manx National Heritage
22: Portrait of 7th Earl and Countess Derby – F.C.L.
22, 24, 25: Daniel King illustrations – Manx National Heritage
27: Eliza Murrey's sampler of Ronaldsway House, 1793 – by kind permission of Mrs J. P. Holt
28: From a drawing by J.M. Nicholson of the portrait of William Christian in the Manx Museum – M.N.H.
32: Plan of The Close, Braddan – M.N.H.
33: Map of Watch and Ward – M.N.H.
34–35: Bishop Wilson and church illustrations – M.N.H.
35: Drawing of Castletown Grammar School, 1902, by Flaxney Stowell – M.N.H.
36: Drawings by Susan Jones
40: Plan of Manx Cottage by Susan Jones
42: From an engraving – M.N.H.
43: Bishop Hildesley and Frontispiece of Manx Bible – M.N.H.
44: Naval cutter in Irish Sea – F.C.L.
47: From a watercolour painting of Castle Rushen by Moses Griffiths, 1774 – M.N.H. Portrait of Sir George Moore – M.N.H.
48: Coin illustrations – F.C.L.
50: John Wesley, from a bust modelled from life by Enoch Wood – F.C.L.
51: The Brig Caesar – M.N.H.
52: St. George's Church and St. Matthew's Church (after a drawing by George Pickering) – F.C.L.
54: Map of Isle of Man by Peter Fannin, 1789 – M.N.H.
55–56: From 'Views of the Isle of Man,' 1795, by John 'Warwick' Smith – M.N.H.
58: Portrait of Nessy Heywood and the Nunnery Mansion – F.C.L.
60–61: Illustrations from 'A Tour Through the Isle of Man' by David Roberston, 1794
62: Detail from Peter Fannin's Map of the Isle of Man, 1789 – M.N.H.
63: Elevations by George Steuart – M.N.H.
64: Royal Bounty poster – M.N.H.
66–67: Castle Mona and Meridith's detailed drawing of Douglas – M.N.H.

In 1899 Tynwald gave approval to a law permitting the new 'horseless carriages' to travel on Manx roads at a maximum speed of 14 miles per hour, thus exempting them from the Highway law for steam rollers which are restricted to 4 m.p.h., with someone walking in front waving a red flag. The few owners of a motor car, such as the 5 horse power Deauville seen here, are delighted at the prospect of travelling about the Island at such speeds though already some have been accused of 'furious driving' which creates clouds of dust and frightens horses. The 450 operators of horse drawn carriages have also expressed great alarm at the prospect of losing their livelihood after the internal combustion engine has already demonstrated it has the power to climb the steepest hills without the assistance of passengers having to push the vehicle.